The Muses' Library

★

THE
COLLECTED POEMS
OF
CHRISTOPHER SMART

THE
COLLECTED POEMS
OF
CHRISTOPHER
SMART

edited, with an introduction
and critical comments
by

NORMAN CALLAN, M.A.

VOLUME TWO

LONDON
ROUTLEDGE AND KEGAN PAUL LTD

First published in 1949
by Routledge and Kegan Paul Ltd
68–74 Carter Lane, London E.C.4
Printed in Great Britain
by Butler and Tanner Limited
Frome and London

CONTENTS

RELIGIOUS AND DEVOTIONAL POEMS

RELIGIOUS AND DEVOTIONAL POEMS

A Translation of the Psalms of David

PSALM I

THE man is blest of God thro' Christ,
Who is not by the world intic't,
    Where broader ruin lies;
Nor has descended to a seat,
Where scoffers at the gospel meet,
    Their Saviour to despise.

But for himself is wise to chuse
God's holy law, which he pursues
    With all his means and might;
This as his exercise he takes,
And working morn and midnight makes
    His duty his delight.

He like the tree, that bow'ring wide
Upon the river's sunny side
    Has timely fasten'd root;
Shall duly each succeeding year,
In beauty and abundance rear
    His bud, his bloom, and fruit.

His leaf shall spread a lasting shade,
Of ever-green that may not fade,
    Or wear a languid hue;
And look ye forward to his end,
Success shall every work attend,
    He takes in hand to do.

But otherwise with those it fares,
Whose life against the gospel dares,
    And with their impious race;

385

They like the chaff from off the land
Shall by dispersing winds be fann'd,
    From earth's offended face.

The sinners therefore shall be far
From confidence, when at the bar
    Of God's tribunal tried;
Nor can the folk, with hearts unsound,
Assemble to maintain their ground
    With men to Christ allied.

For God his special grace bestows
On him, whose work and way he knows,
    The perfect man and just;
But not a path of the profane,
Nor shall a monument remain
    To frowardness and lust.

PSALM II

WHY do the heathen zealots rage,
    So boist'rous and so blind;
And all the people pre-engage
    To vanity their mind?

The kings upon their God have warr'd,
    Assembling all their might;
And worldly pow'rs against the Lord,
    And Christ his Son unite.

Let us, each impious rebel cries,
    Their bonds in sunder break;
We will not hold us to their ties,
    Nor such salvation seek.

He that in heav'n supports his reign,
 Of spotless virgin born,
Shall give them blessing for disdain,
 And charity for scorn.

Then shall he make his day-spring shine
 In evangelic peace;
And sinners from the wrath divine,
 Thro' faith in him release.

I chose my king, whose worth and weight,
 Have all compeers excell'd;
And, Zion, on thy topmost height
 His coronation held.

This is my gospel and my lot,
 That God himself should say—
'Thou art my Son whom I begot,
 And magnify this day.'

Desire, and I thy boon will bless,
 And open to thy knock;
All earth thy pasture to possess,
 And all mankind thy flock.

Their fictious gods of brass and stone,
 Thine iron rod shall wound;
Like vessels of dishonour thrown,
 And trampl'd on the ground.

Be wise now therefore, O ye kings,
 From blood and rapine pause;
And come to learn celestial things,
 Ye judges of the laws.

Come in the Christian cause sincere
 Your services employ,

With godly love, and manly fear,
　·And with angelic joy,

Embrace the doctrine and the priest,
　In which ye shall not die;
And bidden to the bridegroom's feast,
　With lively faith comply.

PSALM III

LORD, how my bosom foes increase,
　How num'rous their allies;
The troublers of my peace
　In multitudes arise!

For many a taunting wretch I grieve,
　That scoff at God, and say,
'Tis hopeless to believe,
　Nor is there fruit to pray.

But thou, Lord Jesus, art my fort
　From every hostile dread;
My worship and support
　Of this my drooping head.

When to the Lord my voice I sent
　My hardships to recount,
A gracious ear he lent
　From out his holy mount.

For due repose my couch I press'd,
　And rose to pray'r again;
For God my slumbers bless'd,
　My spirit to sustain.

Thro' him I will not be dismay'd,
 Tho' thousand thousands rage;
And rank and file array'd
 Domestic warfare wage.

Up, Lord, and as my foes rebel,
 Let thy controuling might
Their fierce attacks repel,
 And disannul their spite.

Salvation is from God to man,
 Whom he delights to spare;
Our host from rear to van
 His gen'ral blessing share.

PSALM IV

To the call of pressing need,
 Christ my righteousness repair;
Thou, whose blood my bondage freed,
 With compassion hear my pray'r.

O ye sons of sinful dust,
 Will ye still my fame belye;
As for vanities ye lust,
 And to fond delusion fly?

Know ye this, that God has made
 Men of piety his choice;
Wherefore, when I call for aid,
 He will hearken to my voice.

Flee from sin, and stand in awe,
 Sift thyself to curb thy will;
To thy private pray'r withdraw,
 To thy conscience and be still.

Offer thou the righteous gift,
    Which sincerity bestows:
All your thoughts to Jesus lift,
    And in God your trust repose.

Some have made an impious doubt,
    And descending grace withstood;
Saying, who shall help us out,
    And describe the way to good?

Lord, do thou the blind illume,
    From thy glorious presence dart
Rays of light to clear the gloom,
    That surrounds the harden'd heart.

Thou hast made my joy compleat,
    Since thro' thee my people thrive;
Such a crop of choicest wheat,
    So much wine and oil they hive.

On my peaceful pillar thrown,
    I myself of rest assure;
For 'tis thou, O Lord, alone,
    In whose help I dwell secure.

PSALM V

WEIGH the words of my profession,
    Lord, in thine indulgent scale;
Of a father's prepossession,
    Let my thoughts themselves avail.

Give my suppliant voice the hearing,
    To mine orisons repair;
For my God, my king appearing,
    At thy shrine I make my pray'r.

At the dawn of morning soaring,
    Thou shalt hear my voice betimes;
Lifted eyes and hands imploring,
    As my soul herself sublimes.

For thou hast no inclination
    To the vicious and the vain;
Nor in thy blest habitation
    Shall a wicked thought remain.

Worldly fools and self-deceivers
    Shall not rank within thy sight;
Impious men and unbelievers
    Are offensive to the light.

Him that makes a lye his study,
    And against his Saviour wars,
Men of subtle minds and bloody,
    In his nature God abhors.

But my soul, in full persuasion
    Of thy mercy, shall be meek;
And at all times take occasion
    In thy church thy grace to seek.

In thy righteousness direct me,
    Lord, because my friends are few;
Clear my passage, and protect me,
    In the path that I pursue.

For with faithless lips they flatter,
    And their speeches frame with art,
Clean without the cup and platter,
    Foul within the head and heart.

With their breath their throats are tainted,
    To the quick their conscience stung;

Yet like tombs inscrib'd and painted,
 They dissemble with their tongue.

Save them, Jesu, lest they perish
 Thro' their own debas'd conceit;
Give them Christian hope to cherish,
 And the tempter to defeat.

And with thanks their praises blending,
 Let thy faithful saints be glad;
For their innocence defending,
 Thou their souls in joy hast clad.

To the good thou wilt be gracious,
 In the fort or in the field;
And with kindness efficacious
 Shalt protect him as a shield.

PSALM VI

O GRACIOUS God, rebuke me not,
 What time thy wrath is at the height;
Nor as resentment waxes hot,
 Let David feel its weight.

O Lord, have mercy on my groans,
 Let mine infirmities be spar'd;
My Saviour heal me, for my bones
 Are harrass'd and impair'd.

My troubled spirits also droop
 With all that puts my frame in fear;
But how much longer must I stoop
 To trials so severe?

O captain of salvation, turn
 My vessel from the nether lake,
Let mercy stand upon the stern
 For my Redeemer's sake.

For all that grace and goodness gave,
 What man in death a sense retains;
And who from forth th' ungrateful grave
 Shall raise the sacred strains?

In this my lamentable plight,
 Ev'n unto weariness I weep;
And all the melancholy night
 My couch in tears I steep.

My healthy bloom thro' such excess
 Of grief is wasted and declin'd;
Because of all the woes that press
 At once upon my mind.

Away, and let my coast be clear'd
 Of all the worldly men and vain;
For God, thro' Jesus Christ has heard
 My voice as I complain.

God has received my soul's appeal,
 And does her faithfulness allow;
God shall with David kindly deal,
 And sanctify his vow.

But all that my good works defame,
 Shall shame and terror overtake;—
And may that terror and that shame
 For true repentance make.

PSALM VII

O Lord, my God, I ground my creed
    In thine almighty pow'r;
Preserve me, and their course impede,
    Who chase me to devour.

Left like the lion and the bear,
    That came upon my fold,
They set about my soul to tear,
    By no rebuke controul'd.

O Lord, if I have done the crime
    Whereof I stand accus'd;
Or hand or heart at any time
    To mischief have abus'd;

If e'er with them that well deserve
    I treacherously deal;
Yea, rather if I cease to serve
    My causeless foe with zeal;

Then let mine enemies be sped,
    Nor give me to respire;
Yea, let them take my life, and tread
    My trophies in the mire.

Stand up, O Lord, and plume thy crest
    Against my rival's rage:
Arise—thy judgment be the test,
    As we the contest wage;

So shall thy congregation make
    Toward thy hallow'd fane;
And therefore for thy people's sake
    Exert thyself again.

The Lord shall judge the common cause,
    My plea, O Christ, admit;
As I have kept thy holy laws
    Mine innocence acquit.

O let all wickedness and lust,
    In penitence conclude;
But govern thou the good and just,
    With grace and peace renew'd.

For God in righteousness explores
    A man's interior part;
The reins, and all the secret pores
    Of his deceitful heart.

My sole security from force
    In God's assistance lies;
To his defence I have recourse,
    Who saves the good and wise.

God is all-gracious to decide
    For those that weep and pray;
Strong in his patience, which is tried
    By sinners every day.

Yet e'en to those that love the dark,
    His vengeance will be slow;
For pity built the floating ark,
    And goodness bent his bow.

His swords are turn'd to shepherd's crooks,
    The breast-plate and the helm;
His darts and spears to pruning hooks,
    To dress the vine-clad elm.

Behold a virgin has conceiv'd,
    By congress undefil'd,

And lost Jeshurun is retriev'd
    By an almighty child.

Lo! he has dug the grave of death,
    Destruction to destroy;
And open'd by his HOLY BREATH
    The way to endless joy.

And all the labour of his love
    To glory shall redound;
In earth beneath, in heaven above
    His truth shall be renown'd.

To this his righteous word reveal'd,
    I will in thanks reply;
And faithfully for ever yield
    That CHRIST is God most high.

PSALM VIII

O LORD, that rul'st the human heart,
How excellent thy name and art,
    In all the world renown'd!
The glorious pillars of thy reign
No flight can reach, nor heav'ns contain,
    Nor exaltation bound!

The very babes and sucklings cry,
Almighty Father, God most high!
    Whom blasphemy profanes—
Thou hear'st and tak'st them by the hand,
Nor can the silenc'd fiend withstand
    The strength that Christ ordains.

I will my soaring thoughts exalt
To yonder heaven's cerulean vault,
    Whose height thy fingers form'd;

The moon attended at thy call,
Made marvelously fair, and all
    The stars around her swarm'd!

Lord what is man, that he should find
A place in his Creator's mind
    Or what his whole increase—
A race of rebels vain and weak,
That he should for a moment break
    Upon his Saviour's peace?

An angel quite thou mad'st him not,
A little lower is his lot,
    On earth thou set'st him down;
There his dominion and degree,
To glorify and worship thee
    For glory and a crown.

Him thou deputed to review
The scenes of nature, and subdue
    Thy creatures to his will;
Whose motley numbers own his sway,
And by his strength compell'd obey,
    Or disciplin'd by skill.

All flocks of sheep and droves of kine,
Which as his olive and his vine,
    To man their goodness yield;
And not a beast that can be nam'd,
But may be taken or be tam'd
    In woodland or in field.

In air, in ocean he controuls,
The feather'd millions, finny shoals,
    From minnows to the whale;
Whate'er beneath the waters creep,
Or glide within the yielding deep,
    Or on the surface sail.

O thou that rul'st the human heart,
Supreme of nature and of art,
 How is thy name renown'd!
How blest thy providential care,
In heav'n above, in earth and air,
 And in the vast profound!

PSALM IX

WITH my heart's sincere intention,
 Lord, my prayer shall be preferr'd;
I will make melodious mention
 Of the wonders of thy word.

Tow'ring with a previous relish
 Of celestial joys I fly;
And my songs I will embellish
 With thy name, O thou most high!

While mine enemies are routed,
 Punished for their causeless strife;
They shall dread the God they doubted,
 And reform their wicked life.

For by thy divine protection,
 My just cause thou shalt maintain;
On a throne of true perfection
 Thou support'st a righteous reign.

Thou hast check'd the heathen fury,
 By thy hand the godless bleeds;
Thou hast driv'n them far from Jury,
 To repent them of their deeds.

O thou enemy, destruction
 Is with thy destroyer dead;

And the cities, whose reduction
    Thou accomplish'd, are not read.

But o'er infinite duration
    God th' eternal sceptre bears,
And for catholick salvation,
    He his judgment-seat prepares.

For with merciful decision
    He shall try his sinful foes,
And in judgment make provision
    For his love to interpose.

God shall likewise be propitious
    To the poor in their distress;
And from men and times malicious
    With a shelter he shall bless.

And the men of godly science,
    In thy name shall put their trust;
For the Lord has made alliance
    With the pious and the just.

Praise the Lord, whose fair pavilion
    Is on Zion's hill display'd;
Shew the people every million
    Of the works, which he has made.

When he makes his inquisition
    For a bleeding martyr'd saint,
He forgets not their petition,
    Which in hardship make complaint.

Lord, let what I bear atoning
    For my sins, thy servant save:
Thou that liftst my spirit, groaning
    On the verges of the grave.

That I may thy praise illustrate,
    Where fair Zion's daughters dwell;
In thy son, whose birth shall frustrate
    Satan's wiles, my joy shall swell.

Their own pit has gap'd to smother,
    Those that made it yawn so deep;
From the net they hid for other,
    They their steps can scarcely keep.

But the Lord is known by sparing
    Sinners thrown on rocks and shelves,
And ungodly self-ensnaring,
    He delivers from themselves.

Men, whose ways are so perverted,
    That in terror they would end;
Shall, thro' Christ, be disconcerted,
    And by grace to bliss ascend.

As for those who, meek and lowly,
    Are in worldly goods forgot,
They shall have from God most holy
    An eternal glorious lot.

Lord, arise, let carnal traitors
    Have no more the upper-hand;
Let thy spirit conquer natures,
    That thy saving health withstand.

Those who, thy remonstrance scorning,
    Still continue in their lust,
Lord, remind with early warning,
    That they are but mortal dust.

PSALM X

LORD, in this disastrous season
    Why dost thou at distance keep?
Times of turbulence and treason
    Loudly for thine absence weep.

Worldlings for their own false pleasure
    Cruelly the poor intreat;
Deal them not, O God, the measure
    They in craft to Christians mete.

For the self-applauding vicious
    Speak the bravest and the best
Of the griping avaricious,
    Whom God's bounteous laws detest.

There is infinite alliance
    'Tixt ungodliness and pride;
In their thoughts they bid defiance
    To the God their words deride.

Hard their ways are, disregarding
    In what throngs opposers bleed,
While thy love, thy bolts retarding,
    Gives them courage to proceed.

For they've to themselves suggested,
    Tush! we are not like to fall;
Nor shall ever be molested
    With the common lot of all.

Fraught with double-tongu'd expression
    Are their mouths and base deceit;
With vain lies and lewd transgression,
    Thought and speech they are replete.

In the thievish corners lurking,
 They th' unmansion'd poor prevent:
Blood-shot eyes with terror working
 On the private stab intent.

Like a lion fierce and greedy,
 Couchant in his secret den,
They're in wait to grind the needy;
 All is prey within their ken.

And without remorse they grind him
 With their teeth for slaughter set;
Whensoe'er the traitors find him
 Caught within their cover'd net.

Formal, with affected meekness,
 Each a seeming saint behaves;
That the poor, thro' want and weakness,
 May become their captain's slaves.

In their hearts themselves they flatter;
 Tush! the Lord beholds us not;
And the knowledge of the matter
 Christ himself has quite forgot.

Rise, O Lord, the cause examine,
 And thy mighty hand uprear;
In the day of war and famine
 For the poor in pow'r appear.

Why should every impious traitor
 Such a foul presumption dare:
Tush! for God, the great Creator,
 Will not for his creatures care.

Murder, theft, and devastation,
 Thou hast seen their ruins lie,

For thy chosen church and nation
    Are for ever in thine eye.

To thy goodness for their trial
    The poor destitute appeal;
For with thee is no denial,
    When for aid the friendless kneel.

Take from malice thy protection,
    Throw the light on dark disguise,
Purge away each foul affection
    And the wicked shall be wise.

Christ his crown of palms is wreathen,
    And for ever, ever blooms;
King alike of Jews and heathen,
    He th' eternal reign assumes:

Thou hast heard the poor's petition
    Thou establishest their heart;
And the cry of their condition
    Has ascended where thou art.

That with thy benign compassion
    Thou thine orphans may'st redress;
From the men of worldly fashion,
    Who are proud when they oppress.

PSALM XI

In Christ, his work and word
    I trust, why should ye say,
That like a tim'rous bird
    My soul must wing her way,
And flee from those, whose deadly skill
At worst can but the body kill ?

For, lo! the godless bend,
    And expedite their bow;
At me the darts intend,
    They in their quiver stow,
That they with private aim may wound
The men of upright heart and sound.

If thus the wicked spurn
    At fundamental points,
The house they overturn,
    And put it out of joints:
And what have pious Christians done,
That they such lawless lengths should run!

The Lord is in his church
    Her pillars to sustain;
And there his cherubs perch,
    And there his saints remain:
But his exalted glory dwells
Where heaven's interior convex swells.

The Lord directs his eyes
    .   To where the poor man prays,
And to distress applies
    Their charitable rays:
Our hearts his eyelids, as they move,
With infinite discernment prove.

The God of truth allows
    The righteous man's pretence,
And ratifies his vows;
    But every slave of sense
That on his holy spirit wars,
His perfect excellence abhors.

Yet tempest, fire and snares,
    And brimstone of the lake,

Which vengeance still prepares,
 And wrath and terror make,
He shall from penitents avert,
Thro' Christ his infinite desert.

For God, which is the light
 And rectitude, receives
The man that acts aright,
 And lives, as he believes;
The fair and equal he respects,
And with his countenance protects.

PSALM XII

Assist, O Lord, for all have sinn'd,
 And war with goodness wage;
For faithfulness is thinn'd
 From every rank and age.

The conversation is in vain
 Which friends and neighbours hold;
Their hearts within them feign,
 Their flatt'ring lips are sold.

The Lord, which came from heav'n to speak,
 His purpose has avow'd;
'I magnify the meek,
 And I degrade the proud.'

Such as have said we shall succeed
 Against the word of God;
Our province is to plead
 Without a master's nod.

Now for the sake of those that lie
 And void of comfort grieve,

405

And for the bursting sigh,
    Which suff'ring Lazars heave;

I will arise with full amends
    Against the spoiler's claw,
'My brethren, sisters, friends
    Are such as keep my law.'

In purity God's words are weigh'd
    Beyond all specious gloss,
As silver is essay'd,
    And sev'n times purg'd of dross.

The Lord has bless'd their sure effect
    To saints upon their knees,
And promis'd his elect
    To shorten days like these.

The sons of wickedness abound,
    And by the world are priz'd;
When such are chair'd and crown'd,
    An honest man's despis'd.

PSALM XIII

How long, O my God, shall I plead,
    Nor thou for thy servant declare,
And wilt thou for ever recede,
    For ever be hid from my pray'r?

How long shall I seek to my breast
    For counsel in anguish of heart;
How long shall the rebels profest
    From insult to triumph depart?

406

Consider, my God, and assist,
    Thine ear, O my Saviour, I crave;
Enlighten mine eyes from their mist,
    My sleep from the dread of the grave!

Lest they, mine oppressors, should vaunt,
    And say to our arms he has bow'd;
For if my good courage they daunt,
    Their joy will be furious and loud.

But I to thy dictates agree,
    Which save me from Satan and Saul,
My trust in thy goodness to me,
    My joy in thy mercy for all.

To Christ I my song will recite,
    Whose grace, O my soul, is thy dow'r;
Most high in the regions of light,
    Most mighty in love and in pow'r.

PSALM XIV

THE fool and fond of Mammon's leav'n
    Has said it in his heart,
There is no God in Heav'n
    To take fair virtue's part.

The worldly men themselves abuse,
    In every course they run;
Forbidden things they chuse,
    Nor is the needful done.

The Lord came down from heav'n, and said
    The heir they will revere—

407

But his report he made,
    'My kingdom is not here.'

For all the race is gone astray
    From Eden to the wild;
Not one to fast or pray,
    Not one but is defil'd.

Their cursing throats are baleful deep,
    Like sepulchres that yawn,
And aspick poisons steep
    The lips with which they fawn.

In blasphemy their voice they lift,
    Their mouths are fill'd with gall;
Their devious feet are swift
    To work their neighbour's fall.

Ruin and wretchedness attend,
    Their feet by Satan shod;
They have no peace or friend,
    No fear or hope in God.

Have they no thought that they inure
    Their souls to sin alone;
And grind my helpless poor,
    And daily pray'r postpone?

Hence guilt in pow'r with terror shakes,
    Ev'n when no dread is nigh,
For God himself betakes
    To where the righteous cry.

The poor and meek they mock'd and scourg'd,
    And crucified and slew—
'Forgive them, sire, was urg'd,
    They know not what they do.'

Thus Christ has brought a change about,
 And bore our sins away;
Let Israel's children shout,
 And Jacob's banners play.

PSALM XV

LORD, who shall dwell in thine abode
 Of holiness and love;
To whom hast thou the grace bestow'd,
 To reach the heights above?

To him who has reserv'd his youth
 From Mammon's baits and spells,
And takes a pleasure in the truth,
 Which from his heart he tells.

Whose tongue's unpractis'd in deceit,
 Whose thoughts all wrong disclaim,
Nor are with virulence replete
 Against his neighbour's fame.

So meek he will not over-rate,
 When he his worth computes;
But glories on the good to wait,
 And further their pursuits.

Whose word of promise is his oath,
 And never made in vain,
Whose honest deed is more than both,
 Tho' he the loss sustain.

Who hoarded money has not lent,
 Exacting by the loan;
Nor took a bribe with black intent
 To cause the martyr's groan.

Who that performs, and this forbears,
    Shall never act amiss,
Nor fall into the worldly snares,
    But speed for endless bliss.

PSALM XVI

PRESERVE me, Lord, in this my state
Of trial, and a longer date
    To my pursuits allow;
Since to thy glory they redoun'd,
For in thy name my hope I found,
    And ratify my vow.

My soul has to the Lord profess'd,
Thou art my God supremely bless'd;
    For whom I have declar'd;
The carnal charms that fools entice,
And all the world is of no price
    When with thy love compar'd.

My soul's first rapture from my youth
Was for the champions of the truth,
    Whose deeds the rest outshine;
Who, God and virtue on their side,
Have Satan and the world defy'd,
    With wrath and zeal divine.

But such as from their colours run
Shall be distracted and undone,
    Of Antichrist the seed;
Who hold idolatrous conceits
And to their images and cheats,
    As priests and gods give heed.

I will not mind their house or hour,
When they their vain libations pour,
    And hands in blood imbrue;
My lips their names shall not pollute,
Whose lives and rites themselves confute,
    Unhallow'd and untrue.

My portion is my Saviour's grace,
Whose invitation I embrace
    To his divine repast;
I drink thy cup my sin to blot,
Thou shalt maintain me in my lot,
    To whom I feast and fast.

My private lot is fallen fair,
And God, thro' Christ, has made me heir
    Of beautiful domains;
To him I give my youth and age,
And lo! a goodly heritage
    My faithfulness regains.

My thanks to God shall be preferr'd,
Who gives me warning by his word,
    And counsels me to good;
Also my reins by night beware
Of Satan's wiles, which are by pray'r
    And vigils best withstood.

My duty lest I should forget,
I still before my eyes have set
    Heav'n's omnipresent king;
And his good angel guides my hand,
I shall not therefore fail to stand
    The mines that traitors spring.

Hence my glad heart is bound to bless,
And her big gratitude express

In all the pow'rs of praise;
Also my flesh in hope shall sleep,
For soul and body from the deep
    Thy conq'ring word shall raise.

Thou shalt not leave my soul in hell,
Nor with the wretched fiends that fell
    Thy holy one to stay:
The third day, and he shall arise,
Nor shall be like to him that dies,
    And turns corrupted clay.

The gates of heav'n thou wilt unfold,
And thy right hand I shall behold
    In triumph o'er the tomb;
There dwell the cherub and his mate,
There plenitude of pleasures wait,
    And joys eternal bloom.

PSALM XVII

In this my cause, O Lord, preside,
    Weigh my complaint and take my part;
Attend my pray'r, untaught to glide
    From lips of practis'd art.

Let me from thee my sentence learn,
    Do thou mine innocence declare;
And let thine equal eyes discern
    The bounds of false and fair.

I stand acquitted in the night
    When my still heart thy spirit proves;
For I am bound with all my might
    To speak as best behoves.

Warn'd by the works that men commit,
    Against the word Jehovah spake,
By grace I kept me from the pit
    Which sin and mis'ry make.

O bear me up as I proceed
    In this my pilgrimage of pain;
And lest I fail in strength or speed
    My heart and feet sustain.

To God my suit I have referr'd,
    And he shall his attention lend;
O grant an audience to the word
    Of meekness which I send.

O thy stupendous goodness shew,
    And all thy copious mildness show'r;
Thou Saviour of the faithful few,
    From such as thwart thy pow'r.

Choice as the lustre of an eye,
    Preserve me with thy precious things,
And let me to the covering fly
    Of thy paternal wings,

To guard me from my foes profest,
    That torture me with endless strife;
My enemies my bounds invest
    To take away my life.

They're swoln with fatness, as their days
    To sumptuous banquets they devote;
Their mouths are fill'd with pompous phrase,
    As on their wealth they glote.

On every side our way they block,
    And turn their eyes on every place,

Our stedfast purposes to shock,
 And to prevent our race.

Like as a greedy lion works,
 His prey from safety to decoy;
Or as his whelp in secret lurks
 The trav'ler to destroy.

Up, Lord, the godless disconcert,
 And to humility controul;
That bitter sword of thine avert
 From David's faithful soul.

The worldly men, who're better sped,
 Who have their portion here below;
Who from thy treasuries are fed
 The prosp'rous carnal foe.

A num'rous offspring they conceive
 According to their gross desires;
And their ill-gotten wealth they leave
 To children like their fires.

Mean while to these my joyful eyes
 Thou shalt thyself in truth present;
And when I in thy semblance rise,
 My heart shall rest content.

PSALM XVIII

THEE will I love, O Lord, my tow'r,
My Saviour of almighty pow'r
 Is God, in whom I dare;
By whom my conq'ring bands are led,
My buckler in the hour of dread,
 And refuge from despair.

I will invoke the great Supreme
Whose matchless merits are the theme
    Of everlasting praise;
So when the furious warriors chafe,
I shall command the battle safe
    From terror and amaze.

The sorrows of a death-like gloom,
And all the visions of the tomb
    Came threat'ning as at hand;
And blood in such profusion spilt
By swords extravagant of guilt
    My trembling heart unmann'd.

Hell with her agonizing pains,
And horror of eternal chains,
    My vestibule alarm'd;
And by my active health forsook,
A ghastly consternation shook,
    And all my strength disarm'd.

Thro' trouble when my members fail,
O Lord, I will myself avail
    Of thy most holy name;
To thee prefer my soul's complaint,
And from diseases and restraint
    Thy blest protection claim.

So that within thy sacred shrine
Thou shalt thy gracious ears incline,
    As I thy help beseech;
Thy psalmist to the height shall soar,
And up at Heaven's interior door
    Shall thine attention reach.

Strong dread redoubled to convulse
All nature's frame at every pulse,

And from their topmost height,
Down to the bottom of their base,
The hills were shaken and gave place,
　　Because his wrath was great.

Out in his presence issue wreathes
Of lucid smoak, and as he breathes
　　Flames from his mouth transpire;
Which rage so vehement and fierce,
The bowels of the earth they pierce,
　　And set her mines on fire.

The empyrean at his frown
Was humbled, and the heav'ns came down
　　With all the host incens'd
Of Michael summon'd from his seat,
And gathering underneath his feet,
　　The darkness was condens'd.

And on the innumerable flight
Of cherubims, the sons of light,
　　He rode in grand career;
And bore on the stupendous force
And speed of winged winds his course,
　　O'er vaulted space to steer.

A thick tremendous veil he made,
The glorious majesty to shade,
　　Where in the midst he storm'd;
And his pavilion was a cloud
Of deepest water, which to shroud,
　　His alter'd face he form'd.

But then the brightness which he beam'd,
As he the copious lustre stream'd,
　　The dusky scene controuls;

And as the gloom around was clear'd,
From out the central blaze appear'd,
    Hail mixt with burning coals.

God also thunder'd—the most high
Pronounc'd his thunder in the sky,
    The rolling pomp to drive;
And at his omnipresent word,
Above, beneath, around occurr'd
    Hailstones and coals alive.

He from his loaded quiver drew
The forked arrows, and they flew
    To make obstruction void;
He bade the heathen wrath avast,
And with the lightning that he cast,
    Their menaces destroy'd.

The secret water springs the while
Were seen ev'n to the source of Nile,
    And in the world beneath,
The pillars of th' inferior arch
Stood naked at the fires that search,
    And his strong vengeance breathe.

His blessed angel he shall send
To fetch me, and in pow'r defend
    From his terrific scourge;
With which he visits all around,
And from the floods of the profound
    I shall to peace emerge.

He shall in love prevent my fall,
Till my worst enemy of all
    With guilty shame shall blush;
And save me from the gross disgust
Of men with ruffian rage robust,
    Whose furious weight would crush.

In that sad hour of pinching need,
They strove my progress to impede,
    And from my point debarr'd;
But Christ the Lord, to whom I pray,
Upheld my goings in the way,
    At once my guide and guard.

He saw my jeopardy discharg'd,
And freedom's ample walk enlarg'd
    With plenty and content;
He set me in a spacious place,
Because I found peculiar grace,
    When kneeling to repent.

The Lord shall my reward prepare,
Because my dealings have been fair,
    And from all treach'ry free;
According to the spotless hue,
With which these harmless hands I shew,
    My recompence shall be.

For I with courage have abode
By God and truth, and kept the road
    Which goes to endless bliss;
Nor have deserted from his cause,
Like men that have not known his laws
    The godless and remiss.

Because with application strict
I to thy laws my mind addict,
    Their import to discern;
Nor poorly single out a part,
But keep them all with all my heart
    As of the last concern.

I likewise found myself intire,
And pure from every vain desire,
    Lascivious and unclean;

My former follies I eschew'd,
And all the past of life review'd,
   My thoughts from vice to wean:

Wherefore the Lord, whom thus I please,
And which my righteous dealing sees
   With his paternal eyes,
According as my hands are pure,
Shall to my soul in heav'n secure
   The blest immortal prize.

Where saints and holy angels dwell,
Thou shalt in holiness excell,
   And shalt have perfect peace;
Where perfected beyond the sketch
Of Nature, to their utmost stretch,
   Faith, hope and grace increase.

In living waters thou shalt bathe,
And God with purity shall swathe
   Thy loins as with a girth;
And with the clean and undefil'd,
Thou shall be number'd as a child,
   In this thy second birth.

For thou shalt save the poor oppress'd,
And have his grievances redress'd,
   By thine immediate aid;
And pompous pride, that is above
The works of charity and love,
   Thou shalt to want degrade.

Thou shalt indulge a farther length
To David's life, and with new strength
   My blazing lamp shall burn;
Again my vessel shall embark,
And God shall dissipate the dark,
   And urge the day's return.

Thro' thee I shall maintain my post,
Nor of the fury of an host,
    Or numbers, make account;
And, as thy present help supports,
Shall leap o'er battlements and forts,
    And every bar surmount.

God's way is just, his word the same,
And proof against the sev'nfold flame,
    When challeng'd to the test;
He is the Saviour and the shield
Of all that in his truth reveal'd
    Their firm affiance rest.

For what is the Supreme, or who
But God Almighty, and all-true
    On his eternal throne;
What is this pow'r and strength of ours,
And what is strength, or what are pow'rs
    But God's, and God alone?

It is the Lord that girds my sword,
Whose grace and might their help afford,
    Calm thought with wrath to mix;
Against each giant foe of Gath,
'Tis he alone directs my path,
    His champion's fame to fix.

His mandates to my feat impart
The swiftness of the nimble hart,
    To run with them that fly;
He takes me up from off the ground,
On which with active speed I bound,
    And sets me up on high.

The Lord has with my forces fought,
And these my hardy members taught
    The battle to sustain;

My hands are practical and apt,
And with their vigour I have snapt
   A bow of steel in twain.

Thou'st plac'd salvation's glorious helm
Upon thy servant, and his realm
   E'en to remotest Dan;
I rise augmented from thy rod,
And thy kind chastisement, O God,
   Shall magnify the man.

Thou shalt enlarge me round about,
And wheresoe'er I take my rout,
   My pilgrimage equip;
By thee directed I shall move,
And thou shalt keep as in a groove.
   My footsteps lest they slip.

With God and Israel's cause at stake,
I shall their armies overtake,
   Which our perdition seek;
Nor will my rapid courses slack,
Nor bring Jehudah's standard back,
   Till I have made them meek.

I will attack them sword in hand,
Nor shall they my sure stroke withstand,
   While God my arm uplifts;
One shall his thirst of glory glut
With hundreds vanquish'd—ten shall put
   Ten thousand to their shifts.

Thy pow'r shall gird and brace my loins,
Whene'er the fierce encounter joins,
   Thine angel shall aggrieve
The foe that Israel's coast alarms,
Till I by my victorious arms
   Immortal fame atchieve.

421

Thou'st made mine enemies retreat,
Nor could they, previous of defeat,
    My fair battalia front;
And I shall quell their boistrous boasts,
Invested by the Lord of Hosts,
    With brav'ry scorners want.

Their clamours shall ascend the skies,
But none shall stay to hear their cries
    Of angels or of men;
To God they shall address their suit,
Yet they shall have but little fruit,
    To their devotions then.

They came in number, like the dust,
Their weapons in our heart to thrust,
    Like dust they shall recede;
Or crumbled clay before the wind,
Nor shall an atom stay behind,
    To signify their deed.

Thou shalt preserve thy servant's life
From faction and domestick strife,
    However rais'd or spread;
And fresh from every clime and shore,
The heathen shall thy name adore,
    With David at their head.

My swelling sails shall be unfurl'd,
And to reform a distant world,
    Thou shall my fleets convoy;
And nations from thy word remote,
I to thine honour will devote,
    And in thy ways employ.

Soon as my precepts they imbibe,
They shall to their good truth subscribe,
    And their rude manners change;

Yea perjured hypocrites shall throng
To God and Jesus, whom they wrong
    As they themselves estrange.

The stranger shall be taken in,
Redeem'd from slavery and sin,
    Their Saviour to invoke—
Their nature shall no more despond
Of mercy, but embrace the bond
    Of peace and Christ his yoke.

The God of all perfection lives,
And reigns o'er all things, and he gives
    The laurel to my lance;
And I will bless him and applaud
His pow'rful succour, and his laud
    And magnitude advance.

E'en he whose holy angels wage
Their warfare with me, and engage
    Against the strength of stealth,
Of hate and falshood, and confirms
My people in submissive terms
    By plenty, peace and wealth.

He shall my soul's salvation set
O'er those that cruel men abet,
    Still pouring fresh and fresh;
And for my safety shall provide
From every loud blasphemer's pride,
    And from an arm of flesh.

I therefore will my Saviour thank,
And from a faithful heart and frank
    The song of praise produce;
And to the Gentiles will I sing
Of him who guides the warrior's sling,
    Or fills the peaceful cruse.

Great things and prosperous hast thou done
In love to David—and his Son
    Shall ride the royal mule;
King David thy free choice appoints,
And from his loins thy seer anoints
    A man thy tribes to rule.

PSALM XIX

THE glory of the Lord appears,
In heav'n and all the clust'ring spheres,
    Which in rotation shine;
The fleecy clouds and colour'd bow,
And arch of vaulted azure show
    The handy work divine.

Day tells to day—as one recedes,
For early prayer the morrow speeds
    In harmony to come;
To night the night succeeding chimes,
Sweet are the numbers and the times
    That fill their annual sum.

There is no nation, clime or tongue,
Where their first mattins are not sung,
    And in the spirit caught;
There is no language, sound or speech,
But their melodious vespers reach,
    And warble to the thought.

The soothing symphonies, they frame,
O'er spacious nature are the same,
    Isle, continent or main;
And their sweet notes, as on the wing,
The constancy of God they sing,
    To farthest earth pertain.

Amidst their motions he displays
A grand pavilion, for the blaze
    And rapture of the sun;
Who sallies forth as from a bride,
Or, as a giant in his pride,
    The stated race to run.

From one extreme of heav'n he vaults,
Whence he his topmost height exalts
    His fiercer darts to beam;
There's nothing hidden from his heat,
While his vast circuit to compleat,
    He makes the far extream.

The law of God is passing pure,
By which such learning I procure,
    As shall my soul renew;
His statutes are of endless trust,
And with the wisdom of the just,
    The simple mind endue.

The statutes of the Lord are right,
And fill with gladness and delight
    The good ingenuous mind;
The current tenour of his laws
Is plain and clear in every clause,
    And lightens e'en the blind.

Clean, and most holy from offence,
Is God's religion, and from thence
    Eternal and unchang'd;
His faithful judgments are above
All errors, founded by his love,
    And in his truth arrang'd.

More precious are they thousand fold,
And more desirable than gold,
    Yea than the purest ore;

And with more sweets the heart content,
Than honey, which from heav'n is sent,
    Or bees imblossom'd store.

And from the truths that they convey,
I likewise learn the readiest way
    To please and serve the Lord;
And in observing of the ties
Which they inforce, there is a prize
    Of infinite reward.

Who can his own offences tell,
How oft the busy fiend of hell,
    His subtle snare intrudes?
O cleanse me from my wicked works,
And from the secret sin that lurks,
    And all my search eludes.

And keep thy servant from the sin
Of gross presumption, lest it win
    An empire in my breast;
So should I be defil'd, and fall
Into the blackest crime of all,
    Ingratitude profest.

To these my words, in which I couch
My pray'r, and thy blest name avouch,
    The pious sighs I heave,
And all the musings of my heart,
Attend, and in the better part,
    Do thou from heav'n receive;

O Lord, the strengthner of my soul,
My final comfort, and the goal
    Of every course I take;
Behold I ask, I seek, I knock,
Do thou comply, divulge, unlock,
    For Jesus Christ his sake.

PSALM XX

In time of need the Lord allow
Thy pray'r, and ratify thy vow;
May Jacob's God admit thy claim,
And save thee in his holy name.

Christ Jesus from his bosom send
Assistance, and thy peace defend;
From heavenly Zion midst the throng
Of cherub angels make thee strong.

Remember thy devoted gift,
And all thine orisons uplift;
His face to bless thy censer turn,
And meet thine odours, as they burn.

To thy good purposes aspire,
And grant thee all thy soul's desire;
To his commands direct thy will,
And all thou hast at heart fulfill.

We will rejoice in God's applause
To thy good work, and in his cause,
While we the streaming flags unreef,
Proclaim the Lord, accept our chief.

Now know I that my pray'r has place,
And God presents me with his grace,
That from the holiest heav'n he hears,
And his right hand my vessel steers.

Some on the prancing steed confide,
And some in chariots proudly ride;
But we to great Jehova trust,
And prostrate to the Lord our dust.

They that on helps like those rely,
Or shameful fall, or fearful fly;
But we, thro' Christ our hope renown'd,
Rise manful and maintain our ground.

Save, Lord, and hear us, we beseech,
Extend thy grace for all and each;
O king of sempiternal sway,
From heav'n regard us, as we pray.

PSALM XXI

KING David shall rejoice
        In thee, O Lord, his tow'r,
The man of God's own choice,
        Whom grace and might impow'r:
But when his Saviour he shall plead,
His joy to transport shall exceed.

Thou hast indulg'd thy gift,
        And his petitions blest,
Acording to the drift
        Of his supreme request.
Thou hast accepted, nor oppos'd
The name, in which his pray'r he clos'd.

Henceforth thou shalt prevent
        By grace his heart's desires,
Thy blessing shall be sent
        Or e'er his pray'r aspires;
His crown shall be of purest gold,
And Judah's sceptre he shall hold.

He with devotion su'd
        For health and length of years,
And thou his life renew'd,
        And freed him of his fears;

Thou shalt eternalize the grant,
And to perpetual bliss transplant.

The rays of his renown
        From thy salvation beam,
Thou shalt his greatness crown
        With grace and high esteem;
And glories which from heav'n advance
Upon his lifted face shall glance.

For thou shalt give him taste
        Of everlasting bliss,
And from the carnal paste
        Thou shalt his soul dismiss,
That he in heav'n may take his place,
And see his Saviour face to face.

And this because the king
        Has his affiance built
On him, which o'er the sting
        Of death and lures of guilt
Shall ever in the height prevail,
And in such hope he shall not fail.

Thine enemies shall find,
        In spite of unbelief,
That thou art loving kind;
        Th' adult'ress and the thief
Shall shed a penitential flood,
And own thine all sufficient blood.

From everlasting death
        Thou shalt their souls reprieve,
And from thy blessed BREATH,
        Thy grace they shall receive;
The flames of hell thou shalt abate,
And blunt the darts of mortal hate.

Their children shall be taught
    And nurtur'd in the right;
For with the price they're bought,
    And Christ's eternal light,
Which beams from his victorious tree,
Shall of his burden make them free.

And all this mighty good
    They shall from thee obtain;
Tho' they thy word withstood,
    And tho' the Lamb was slain
By their confederate fraud and force,
Foul hands and hearts without remorse.

But thou shalt make them turn
    Their backs upon their crimes;
And by repentance spurn
    The filth of former times;
And to their rapture thou shalt show
The waters of thine em'ral'd bow.

Let exaltation pil'd
    On exaltation bless
The man so much revil'd
    For meekness in excess.
'Why callest thou me GOOD'—adore,
Sing praise and magnify the more.

PSALM XXII

O MY God, my God, receive me,
    Why am I no more thy care,
Why dost thou recede to leave me
    In a state of pain and pray'r?

Lord, thou hearest not, thro' illness
    As I weep upon my knees;
All the day, and in the stillness
    Of the night I have no ease.

But there is no diminution
    Of thy holiness and grace,
Through all change and revolution,
    O thou praise of Jacob's race.

Faithful were our sires, and steady
    To the hope they built in thee;
And thy gracious hand was ready
    To support and set them free.

By thine angel they were aided
    As they call'd upon thy name,
And of thy good truth persuaded,
    They escap'd disgrace and shame.

But thy servant is neglected
    Like a worm upon the turf;
Scarce a man, and disrespected
    By the very scum and scurf.

All with smiles of scorn exploding,
    As with taunts their spite is fed,
And with ignominy loading,
    Shoot their lips and shake their head.

'On the Lord for help he waited
    Let the help attend his call,
If a wretch so vile and hated
    Be of any price at all.'

But thy pow'rful love embrac'd me
    Soon as from the womb I sprung;

And in thy remembrance plac'd me
    When upon the breasts I hung.

I have walk'd by thy direction
    Ever since my natal hour;
Thou the God of my protection,
    From my mother's womb, in pow'r.

Keep not mercy at a distance
    Now when trouble presses hard;
For I fail of all assistance,
    If the Lord will not regard.

Youthful insolence confounds me,
    Striplings of the hostile seed,
And maturer strength surrounds me,
    Pride of Bashan's brawny breed.

Stalking to the gates of Zion
    They my face with wrath behold,
Like the ramping roaring lion,
    When he came upon my fold.

Loose, as to a fluid turning,
    Are my bones, my joints relax,
And my heart, within me burning,
    Is become like melting wax.

Like the fragments of a potter,
    All my strength is dried and broke,
Parch'd my organs, and I totter,
    As thou gave the final stroke.

For with mows of malediction
    Crowds against my peace consent,
And with dark disguise and fiction
    Artful traitors circumvent.

For my death their cross erecting,
    Both my hands and feet they wound;
I can tell my bones projecting
    To the staring crowd around.

As a spoil my garment's taken,
    Into shares their band divide,
For my vest their lots are shaken,
    Their contention to decide.

But, O Lord, by long secession,
    Leave me not with woe to waste;
Thou my helper in oppression,
    Quick to my deliv'rance haste.

From the weapons of the cruel,
    Take my soul to life and light;
Mine inestimable jewel
    From the carping pow'rs of spite.

From the tyrants that arraign me,
    Speed me to thy righteous throne,
Thou that didst by grace sustain me
    In the wilderness alone.

Jesus in my private station,
    With my brethren will I praise;
And before the convocation,
    Will his peerless marvels blaze.

Praise the Lord all ye that fear him,
    And exalt him voice and mind;
You of Jacob's seed revere him,
    And in Abr'ham all mankind.

For the friendless and unable
    He disdains not to supply,

Nor rejects them from his table,
    But attends whene'er they cry,

With communicants assembling
    To thy church, my praise is thine;
And my vows with fear and trembling,
    To their pray'rs I will subjoin.

God shall give the poor in spirit
    Bread with everlasting peace;
Faith and praise shall realms inherit,
    Where their pow'rs shall never cease.

Christ, by farthest earth asserted,
    Shall remind them of their end;
All mankind shall be converted,
    And the Christian Church attend.

For to Jesus is dominion,
    Him all tongues and climes obey;
Wanton will and vague opinion
    To the truth in Christ give way.

Such as in the world have flourish'd,
    Whom true worth and fame reward,
Have been in the spirit nourish'd
    By the nurture of the Lord.

Every saint that serves his Maker
    Unto death, he shall restore
With his Son to be partaker
    Of a life to die no more.

As for me and my descendants,
    We will reverence his laws;
Reckon'd as the chief dependents
    On his honour, house and cause.

My posterity shall glory,
    As the heavens declare his reign,
Preaching his stupendous story
    To the souls he shall regain.

PSALM XXIII

THE shepherd Christ from heav'n arriv'd,
    My flesh and spirit feeds;
I shall not therefore be depriv'd
    Of all my nature needs.

As slop'd against the glist'ning beam
    The velvet verdure swells,
He keeps, and leads me by the stream
    Where consolation dwells.

My soul he shall from sin restore,
    And her free pow'rs awake,
In paths of heav'nly truth to soar,
    For love and mercy's sake.

Yea, tho' I walk death's gloomy vale,
    The dread I shall disdain;
For thou art with me, lest I fail,
    To check me and sustain.

Thou shalt my plenteous board appoint
    Before the braving foe;
Thine oil and wine my head anoint,
    And make my goblet flow.

But greater still thy love and grace.
    Shall all my life attend;
And in thine hallow'd dwelling place
    My knees shall ever bend.

Or this.

CHRIST Jesus has my name enroll'd,
And to his own peculiar fold
    Above all want consign'd;
Thou hast to ghostly welfare brought
The sheep, thy precious blood has bought,
    O shepherd of mankind.

Me plac'd beneath the blue serene,
In pastures ever fresh and green,
    Where all is peace and still,
He feeds—and sets me on the brink
Of living waters, there to drink
    Of comfort and my fill.

He shall convert my carnal heart,
And every Christian grace impart,
    To fix me in his way;
For by his hallow'd name he swore,
And for the sake of that no more
    Shall David ever stray.

Yea tho' from hence my journey lies
Down thro' the vale of tears and sighs,
    And up the steep of pain,
No terror shall my course withstand;
Thy rod and staff are still at hand
    To check me and sustain.

Thou shalt add plenty to thy grace,
And heap my board before their face,
    My troublers to confound;
The head that thou hast lifted up,
Thou hast anointed, and the cup
    Of my salvation crown'd.

The goodness and the grace divine,
Shall constant all along the line
    Of utmost life extend;
And I shall in thy temple dwell,
In thankful psalmody to tell
    Of transport without end.

PSALM XXIV

THE earth is God's, with all she bears
    On fertile dale or woody hill;
The compass of the world declares
    His all efficient skill.

For her foundations has he laid,
    The flowing waters to restrain,
And all her firm consistence made
    Upon the mighty main.

Who shall have strength and grace to climb
    Up to the sacred mount of God?
And for the holy place sublime,
    What pilgrim shall be shod?

Whose hands are clean, and heart is whole,
    Whose mind and tongue vain thoughts
        suppress,
Nor stain with perjury his soul,
    His neighbour to distress;

The Lord shall bless, and give him fruit
    In heav'n as his salvation speeds,
And God shall righteousness impute
    To his accepted deeds.

Such is the nature and reward
  Of all the children of his grace,
E'en them, who zealous for their Lord,
  O Jesus, seek thy face.

On golden hinges as ye swing,
  Ye gates, ye doors of endless mass,
Lift, lift your arches, and the king
  Of glory shall repass.

Who is the king of glory, who
  Is worthy of so great a name?
E'en Christ all pow'rful to sudue,
  Of vast victorious fame.

On golden hinges as ye swing,
  Ye gates, ye doors of endless mass,
Lift, lift your arches, and the king
  Of glory shall repass.

Who is the king of glory, say?
  'Tis Christ most worthily renown'd;
He whom the hosts of heav'n obey,
  Is king of glory crown'd.

PSALM XXV

LORD and Master, to thine altar
  In the heav'ns by faith I scale,
Let no terror make me faulter,
  Nor let enmity prevail.

They shall never be confounded
  Who upon thy grace depend,
But false hearts, by conscience wounded,
  That without a cause offend.

In thy sacred institutions,
 Lord, be thou my gracious guide,
Strengthen my good resolutions,
 By thy canons to abide.

With a Christian education
 Give my soaring soul her scope;
For thou, God of my salvation,
 Art alone my daily hope.

Lord, with all their sweet effulgence,
 Beam thy mercies on thy fold,
And remember thine indulgence
 Shewn to thine elect of old.

Lord, upbraid not with the sallies,
 And offences of my youth,
But exert that love, which tallies
 With thy goodness and thy truth.

Gracious is the Lord, a lover
 Of the thing that's just and right;
He the wand'rers shall recover
 To the paths of life and light.

Men of gentle disposition
 By his judgments shall he sway;
And for hearts above ambition
 Shall facilitate his way.

Christ is truth with mercy treating
 All his congregated sheep,
Which his liturgy repeating
 All his ceremonies keep.

Lord, for Christ his intercession
 In the blood of every stripe,

Spare and pardon my transgression,
    Gross and for perdition ripe.

Where's the man dispos'd to center
    All his views in God the word,
He shall by his guidance enter
    In the way that Christ preferr'd.

After death his soul surviving,
    Shall in peace her hours employ,
And his seed, thro' promise, thriving,
    Shall their native land enjoy.

All the mysteries and mazes
    Of the providential year,
To the man that fears and praises,
    Clear, as nature's laws, appear.

For the church and constitution
    I my soul by pray'r sublime,
From unequal destitution,
    And the snares of men to climb.

Turn again, O Lord, restore me,
    Let my breathings have access;
For the gloomy scenes before me
    Are desertion and distress.

Sorrows in my heart are heighten'd,
    And upon my spirit fall:
In afflictions am I streighten'd,
    Lord, deliver me from all.

Look upon the fierce invasion
    Of the powers that war within,
Mov'd from thence to take occasion
    Of forgiveness to my sin.

See my foes, how much recruited,
    To what swarms their musters swell,
Who my prowess have disputed,
    And in tyrant hate rebel.

From the fury, that has thirsted
    For my soul, O set me free,
Let me not be sham'd and worsted,
    Since I put my trust in thee.

Let fair dealing and perfection
    Steer me, as my course I run,
For my calling and election,
    And my hope is Christ, thy Son.

All thy flock, which travel weakens,
    Lord, by daily grace refresh;
Save the bishops, priests and deacons,
    From the devil, world and flesh.

PSALM XXVI

BE thou my judge, O Lord, of all
    Mine innocence to clear;
My trust is I shall never fall,
    If that through Christ appear.

Examine me, and take the part,
    O Lord, so much thine own;
Try out my reins, and prove my heart,
    Which thou canst know alone:

Because thy loving kindness stands
    For ever full in view,
And in the truth of thy commands
    My path I still pursue;

441

I have not for companions chose
· The idle and the vain;
Nor love the neighbourhood of those,
　　Who teach an art to feign.

Where wicked men in parties meet,
　　I have the place abhorr'd;
Nor will I stoop to take a seat
　　With those that hate the Lord.

My hands already wash'd more clean
　　Mine innocence shall make;
And so prepar'd will I be seen
　　Thine eucharist to take.

That with exemplary delight
　　I may my thanks profess,
And raise my voice with all my might
　　Thy wond'rous works to bless;

Lord, I have made thy house my home,
　　And love to keep my post,
Where dwell beneath the hallow'd dome
　　Thine honour and thine host.

Shut not my soul amongst the cries
　　Of Anti-christ's domain,
Nor where they blood and burnings prize
　　Let me my life retain.

Whose hands at all times ready skill'd
　　To deeds of shame subscribe;
And their right hands display'd and fill'd
　　With Mammon's deadly bribe.

But as for me I will proceed
　　To run a virtuous race;

O Jesu Christ, let me be freed
    By mercy from disgrace.

My stedfast foot I firmly fix,
    And will maintain my ground,
And with the congregation mix
    Thy glory to resound.

PSALM XXVII

THE God of Jacob's host
    Is my defence and light,
Why should I quit my post,
    Or shun the day of fight?
Christ Jesus is my strength and aid,
Why, therefore, should I be dismay'd?

When wicked men advanc'd
    Embattel'd troops and bands,
And impious words inhanc'd
    By violence of hands;
The Lord abash'd the pow'rs of hell,
And back they went, and down they fell.

Tho' hostile pow'rs increase,
    Conspiracies to plan
Against my realm and peace,
    I will asert the man;
Tho' war against me be declared,
My faith shall never be impair'd.

I have desired a boon,
    By which I will abide,
With angels to commune,
    And in thy house reside;
With champions in their Saviour bold,
Which now God's beauteous face behold.

For tho' the heathen chafe
    And troublous times predict,
The Lord shall keep me safe
    From these that would afflict;
Yea he shall in his temple seat,
And place upon a rock my feet.

And while my threatners halt,
    That come so big with dread,
My Saviour shall exalt
    The honours of my head,
To baffle the surrounding foes,
Who seek thy servant to depose.

I therefore will devote
    In joyfulness divine,
Instead of ram or goat,
    Myself before thy shrine.
With songs I will thy praises chant,
And in familiar talk descant.

To these my pray'rs attend,
    As in thy house I kneel;
In pity condescend,
    O Lord, to my appeal;
In mercy to my fervent suit
Thy blessed Comforter depute.

The holy spirit proves
    The workings of my breast,
And as its impulse moves,
    My heart is thus addrest.
'Seek ye my face'—resign'd and meek,
Thy face, Lord Jesus, will I seek.

O do not disengage
    From my request thine ear,

Nor in this vicious age,
From David disappear,
Nor cast the servant of thy crust
From his dependence in disgust.

Thou hast from spite and spies
Been still my soul's resource,
And thy benign supplies
Have kept a constant course:
O leave me not—my measure still,
Thou God of my salvation, fill.

When all the ties direct
Of love no longer bind,
When fleshy sires neglect
And mothers prove unkind,
Then God receives me as his ward,
The child and orphan of the Lord.

O train me in the track
Of thine eternal way,
O Lord, and lead me back
From whence I went astray;
Because the traitors over-reach
Thy servant, and his truth impeach.

Surrender not my cause
To prejudice, the hate
Of rebels to thy laws
From virulence innate;
For on my fame they have let loose
False accusation and abuse.

I should have been depriv'd
Of spirits in my need,
But that I strength deriv'd
From this my steadfast creed;

That I shall God's perfections know,
Where life is in eternal flow.

O tarry thou in hope,
        Expecting God's good hour,
And pray for strength to cope
        With every adverse pow'r;
And he, the Comforter, shall bless
Thy soul, which in thy faith possess.

PSALM XXVIII

To thee I pour my wailings out,
O Lord, my strength and my redoubt,
        Nor my petition scorn;
Nor make as tho' thou hearest not,
Lest I be liken'd in my lot,
        To men of hope forlorn.

Hear thou the language of my woe,
When to thy holy shrine I go
        In meekness and in pray'r;
And as I lift my hands on high
Towards thy mercy-seat, reply
        To my confession there.

O pluck me not in wrath away
With godless men, that disobey
        Thy laws so much profest;
Who with their neighbours mildly treat,
But cherish mischief and deceit
        Within a treach'rous breast.

Yet do not thou, O Lord, requite
My foes according to their spite,
        But bless them to repent;

446

Nor give the sinners like for like,
The measure they for others strike,
    And frauds that they invent.

Retaliate not their mighty wrongs,
Nor recompense them as belongs
    To these their works malign;
The wages of their sin remit,
And keep their souls from out the pit,
    Which they for others mine.

Tho' they regard not in their mind,
The works omniscient love design'd,
    And hands almighty skill'd,
Yet may they for their crimes atone,
And all on Christ the corner stone
    In clemency rebuild.

The Lord with adoration hail,
For he has made my pray'r prevail,
    As I from wrath abstain;
And my humility succeeds,
And that request which pity pleads,
    I from his mercy gain.

God is my courage and my shield,
And to his name I have appeal'd,
    And trusted in his aid;
Wherefore my heart with gladness springs,
While to his praise with voice and strings
    The sweet oblation's paid.

God is my fortress and ally,
In whose strong prowess I defy
    The sword and pointed shaft;
And all salvation and defence
Is from him, and for innocence,
    To frustrate force and craft.

O save thy people and enlarge,
The flock of thy peculiar charge
    From all the bonds of sin;
Feed them and in thy pasture place,
And grant them thine especial grace,
    The topmost height to win.

PSALM XXIX

YE men of birth and high renown,
Who, zealous for the heav'nly crown,
    Have gallant deeds atchiev'd,
The Lord with thankfulness adore,
The strength, the praise to him restore,
    From whom ye both receiv'd.

Give to the Lord's most holy name,
The honour which his merits claim,
    In meekness as ye kneel;
With reverence pay your daily vow;
In seemliness and order bow
    With lively faith and zeal.

The word of infinite command,
August, adorable and grand,
    The water-flood controuls;
And in terrific glory breaks
Upon the billows, and he speaks
    The thunder as it rolls.

The voice of God and pow'r are one,
The mandate which he gives is done
    In all the dread profound;
Vast operative strength and skill,
The proclamation of his will,
    Is of majestic sound!

The voice of God in anger drives
The tempest to the mark, and rives
    The cedar-trees in twain,
Yea Lebanon, with all his growth,
Was rifted when the Lord was wroth,
    And strawn along the plain.

The lofty mountains huge and steep,
At voice of his commandment leap
    Like calves upon the sod.
And Libanus and Sirion too
Bound like young unicorns to do
    Obeisance to their God.

The voice of God divides the flakes
Of torrent fire, his mandate shakes
    The wilderness with fear;
Yea Kadesh with his voice he shocks,
And caverns, mountains, woods and rocks
    With dreadful trembling hear.

The voice of God upon the lawn
Descends and causes hinds to fawn,
    The thicket disarrays;
With terror strikes the human race,
Who that tremendous time embrace,
    For publick pray'r and praise.

The Lord in highest heav'n ascends,
The while his stedfast course he bends
    All ocean's depth to ford;
From eastern to the western beam,
The Lord is evermore supream,
    Is evermore ador'd.

The Lord shall make his people strong,
With corn and wine our lives prolong,
    And cloath us with his fleece;

He shall the bonds of sin unloose,
And on our consciences diffuse
    The blessing of his peace.

PSALM XXX

O LORD, I will thy pow'r exalt,
    Which hast advanc'd me far from shame,
And check'd my foes in their assault
    Upon my realm and fame.

O Lord, the God of my belief,
    To thee I sent the plaintive sounds,
And thou wert mov'd to sooth my grief,
    And heal my gaping wounds.

Thou, Lord, hast brought my soul from hell,
    And hast my fault'ring life sustain'd
From those that in the darkness dwell,
    And in the pit are chain'd.

Give praises, O ye blest above,
    And grateful songs to God combine,
For a memorial of his love,
    And sanctity divine.

Wroth but the twinkling of an eye,
    Pleas'd, and his smiles all nature buoy;
A night in heaviness we lie,
    But morning teems with joy.

And in my prosp'rous hour I said,
    My wealth is in a settl'd state;
Thou, Lord, hast of thy goodness made
    Mine eminence so great.

But thou, to curb my growing pride,
   The fost'ring radiance of thy face
Didst in thy just displeasure hide,
   And I was in disgrace.

Then cried I, for I could not brook
   God's dispensations in extreams,
And to the Lord myself betook
   In meekness, as beseems.

Can there emolument arise
   To God or man from out the pit,
When this my body they despise,
   And to the dust commit?

Shall gratitude be mixt with clay,
   And still retain her thankful powr's,
Or shall the man thy truth display,
   Whose tongue the worm devours?

O Lord, attend and hear me out,
   Be merciful, O most ador'd,
And to thy servant, thus devout,
   Thy timely help afford.

Thou'st turn'd my heaviness to mirth,
   And put off all my weeds of woe,
And shalt thy gladness, as a girth,
   About my loins bestow.

Wherefore there is exceeding cause,
   O God, that pray'r should never cease,
And I will praise thee without pause
   In everlasting peace.

PSALM XXXI

In thee, O righteous Lord, I lay
    The ground of all my creed;
Let not confusion disarray
My well form'd thoughts, but as I pray
    My soul unto her safety speed.

From heaven's interior shrine mature,
    Thy favourable aid
Admission there let me procure,
In condescension to the poor,
    When his remonstrances are made.

Be thou my bulwark to defend,
    Like some strong bastion's mole,
That every sense of fear may end,
When on thy succour I depend,
    To shield my body and my soul.

For thou art my munition strong,
    And citadel of might;
Be my companion and my song,
To lead me safe thro' life along,
    And for thy name's sake set me right.

Extract my soul from out the net,
    Which they with secret spleen,
And as each other they abet,
With joint antipathy have set,
    For on thy mighty pow'r I lean.

To thy good keeping I commit
    My spirit, as is due,
For thou shalt of her sins acquit,
And save my soul from out the pit,
    O Lord, thou God supremely true.

I scorn the fools that put their trust
    In superstitious craft;
That worship vanities and lust,
And bow themselves before a bust,
    But to the Lord my sighs I waft.

I will with joy and gladness hail
    Thy charitable care;
Thou'st put my troubles in thy scale,
And made thy mercies countervail,
    My tottering fabrick to repair.

Thou hast not given me up, nor bound
    Within the stranger's hand,
Nor in the streights hast run aground
My vessel, but secure and sound
    Hast brought her to a spacious land.

Lord, let thy beams of mercy shine,
    For terror and distaste,
And every bitter woe is mine;
My eyes to see such objects pine,
    Yea both my flesh and spirit waste.

My life within my veins is cold
    With heaviness and tears,
And I with mourning am grown old,
Ere yet succeeding times have roll'd
    The stated complement of years.

My strength my wasting frame forsakes
    Thro' sin and rank abuse;
Each member with convlsion shakes,
My bones with various pains and aches
    Are robb'd of their nutricious juice.

My name was nam'd as a reproof,
    That neither friend nor foes,

Nor neighbours came beneath my roof,
And my companions kept aloof,
    As other company they chose.

The world have all my deeds forgot,
    And I am in the place
Of one, whose memory is not,
Whose body damps sepulchral rot,
    And like an useless broken vase.

For I have heard the godless crowd
    In blasphemy and strife,
And fear on every side's avow'd,
While fraud and faction are allow'd
    To meet, and scheme against my life.

But thou, Lord, art my corner-stone,
    I put my trust in thee,
And I thine omnipresence own,
O Christ, thou art my God alone,
    To whom I bow the faithful knee.

In thy dispose is every hour
    Of mine allotted time;
Save me from their confed'rate pow'r
Whose bands with steadfast malice show'r
    Their darts, and from rebellion's crime.

Thy lustrous countenance reveal,
    My watchings to reward,
And by thy gracious mercies heal
The cruel agonies I feel,
    Thro' Jesus Christ, our blessed Lord.

O Lord, let no foul shame abash
    The man that pays his vows,

But rather let confusion dash
The wicked, profligate and rash,
    And thus a sense of guilt arouse.

The lying lips, O Lord, refrain,
    That in despite extream,
And cruelty and sour disdain,
First take their Saviour's name in vain,
    Then all his righteous sons blaspheme.

O how abundant is the store
    Thy bounteous love provides
For all that thy commands adore,
Ere yet the course of life is o'er,
    With wealth, and bliss in heav'n besides.

Thou in thy bosom shall protect
    Their souls from kindling ire,
And to their peace have such respect,
That in thine house thou shalt select
    A place for virtue to retire.

With thankful heart and willing mind,
    I will the Lord renown,
Because he has been loving kind,
And to my need a fort assign'd
    Within a strong rodoubted town.

In that precipitate pursuit,
    When I was forc'd to fly,
I said my pray'r has cast its fruit;
The Lord will not my strength recruit,
    Nor watch me with his gracious eye.

Yet not the less thou didst accept
    The voice that I preferr'd;

Thou heardst the cries with which I wept,
And God amidst my doubtings kept
    The purpose of his holy word.

O love the Lord all ye his sons,
    On whom his angels smile;
For God preserves the man that runs
His race with faithfulness, and shuns
    The commerce of the proud and vile.

Be strong and of a manly heart,
    Ye champions of the cause,
And God new courage shall impart,
To parry every sword and dart
    From those that triumph in his laws.

PSALM XXXII

THE man is blest that is asham'd
Of vice, and by the Lord reclaim'd,
    Anew his life begins;
Who by his penitence abides,
Sav'd by that charity that hides
    The multitude of sins.

The man to whom the Lord remits
His foul transgression, and acquits
    Of all his evil ways;
In whose serene ingenuous smile
Is no deception, and no guile
    In that he thinks or says.

When on the ash myself I cast
With sharp remorse for errors past,
    And grief too great to speak;

Upon my pangs my lips were seal'd,
With groanings not to be reveal'd,
 My flesh and bones were weak.

For in the day, and on my bed,
Thy hand lies heavy on my head
 My failings to chastise;
My moisture scarce affords a tear,
Like earth what time the sultry year
 Her bursting bosom dries.

I will acknowledge mine offence,
And wail my forfeit innocence,
 As I thy grace invoke;
The base injustice of my deed
I said, nor with myself agreed
 Its heinous filth to cloak.

I said I will redeem the time,
And to the Lord confess my crime
 In that I have transgress'd;
And Christ, of peerless pow'r to save,
All mine iniquity forgave,
 And my contrition bless'd.

By this the pious shall be warm'd,
And many a righteous vow perform'd
 Where thou art to be found;
But conscious sinners from thy fane
Through overwhelming guilt abstain,
 And fear themselves to sound.

Thy bosom is my soul's retreat,
And there she would herself secrete
 From all this world of woe;
Thou shalt inspire me to prevail,
And songs of gratulation hail
 My triumph as I go.

I will to thee my ways unfold,
And teach thee whence thou shou'dst withhold
 And where thy steps advance;
I thy misdoubtings will decide,
And with mine eye will be thy guide
 From error and mischance.

Be ye not like to horse or mule,
That are not bless'd with reason's rule,
 But restless and untam'd,
Until they're here and there impell'd,
Their mouths with bit and bridle held,
 And feet in trammels fram'd.

A multitude of woes shall wait
Upon the wicked, whose estate
 Is desperate and dread,
But those whom Christ has call'd to grace,
The heavenly mercy-beams embrace,
 And their mild influence shed.

Be glad in God, ye sons of light,
Who think and speak and act aright,
 And you ye sound of heart,
Whom Satan's wiles could ne'er decoy,
In fulness of immortal joy
 Home to your peace depart.

PSALM XXXIII

REJOICE in God, ye saints above
 The wiles and fire of fraud and lust;
For gratitude is fruitful love,
 And well becomes the just.

Praise with the harp the prince of grace,
    Let lutes accord to him that sings,
Adapt the mellow sounding bass
    With ten melodious strings.

Let novelty commend the strain,
    And sing, adoring, as ye kneel,
And swell with all your might and main
    The full resounding peal.

For Christ the word of his command
    Is truth in all its various terms,
And all th' atchievements of his hand
    His faithfulness confirms.

He has his righteousness at heart,
    And love and mercy hold his rod,
And earth abounds in every part
    With goodness and with God.

The firmament and all the host
    Of heav'n by Christ the word were form'd,
And quickning to the Holy Ghost,
    With active heat were warm'd.

In one great magazine compell'd,
    The waters of the main he heaps,
And, as a store by warders held,
    The briny depth he keeps.

Let earth in all her throng'd abodes,
    And ye, where'er your tents are spread,
Ye people, bless in all the modes
    Of reverence and dread.

With him the word and work are one,
    The moulds were made, the forms were cast,

As he commanded it was done,
    And stood for ever fast.

The Lord abolishes the schemes
    And purposes of heathen sects;
The people's murmurs, prince's dreams
    He quashes and rejects.

The councils of the Lord are sure,
    As infinitely just and sage,
And all his precious thoughts endure
    From age to rising age.

Blest are the people and the realm,
    Where Christ is seated on the throne;
For whom their Saviour holds the helm,
    Elected as his own.

The Lord from heav'n's imperial height
    Beholds the sons of men below,
And thence considers their estate
    Of transient wealth or woe.

By him their hearts are fram'd and turn'd,
    By him the vital fountain plays;
He knows whatere is sought or spurn'd
    In all their works and ways.

There is no monarch therefore sav'd,
    Who has to multitudes recourse,
Nor is the stroke of conquest stav'd
    By numbers or by force.

The horses that the spearmen mount,
    When comes the trying hour of need,
Are of small service or account,
    With all their strength and speed.

Lo! God with fatherly concern,
　　Looks down to see what course we steer,
And blesses those that live and learn
　　A godly hope and fear;

Their souls from terror to redeem,
　　And for their cup and social hearth
To raise the blade and fill the stream,
　　Against the hour of dearth.

Our souls by patience we possess,
　　Untill the Lord his angel send;
For he's our helper to redress,
　　Our buckler to defend.

Wherefore our spirits shall revive,
　　Because our special end and aim
Is still to keep our hope alive
　　By his most holy name.

Lord, let thy gracious love diffuse
　　Its influence on our fervent vows,
Like as our faith all doubt subdues,
　　And we thy cause espouse.

PSALM XXXIV

UNCEASING thanks, as thus I kneel,
　　I will to God return;
And still with eager lips reveal
Th' internal gratitude I feel,
　　And zeal to praise with which I burn.

With confidence in Jesus placed,
　　My soul herself shall plume;

The poor and by the world disgrac'd,
And those that have themselves abas'd,
    Shall hear, and joyfulness assume.

O take the blessed theme of praise
    Our spirits to expand;
And let us our conceptions raise,
God's glorious name together blaze,
    And faithful worship hand in hand.

The Lord my Saviour I besought,
    And he was quickly found,
And in his arms of mercy caught
My spirit, and to safety brought
    From every terror, every wound.

Illumination beams on all
    That to the Lord aspire;
And, when they to the godhead call,
Nought can abash them, or appal
    In such a duty and desire.

Lo! the poor suff'rers importune
    Their Saviour to attend,
And mercy gives them audience soon,
With speed accomplishes their boon,
    And to their troubles puts an end.

The Lord his ever-blessed dove
    Keeps hov'ring with her wings
For all that cherish fearful love,
And buoy their spirits up above
    The peril of all earthly things.

O hear the summons—'Come and see'
    And God's free grace receive;

Exalted to the first degree,
And of eternal worth is he,
   Who stands determin'd to believe.

O to the Lord your God adhere,
   Ye saints, in trembling dread;
For they which his decrees revere,
And nourish reverence by fear
   Are in all exigencies sped.

The lions in the forest roar,
   And hunger as they quest;
But heroes in the Lord, that soar
To heav'n, and there his face explore,
   Shall have no want of what is best.

Come little children and imbibe
   The nurture of my speech;
And I will list you of my tribe,
God's fear within your heart inscribe,
   And early your Redeemer preach.

What man is he that would prolong
   His pilgrimage on earth,
And live in lusty health and strong,
To see each day the theme of song
   And full of melody and mirth.

O'er all thy craving members reign
   Lest they thy soul defile;
Thy tongue with diligence restrain,
And thine unguarded lips contain
   From idle words and active guile.

All evil thoughts and speech avoid,
   And in the Christian race
Be with perpetual good employ'd,

Seek peace, nor ever be decoy'd
    With ought that leads you from the chace.

The Lord his omnipresent eyes
    From highest heavens ascent,
The good and righteous supervise,
He hears their pray'rs as they arise
    Towards his throne with ears intent.

God cannot countenance the deeds
    Of them that act amiss,
But from their commerce he recedes,
Until their Saviour's merit pleads
    To reinstate their souls in bliss.

Whene'er the righteous make complaint,
    From heav'n attention stoops;
God has respect unto his saint
The more when he thro' grief is faint,
    And wholly saves him ere he droops.

Christ is the neighbour of the meek,
    Whose nature is renew'd,
And those that by contrition seek,
And with their tears his love bespeak,
    He will within his fold include.

The crosses of the Lord's elect
    Are grievous here below;
But God gives all his pray'rs effect,
And shall his ministers direct
    To snatch him out of all his woe.

He keeps his bones and all intire
    From fracture and mischance,
So that his foes, when set on fire
Of hell, they cruelly conspire,
    Can only pierce him with a lance.

But mischief from the pit pursues
    The wicked as they tread;
And who the grace of God refuse,
Their way from every virtue lose,
    To death and desolation led.

The Lord his meritorious cross
    Shall ransom all our souls,
And purify our filthy dross,
And they shall not be at a loss,
    Whose faith he in his book enrolls.

PSALM XXXV

O my God, my cause espousing,
    From mine enemies protect;
On my side thy might arousing,
    Let their insolence be checkt.

Take the weapon of the spirit
    Faith's invulnerable shield,
Rear the standard of thy merit,
    And assist me in the field.

Couch thy spear, and stand to parry
    Every lance opposers send;
Say thy suit shall not miscarry,
    I thy Saviour am thy friend.

Let their efforts be diverted,
    Hunting souls and finding shame,
And their schemes be disconcerted,
    Which at me direct their aim.

To the wind the dust condenses,
    Settles when the skies are clear;

Thus let them and their offences
    At thy bidding disappear.

To the thorny way, that narrows
    Into final comfort, lead;
And let vengeance sheathe its arrows,
    As they on their travel speed;

That no more, by dark combining,
    They their secret nets may lay;
Nor by falshood undermining,
    Me without a cause betray.

Let no violent perdition
    Come upon them unaware;
Let them scape by true contrition
    Every terror, every snare.

And my soul with exultation,
    Shall the Lord in truth profess;
And rejoice in his salvation,
    Who delights to bear and bless.

All my frame shall sing in rapture,
    Who, like God, shall things adjust,
When the poor is made the capture
    Of the man of lawless lust?

By false witnesses convicted
    That against me were suborn'd,
I was punish'd and afflicted
    For the very things I scorn'd.

For good offices, ungrateful,
    They could evil things return,
In despite of kindness hateful
    To my sorrowing soul's concern.

Yet when they were sick and ailing,
    I was clad in weeds of woe;
But my service unavailing,
    Shall into my bosom flow.

I behav'd as for a brother,
    Or a dear familiar friend,
As one mourning for his mother
    Just approaching to her end.

But in my distress they jested,
    Yea the very abjects met,
Making mouths, my peace infested
    Without ceasing or regret.

Fawning gluttons, in conjunction
    With the mimicking buffoon,
Gnash their teeth without compunction,
    And my miseries importune.

How long will my Saviour leave me
    To the mercy of such men;
O from lions fierce reprieve me,
    And my darling from the den.

So with thanks thy Godhead greeting,
    In thy church I will adore;
And frequent the gen'ral meeting,
    There my praises to restore.

O! let not my foes exulting,
    In defiance of thy laws,
And with nods and winks insulting,
    Bear me down without a cause.

For the scope of their communing
    Is not insolence to curb;

But their tongue with treach'ry tuning,
    They the publick peace disturb.

With distended mows censorious,
    Every rank offender cries,
Fie upon thy crimes notorious,
    We have seen them with our eyes.

All their impudent behaviour,
    Thou, O God, from heav'n hast view'd;
Be not silent, O my Saviour,
    Nor my just complaint exclude.

Rise, O Lord my God, attending
    To the drift of this dispute,
And my righteous cause defending,
    All mine enemies refute.

Judge me, O my God, to spare me,
    As thy mercy is for all;
Let not clamour overbear me,
    Nor exult upon my fall.

'All that we surmise has follow'd,'
    Let them not with triumph boast,
'His remains the gulph has swallowed,
    He has given up the ghost.'

Make them blush with shame ingenuous,
    Which at my distress rejoice;
Who against the truth are strenuous,
    Give them grace to hear her voice.

Let them say, which like the measure,
    That in charity I deal;
Blessed be the Lord, whose pleasure
    Is his servant's bliss to seal.

As for me in heavenly phrases
    I will harmonize my tongue,
Day by day Jehovah's praises
    Shall in sweeter notes be sung.

PSALM XXXVI

My heart within me is advis'd,
    And but too sure conviction finds,
How little God is fear'd or priz'd
    By men of worldly minds.

For they 're self-flatterers to the last,
    And supple servants of the times,
Till that, which sets them most aghast,
    Detection blaze their crimes.

Their words are foolish and unfair
    And full of falsehood and deceit;
Each act of wisdom they forbear,
    With all that's good and meet.

They mischief on their couches plan,
    The broader way of ruin chuse,
Nor that, whose touch defiles a man,
    Do they at all refuse.

Thy mercy to thy people's faults
    Thou hast in highest heav'n avow'd;
Thy faithfulness itself exalts
    Beyond the topmost cloud.

Thy truth's like mountains strong and steep,
    Which stand with rock-work for their
        ground,
And all thy judgments dreadful deep
    Are like the vast profound!

Thou, Lord, shalt save both man and beast,
    O how transcendent is thy grace:
Beneath thy wings from first to least
    All flesh themselves shall place.

They from thy stores replenish'd still
    Shall in thy spacious dome be fed;
And of thy·pleasures take their fill
    As from the fountain-head.

For in the holiest height with Thee
    In heav'n is life's perennial well,
Light in thy light we there shall see,
    And thence irradiate dwell.

O! with thy charity regal'd
    Let them that know Thee still remain,
And let thy mercy be intail'd
    Upon the good in grain.

O save me from the spurning heel
    Of those, that with proud aspect frown,
Nor let his blow the ruffian deal
    To cast thy servant down.

There are they founder'd in the flood
    Such as were wicked for reward,
For there's no hope, save in the blood
    Of Jesus Christ our Lord.

PSALM XXXVII

FRET not thy self to find
    How wicked worldlings thrive,
    Nor with the hoards they hive
Bear thou an envious mind.

For soon they shall decay,
    And be cut down like grass,
    With all that they amass,
And fare like rotten hay.

But thou in God confide,
    And deal with bounteous hand
    The product of the land,
And thou shalt be supply'd.

Delight thou in the Lord,
    And so thou shalt acquire
    Thy soul's supream desire,
Thy virtue to reward.

Thy way to God commend,
    In him repose thy trust,
    Which all things shall adjust
To crown a blissful end.

He shall thy truth redeem
    To make it clear as light,
    And thy just dealing bright,
As is the noon-day beam.

Be still; with patience wait:
    But grieve not at the course
    Of those whom fraud and force
Have made ungodly great.

Leave off ere you begin
    From rage and discontent;
    If thou thyself torment
Thou shalt be mov'd to sin,

The wicked branch and root
    Shall be from earth remov'd;

But men in patience prov'd
Shall bear and gather fruit.

But yet a little space
   And guilt shall have its due,
   You shall the men pursue
And hardly find their place.

But men resign'd and meek
   Such shall possess the earth,
   And in their second birth
The prince of Salem seek.

Disguise against the truth
   For matter is in quest,
   To rail the wise and blest,
And gnash with angry tooth.

The Lord with high disdain
   Shall scoff at all they lease;
   For he from heav'n foresees
The doom of the profane.

The wicked man is fierce,
   Drawn swords and bended bows
   To slay the poor, and those
Which with their God converse.

The prince of peace and light
   Shall parry every sword,
   When all things are restor'd,
And break the darts of spite.

The pittance of the good
   Is better than the wealth
   That comes by fraud and stealth,
When rightly understood.

For men in sin grown bold
   Christ Jesus shall reduce,
   And for a blessed use
The righteous man uphold.

The righteous Lord approves
   The godly all their days,
   And for eternal praise
To endless joy removes.

Such shall no foe confound;
   But in the day of dread
   To peace they shall be sped,
And e'en in dearth abound.

But vengeance shall consume
   The sinners and self-will'd;
   Yea tho' the LAMB was kill'd
To stave their day of doom.

When bad men run in debt
   At payment they repine;
   The gen'rous and benign
A better pattern set.

The men of virtuous fame
   God's Canaan shall possess;
   But such as will not bless,
Shall be expell'd with shame.

The Lord himself directs
   The righteous in the road,
   And to his own abode
His pilgramage protects.

Though in the way they err,
   They shall not lose their all:

473

The lost shall God recall
And to his fold refer.

Youth was, and age is come;
    I never saw the race
    Of virtue in disgrace,
Or begging for a crumb.

The righteous is humane
    And ever lends to need,
    And his unnumber'd seed
Are blest and good in grain.

All evil acts avoid,
    Persist in doing well,
    So shalt thou surely dwell,
And be in heav'n employ'd.

God to the truth is love,
    Nor e'er the good forsakes,
    But him and his he takes
Up to the bliss above.

The wicked shall be scourg'd—
    But yet his helpless seed
    Their Saviour Christ may plead,
By due contrition purg'd.

The righteous are the heirs
    For whom the Lord provides,
    And all their stock resides
'Midst ceaseless hymns and pray'rs.

The righteous man's discourse
    In wisdom is ad·is'd,
    In judgment exercis'd,
Whose words the truth inforce.

The word is in his heart,
  And on his faithful lip;
  His footstep shall not slip,
Nor from God's way depart.

The wicked sees the joy
  Attending God's free laws,
  And grudging seeks a cause
Th' observer to destroy.

The Lord will not expose
  His servants to the chair
  Of judges so unfair,
Nor with their sentence close.

Hope—and the Lord adore,
  And thee he shall promote,
  And to those realms devote,
Where sin shall be no more.

I with these eyes have seen
  The proud his pow'r display,
  And flourish, like the bay,
So goodly and so green.

I went again to view
  His wretched flatt'rers fawn;
  But lo! the man was gone,
His place was made anew.

Thine innocence hold fast,
  Beware of craft and guile,
  And dying thou shall smile,
That there is peace at last.

But those that still transgress,
  And all the sons of scorn,

Their hope is but forlorn,
To those that bear and bless.

Salvation of the soul
    Is from the Lord of pow'r,
    Which in his adverse hour
Can make the sufferer whole.

The good shall Christ assist,
    And save them from the paws
    Of rav'nous wolves—because
They in his band inlist.

PSALM XXXVIII

LORD, rebuke me not, nor hasten
    In thine ire my day of doom;
Nor in hot resentment chasten
    Him whom pain and grief consume.

For thy poignant arrows thicken,
    And come piercing on my pores;
By thine angel am I stricken
    With innumerable sores.

For my sin and thy displeasure
    All my flesh with anguish groans,
And tormented out of measure,
    There's no quiet in my bones.

For my wickedness excessive,
    Now come down upon my head,
Is a burden too oppressive
    For a sinner in his bed.

For my running wounds are fetid,
   And the filth inhances pain,
Thro' my follies oft regretted,
   And as often play'd again.

Bent and broke with toilsome sorrow
   I am in such evil plight;
From each evening to the morrow
   I go mourning day and night.

For my loins are all infected
   With a noxious plague diseas'd,
Not a single part protected
   Which the poison has not seiz'd.

Weak with this thy visitation,
   And inflamed in every part,
I have roar'd in rank vexation,
   And disquietude of heart.

Lord, thou knowest all the merit,
   And extent of my appeal;
And the groanings of my spirit
   I cannot from Thee conceal.

Strength is gone, and throbbing pulses
   Shake my heart strings with dismay,
And the pain my sight convulses
   That I cannot bear the day.

There is none to give assistance,
   Friends and neighbours stand and look;
And my kinsmen keep their distance,
   Nor can my misfortunes brook.

This was deem'd a lucky season
   For my foes to lay their snares;

And they went about with treason
   Breaking bounds and sowing tares.

As for me, with inattention
   I was deaf to what they said,
Like the dumb, by whom no mention
   Of his miseries is made.

       •

I became as one astonish'd
   Who to nothing gives his heed;
And whose foes are not admonish'd
   From their purpose to recede.

For in Thee, O Lord, confiding
   I with meekness kiss the rod;
Thou shalt plead for my back-sliding,
   O my Saviour, O my God.

I have made my soul's petition
   That my foes no more should swell,
For well pleas'd with my condition,
   They exulted when I fell.

And, in truth, I am surrounded
   As the plagues come on apace,
And mine aching sight is wounded
   While they stare me in the face.

For with penitent confession
   I my worship will begin;
And acknowledge my transgression,
   And be sorry for my sin.

But mine enemies surviving
   Their own malice are in pow'r,
Hatred from no cause deriving,
   Grow more num'rous every hour.

Those increase my persecution
  Who for good the worst return,
To dismay my resolution
  As with zeal for God I burn.

Let me, Lord, at this incursion
  Of my foes thy succour prove;
Nor in anger or aversion
  From thy supplicant remove.

O thou God of all perfection,
  As my plaintive psalm I make,
From all terror and dejection
  Speed me for thy mercy's sake.

PSALM XXXIX

With severest circumspection
  I will guard my ways, I said,
Lest at any time objection
  To my converse should be made.

And my mouth as with a bridle
  I will carefully restrain,
While the reprobate and idle
  In my wearied sight remain.

With such rigour of suppression
  Was I mute, that I forbore
Ev'n from words of good discretion,
  But I was afflicted sore.

As I ponder'd with vexation,
  My sad heart within me burn'd
Till it caused an inflammation,
  When my wonted speech return'd.

Lord, by thy divine monition
    Let me calculate my days,
That their length and their condition
    May have influence on my ways.

Lo! a span is the dimension
    Of my life, and all my reign
Is not worthy thine attention—
    Surely every man is vain.

For in vain himself aggrieving
    'Tis a shadow man pursues,
Gathering riches, nor conceiving
    Who the hoarded heap shall use.

Where is therefore my affiance,
    To what shelter shall I flee?
Truly, Lord, my sole reliance
    And my hope is placed in Thee.

With thy hand of mercy lenient
    Heal me, where my conscience wounds;
Stop the jesting inconvenient,
    Which from thence the scoffer grounds.

I was of my speech divested,
    And no more my lips could move,
For thy pow'r is uncontested,
    When thou wouldst our patience prove.

Cease the stripes of thy displeasure,
    Which I can no longer stand;
I am wasted out of measure
    By thy strict afflicting hand.

Thy severe compunctions goading,
    All our beauties fade and wane,

As the wool by moths corroding;
    Surely every man is vain.

Hear my prayer, O Lord, as falling
    On my face to thee I cry,
Let thine ears attend my calling,
    And to these my tears reply.

For with Thee I am a stranger,
    And a pilgrim's lot I share;
Train'd in hardship and in danger,
    Ev'n as all my fathers were.

For a little space O spare me,
    And my strength a while restore,
Ere thy final sentence bear me
    To be seen on earth no more.

PSALM XL

I TARRIED in the house of pray'r
    To patient hope resign'd;
And God in his paternal care
    To hear my voice inclin'd.

He saved me likewise from the shock
    Of terror and dismay,
And set my feet upon a rock
    To regulate my way.

Such mercies in my mouth inspire
    A song of new delight,
A lesson for th' Hebrean lyre,
    And grateful to recite.

This blessed change beyond their thought
    The multitude shall see,
And put their trust in God that wrought
    This miracle in me.

Blest is the man in God assur'd
    Who has not turn'd his side
To him that has the tale procur'd,
    Or him that hears in pride.

O Lord my God, thy works are plan'd
    How marvellous and great,
Thy careful love and bounteous hand
    What praises shall relate?

If I should set about the task
    Their numbers to recount,
It would such shining talents ask
    As my mean pow'rs surmount.

Fat lambs and firstlings of the year
    Are better fed than slain;
For thou preferst a duteous ear
    To what thy laws contain.

No more the flocks and herds shall die
    For sinners to atone—
Then lo! I come—I come—said I
    To give myself alone.

O God, 'tis written in thy book
    That I should do thy will,
I from my heart have all forsook
    That scripture to fulfill.

Thy righteousness I have declar'd
    Before th' assembled tribes;

O Lord, thou know'st I have not spar'd
    In that thy word prescribes.

I have not been reserv'd to balk
    Thy holy word and ways;
But all the tenour of my talk
    Was how their light might blaze.

I have not hid thy loving grace
    And thine establish'd truth,
But shewn them to the genuine race
    Of Boaz and of Ruth;

God of mine ancestors and arms,
    Do not that truth withhold;
Preserve me in that love, which charms
    Reluctance to thy fold.

Woes multitudinous surround,
    My grief my spirit wears;
My sins my conscious heart confound,
    Out-numbring ev'n my hairs.

O Lord, in thy good pity please
    Thy servant to restore;
And with thy speedy succour ease
    The hardships I deplore.

Give them, O Lord, the sense of shame
    Who seek my soul's distress,
And those with sharp remorse reclaim
    That wish me no success.

Let self-conviction be their lot
    Join'd with the contrite sigh,
Who thus their poison'd bolts have shot,
    'O fie, upon thee, fie!'

Let them rejoice whose final scope
    Is placed in Christ their king,
And all the sons of love and hope
    Their hallelujah sing.

As for my share of all this earth
    It is but mean and poor,
And yet the Lord esteems me worth
    A substance to endure.

Thou art my help, my Saviour thou,
    Of all my goods the sum;
O tarry not, but now, ev'n now,
    O come, Lord Jesus, come.

PSALM XLI

Tune of old xxv

THE bounteous man is blest
    Who feels for want and woe;
The Lord shall save him when opprest,
    And to his need bestow.

The Lord preserve his health,
    And keep him long alive;
Nor open violence nor stealth
    His goodly lot deprive.

The Lord his spirit sooth
    When pain his patience tries—
Yea Christ his bed of sickness smooth
    As languishing he lies.

My state of death reprieve,
    Thou gracious Lord, I said,

O heal and yet again receive,
    For I have err'd and stray'd.

Mine enemies belye
    My fame, and marr my peace,
Enquiring when shall David die
    And his memorial cease?

And if they come or send
    In their officious hate,
Vain talk and false conceits they vend
    To misreport my state.

My foes together swarm,
    And whisp'ring undermine;
For me this evil wish they form,
    This cruelty design.

'The doom of guilt in pain
    Betide his parting breath,
Nor ever let him rise again
    From his untimely death.'

Yea ev'n the man I chose,
    On whom my soul relied,
My daily guest has join'd my foes
    To trample and deride.

But let their rage excite
    Thy mercy, Lord, the more,
And that I may their hate requite
    With love, my strength restore.

By this I rest assur'd
    That I have favour found,
Because thou hast my coast secur'd
    From all the force around.

My health when I am well
    Is from thy bounteous hands,
And thou shalt take my soul to dwell
    Where now my angel stands.

Bless Christ the health of souls,
    And Israel's gracious Lord,
While in immense eternal rolls,
    Let heav'n and earth accord.

PSALM XLII

LIKE as the hart desires the brook
    In summer heat's extream degree,
With panting breast and wishful look,
    So longs my soul for Thee!

O God—my spirit is athirst
    For God in whom we live and move;
When in God's church shall I be first
    My piety to prove?

My tears have been my constant food,
    Which day and night my griefs supply,
While with malevolence renew'd
    Where is thy God, they cry?

Now when I think thereon I shed
    By stealth the show'rs of inward care;
For I before was wont to head
    These multitudes to pray'r.

All in one voice of that delight
    Which from the great thanksgiving flows,
As youths and maids, a goodly sight,
    The festive wreathe compose.

Why do I drag this loathsome load,
   Whence, O my soul, art thou opprest;
And what are these the stings, that goad,
   And wound my tortur'd breast?

O trust in God his pow'r to save
   The cup of thankfulness fulfill,
He keeps thy head above the wave,
   And is thy Saviour still.

O God, internal griefs assail,
   I therefore will direct my thought
To Hermon's hill and Jordan's vale,
   Where thou such wonders wrought.

One sea unto another calls,
   As to the whistling winds they swell;
But at thy word the tempest falls,
   And I am safe and well.

The Lord is good and loving-kind
   Through all the service of the day,
And him which made me man and mind
   By night I sing and pray.

I will inquire of God my strength
   Why hast thou left me thus to go
With such a load and such a length
   Of life in war and woe?

My bones are smitten to the quick
   As with the falchion's keener blade,
While at my face the cowards kick,
   And my distress upraid.

To wit while reprobates intrude
   My soul's deliv'rer to deny,

And with malevolence renew'd
  Where is thy God, they cry?

Why do I drag this loathsome load,
  Whence, O my soul, art thou opprest,
And what are these the stings, that goad,
  And wound my tortur'd breast?

O put thy trust in God again
  The cup of thankfulness fulfill;
He shall thy countenance sustain,
  And is thy Saviour still.

PSALM XLIII

O GOD, give sentence on my side,
  And patronize my righteous cause
Against the sons of sin and pride
  That violate thy laws.

For 'tis thy love which makes me strong,
  Why dost thou then my soul divorce
To drag this load of life along
  Beneath oppressive force?

O issue forth thy radiant beam,
  Thy truth O give me to pursue;
Thy holy hill, thy living stream,
  Thy temple let me view!

O God my God, that I may go
  With joy and gladness to my pray'rs,
And touch, while thankful accents flow,
  The harp's divinest airs!

Why do I drag this loathsome load,
  Whence, O my soul, art thou opprest,
And what are these the stings, that goad,
  And wound my tortur'd breast?

O put thy trust in God again,
  The cup of thankfulness fulfill,
He shall thy countenance sustain,
  And is thy Saviour still.

PSALM XLIV

O God, our ancestors have told
  Of thy stupendous fame,
What deeds thou didst of old,
  And we have seen the same.

For thou didst Canaanites expell,
  And planted Jacob's race;
And how the heathen fell,
  Or fled before thy face.

For they gat Canaan to possess,
  By prowess not their own,
Nor could maintain success
  By human force alone.

But thy right hand their sword renown'd,
  And smiles benignly bright;
As they acceptance found
  And favour in thy sight.

Almighty God, thou art my king,
  To my redemption speed;
Give strength to David's sling,
  And succour Jacob's seed.

Through Thee we soon shall overturn
    Our foes and their allies,
And in thy name shall spurn
    Their armies as they rise.

For when th' assailants give the word
    I will not trust my bow,
Nor vaunt the sword I gird,
    Or glitt'ring spear I throw.

But 'tis that all-sufficient might
    Of GOD THE GOOD AND GREAT
Saves us, and puts to flight
    The sons of sin and hate.

In praising God we make the most
    Of every lengthned day,
And will for ever boast
    The name, to which we pray.

But now thy glory is remote
    From our embattl'd bands;
And headless ranks denote
    The weakness of our hands.

Thou mak'st our standard to give back,
    Nor front the brave dispute;
So that our foes attack,
    And take our goods to boot.

Like younglings to the glutton's tooth
    We're giv'n to be devour'd;
And midst the foes of truth
    Are scatter'd and o'erpow'r'd.

Thine own free men are sold and bought
    And from their homes estrang'd,

Nor is there profit brought,
    Or purchase money chang'd.

Each neighbour licens'd to contest
    Our bounds, his venom spurts,
And we are made the jest
    Of those that haunt our skirts.

We are a laughing-stock become,
    And hear our ill report
From heathen dregs and scum,
    That shake their heads in sport.

Day after day I am confus'd
    While wretches taunt and hiss,
And blush to be abus'd
    At such a shame as this,

And for the voice of them that bear
    False witness and blaspheme,
For foes unus'd to spare,
    And thirst of blood extream.

And tho' thy people are beset
    With woes they cannot stave;
Yet do we not forget
    Thy laws, or misbehave.

Our hearty purpose was not shook
    But to thy truth has stood,
Nor have our steps forsook
    The narrow way to good.

No, not when wrath was ripe to tread
    Our souls where dragons hide,
And darkness overspread
    Where death and night reside.

If we thy truth have disbeliev'd
  Or gone to idol fanes,
God cannot be deceiv'd,
  Which tries the heart and reins.

For we die daily for thy sake,
  And our precarious life
Is every hour at stake,
  Like fatlings for the knife.

Up, Lord, in our behalf arise,
  Thy mercy-beams disclose,
And when thy saint applies,
  No more indulge repose.

Why dost thou hide thee, and neglect
  Our perils to confront,
And will not recollect
  Our wretchedness and want?

For to the ground our spirits fall,
  And rancle with disgust,
And on our hands we crawl
  With bowels in the dust.

Arise, O Lord, and help us now
  Thy honour is at stake:
Save us and hear our vow,
  And that for Christ his sake.

PSALM XLV

EXALTED by a blessed thought
  My soul is on the wing;
I speak, as in the spirit taught,
  The praise of Christ my king.

492

My lips are eager and delight
    Glad tidings to impart,
As is the pen of them that write
    With equal ease and art.

Thy form is fairer than the race
    Of men from Adam sprung;
And God has giv'n eternal grace
    To thy persuasive tongue.

Thy sword's effulgent lightning sheathe
    On thy redoubted thigh;
And crown'd with fame and merit breathe
    The peace of God Most High.

God thy thrice-honour'd mission speed,
    In love and meekness ride
To do the right thy word decreed,
    And truth shall be thy guide.

Sharp is the voice of thy reproof
    When sin thy spirit grieves,
Ev'n underneath the sacred roof
    Amidst the trading thieves.

Thy seat, Lord Jesus, shall remain,
    And endless pow'r is thine;
The sceptre of thy heav'nly reign
    Is rectitude divine.

Thy truth all falsehood disallows,
    Whence God, thy God profest,
His oil has gladden'd for thy brows,
    Above thy fellows blest.

Thy garments of rich cassia smell,
    Of aloes and of myrrh,

From iv'ry rooms, where psalmists dwell
    And joyful pray'rs prefer.

The dames of honour not a few
    Are in thy train enroll'd;
The seat upon thy right stall shew
    Thy spouse in flow'rs and gold.

Consider, daughter, and attend—
    Forget thy carnal sire,
The wealthy pomp, the worldly friend,
    And every mean desire.

Thus shall the prince of peace have joy
    In beauty so supreme;
Thy service and thy song employ
    In Christ thy God and theme.

The daughter of the Tyrian port
    Shall bring her gifts to thee;
The rich of nations pay their court,
    And supplicate the knee.

The bride of Jesus Christ is great
    In glories of the soul,
Of regal gold a precious weight
    Adorns her flowing stole.

Before her Saviour shall she stand
    In needle-work array'd,
And those wise virgins of her band
    With blazing lamps display'd.

In joy and gladness not to cease
    They shall be led along
To Christ the palace of his peace,
    The house of pray'r and song.

Of no terrestial father born,
    Thy servants are thine heirs,
Whom thou shalt leave the world to warn
    By preaching and by pray'rs.

I will thy holy name adore
    As I such hope presage;
Thy saints shall bless thee more and more
    In every world and age.

PSALM XLVI

GOD is our hope, the mighty pow'r,
    From whence the host its strength derives
A present succour in the hour
    Whene'er the battle strives:

We shall not therefore be dismay'd
    Though earth repeated shocks sustain,
And though the hill should be convey'd
    To range the midmost main.

And tho' the billows swell and roar
    And their tremendous tumult make,
Till mountains distant from the shore
    The turbulence partake;

The rivers which the floods supply
    Shall run with sweet composure down
To glad the fort of God most high,
    The place of blest renown.

God in the citadel resides
    Where Zion her strong tow'r sublimes;
He shall assist her in the tides
    Of wealth and woe betimes.

The heathen rages and revolts,
    Whole realms have strange commotions felt;
But God his glorious voice exalts,
    And earth herself shall melt.

The Lord of hosts is with our cause,
    By him are Jacob's legions led,
And Michael with a million draws
    His weapon at our head.

O come ye hither and survey
    Where God his thunderbolts has hurl'd,
With what destruction and dismay
    He hath convuls'd the world.

All tumults at his mandates cease,
    He breaks the bow, the spear he mars,
And to the triumph of his peace
    He burns th' embattl'd cars.

Be still and know the voice divine,
    For exaltation is my due,
And exaltation shall be mine
    O'er Gentile and o'er Jew.

The Lord of hosts is with our cause,
    By him are Jacob's legions led,
And Michael with a million draws
    His weapon at our head.

PSALM XLVII

O JOIN your hands with loud applause,
Ye people, and the common cause
    Of Christian zeal attend:

In voice and spirit sing and shout,
By hearty melody devout,
    And hymns to God ascend.

For a tremendous God is ours,
Most high, most holy, and the pow'rs,
    The majesty, the might,
And all things glorious, all things great
In empire are subordinate,
    And bow to him of right.

The people from his grace remov'd
Shall in our converse be improv'd,
    And to his altars speed;
The Gentiles thus shall he subdue,
And all the runagates renew
    In Abraham's chosen seed.

For his lov'd tribes he shall select
A better country, and direct
    Our travel to his throne;
And Jacob's glory, Jacob's care,
Which is in gratitude and pray'r,
    Shall reckon to his own.

Christ is gone up, the king of kings,
And joyful acclamation rings,
    As thankless earth he spurns;
The marshall'd cherubs stand in rows,
From inmost heav'n the trumpet blows
    While God from death returns.

In Christ your God the song commence,
Which said 'arise let us go hence',
    By flights of lively praise;
To Christ your king in grateful strain
Raise pealing anthems, and again
    The pealing anthems raise.

By God supream all earth is sway'd,
By him administer'd and made,
    Let us perform our part,
Sing vying for th' immortal prize
In high-wrought verse and heed full wise,
    Like masters of your art.

The heathen also he controuls,
In whose obnubilated souls
    His image is effac'd;
God sits upon his throne to bless,
His throne by purest holiness
    And boundless mercy plac'd.

Each rebel Jew the church rejoins,
And every prince from Abraham's loins
    Again his fruit shall yield;
For God, whose exaltation soars
O'er heav'n, and whom all earth adores,
    Shall be himself our shield.

PSALM XLVIII

GREAT is the Lord in every clime,
And worthy of the strain sublime
    Which echoes to his throne;
But chiefest in his holy hill,
In his own city, where his will
    And word are fully known.

Mount Zion! she is passing fair,
Whose noble piles and purest air,
    And stately palms invite;
Salem is on the northern wing,
The city of th' almighty king,
    And all the world's delight.

The sojourner that seeks to God,
And they that flee the tyrant's rod,
    Arrive from every shore;
For known is that benign command
Which blesses every lib'ral hand,
    And hospitable door.

Behold! the kings and their allies
Came to Jerusalem, like spies,
    Our treasures to survey;
They saw our glory with remorse,
And with their vast united force
    The monarchs went their way.

The walls they measured in their mind,
And view'd those ramparts they design'd
    To brave and circumvent;
But troubl'd at the tow'rs in spite
Of malice, multitudes and might,
    They fled with discontent.

For fear took hold upon them there,
And anguish working on despair
    Confounded man and steed;
Such are the terror and the cries
Of some base harlot when she dies
    Of an abortive seed.

The vessels of enormous rate
Conducted o'er their armed freight
    From Tarshish faithless coasts;
He sent upon them, hulk and mast,
The spirit of the eastern blast,
    And overwhelm'd their boasts.

As we have heard it with our ears,
So now thy loving care appears
    Within these sacred walls,

Which thou the God of arms hast made;
He shall be present to their aid
   Whene'er his people calls.

O God, the tribes of thine elect
In trembling fearfulness expect
   Beneath thine hallow'd roof,
Until the word of thy good will
Descend our wishes to fulfill,
   And keep our wants aloof.

O God, thy praise and endless fame
Is as that universal name
   To which all flesh appeals;
By thee remotest earth is bless'd,
And daily bounties heap'd and press'd
   For all thy justice deals.

Let Zion dedicate the day
To mirth, and let the streamers play
   From every goodly spire;
Th' almighty judge is on our side,
And let Judea's blooming pride
   In joy themselves attire.

March out from Zion, walk the rounds,
And measure all her utmost bounds,
   Survey her fort by fort;
Her tow'rs their altitude and strength,
Her villages their breadth and length,
   And make a true report.

The ramparts and the moat review—
The palaces—with caution due
   Apply the reed and line—
Deliver what the Lord has done,
And safely now from sire to son
   The property consign.

For this our Saviour from the rage
Of tyrants is in every age
    Our succour and defence;
Christ o'er his people shall preside,
Christ e'en to death shall be our guide,
    And shall redeem us thence.

PSALM XLIX

O YE people, hear and ponder
    In your ears and in your mind,
All that dwell in homes or wander
    Thro' the world of human kind.

You of high or low gradation
    To my words alike attend,
Men as well of wealth and station
    As the poor without a friend.

I will speak of things essential
    To the folk that would be wise,
And with words and thoughts prudential
    Heart and mouth I will advise.

My harmonius ear inclining
    To the great mysterious verse,
And with harp and hand divining,
    I will oracles rehearse.

Wherefore in these times flagitious
    Should I my good courage lose,
When with practices pernicious
    Guile prepares my heel to bruise?

Some there are that have affiance
    In the goods they get by stealth,

And grow proud by vain reliance
  On the rust of worldly wealth.

But for brotherly affection,
  That in pride and pomp is lost;
Could they buy the Lord's protection,
  They would scruple of the cost.

Deeds of charity and kindness,
  Which would tend their souls to save,
They thro' vice and carnal blindness
  Must relinquish to the grave.

Yea and that tho' God has lengthn'd
  The duration of their years,
And their fleshly veil has strengthn'd
  From the dread sepulchral fears.

For they see the gen'ral sentence,
  Fools and wise together die,
And the rich in late repentance
  With their hoards an heir supply.

Yet they think that their succession
  Shall not be extinct at all;
And the places at discretion
  After their own names they call.

Yet is man from his beginning
  Weak, nor honour long retains,
And degrades himself by sinning
  To the brutes o'er which he reigns.

Thus it is with self-deceivers,
  Fools which heav'nly hope defeat,
And a race of unbelievers
  Praise and practise the deceit.

Such like rotten sheep infected
   Worms their beauty shall devour,
And o'er them the saints elected
   In eternal peace shall tow'r.

But from out the dreary mansion
   God my spirit hath set free,
Height sublime and free expansion,
   Bliss celestial are for me.

Be not daunted at the lustre
   Of thy neighbour's countless store,
At his glory, and the cluster
   Of dependents at his door.

For his wealth and gaudy splendor
   Shall not wait upon his bier;
Pomp and all he must surrender
   When the train of death appear.

While he liv'd, in his adherence
   To the world, he thought him blest:
Long as thou support'st appearance,
   Busy tongues will speak the best.

Soon his father he shall follow,
   In the greedy grave to rot,
And the gulph his soul shall swallow,
   If repentance save him not.

Men of honour and promotion,
   Which of carnal things have far'd,
Model'd to the vulgar notion,
   With the beasts are well compar'd.

PSALM L

The Lord, e'en Christ supremely blest,
    O'er worlds his merit won,
Convokes from east to west
    All flesh beneath the sun.

From Zion in the spirit rais'd
    Amongst the heights above,
Has fair perfection blaz'd
    In glory, peace, and love.

The Lord shall come again to try
    His servant and his foe;
Before his face on high
    The dreadful trump shall blow.

The heav'n and earth he shall arraign,
    And ev'ry cause decide;
His sheep he shall retain,
    And from the goats divide.

Collect my saints from far and near,
    Which, in distress and want,
Were strengthen'd to revere
    Their promise at the font.

And heav'n its verdict shall declare,
    How good thou art and true;
For Christ shall judge to spare,
    And all to love subdue.

Hear my remonstrances, ye tribes,
    I am thy God, improve
By what thy God prescribes,
    And all thy filth remove.

I will not urge your gross defect,
 In that which ye disuse,
And in such sort neglect
 To give the Lord his dues.

I will not take the slaughter'd ox
 For sin, as heretofore;
The fatling of thy flocks
 To me shall bleed no more.

For all the forrest-beasts are mine,
 Whose life the hunter spills,
As are the sheep and kine
 Upon a thousand hills.

I know the fowls that haunt the groves
 Or mountains in their flight,
And all the grazing droves
 Are ever in my sight.

Shall Christ, the bread of life, repeal
 The laws his mercy taught,
And shall he want a meal,
 Which made the world from thought?

Shall God, eternal, self-complete,
 Whom highest heav'n receives,
Obey thy low conceit,
 And eat of kids and beeves?

Not in thine ew'r or dish he dips;
 No—'tis the thankful heart
And homage of thy lips
 That are thy Maker's part.

Whene'er calamities assail
 The suppliant in distress,

Thy Saviour shall not fail
　　To give him cause to bless.

But God disowns the rebel race—
　　My laws why should ye teach,
With hearts deprav'd and base,
　　And ostentatious speech?

Whereas thou hat'st the narrow track,
　　Which saints and martyrs tread,
And turn'st thine impious back
　　To where my word is read.

Thou lov'st the thief where'er he lurks,
　　And traitors to their trust;
Thou hast partook the works
　　Of foul adult'rous lust.

Thy mouth is giv'n to foul discourse,
　　That Christ the Word defies.
Thou hast to fraud recourse
　　To propagate thy lies.

Thou sittest in the seat of shame,
　　And brethren are revil'd,
Nor scruplest to defame
　　Thy mother's duteous child.

These things thou didst, till thou presum'd
　　That God at sin conniv'd—
To death by conscience doom'd,
　　Thou art in Christ reviv'd.

Consider, therefore, and repent,
　　Nor lose, by ling'ring late,
The bridegroom's good intent,
　　Which condescends to wait.

Whom praise and gratitude commend,
 Is fit for heav'ns employ—
'Well done, thou faithful friend,
 Receive thy Saviour's joy.'

PSALM LI

ON a soul with sins encumber'd,
 Lord, have pity and redeem,
As thy mercies are unnumber'd,
 And thy goodness is extream.

Wash me throughly so polluted
 With this hateful filth within;
Let thy merit be imputed
 To my tears to cleanse my sin.

For by faith and fair confession
 I my follies have resign'd,
And a sense of my transgression
 Is for ever in my mind.

Thee, thine awful presence solely
 Has my sin prophan'd, and shown
That thou art most true, most holy,
 When thy words and works are known.

Lo! I was engender'd vicious,
 And the lump within the womb,
Made against the Lord malicious,
 Did false principles assume.

But internal truth demanding,
 Thou hast search'd me to the heart;
And to raise my understanding
 Secret wisdom shalt impart.

With the wholesome hyssop purging,
    Pure again my veins shall flow,
And in springing baths immerging,
    Thou shalt make me white as snow.

Thou shalt make me hear the voices
    Which with joy thy name invoke,
As thy healing pow'r rejoices
    All the bones that thou hast broke.

Turn thee from my foul disgraces,
    Nor my soul in terror plunge;
Spare my sins, and all the traces
    Of my evil deeds expunge.

With another heart endue me,
    And my tainted vitals clean;
In the spirit, Lord, renew me,
    And my troubled mind serene.

Cast me not away for ever
    From the glory of thy face,
Nor my sinking soul dissever
    From the spirit of thy grace.

O console me to inherit
    All my part in thee again,
And confirm me with thy spirit
    Thy true freedom to maintain.

So shall I, so prone to trample
    And thy holy laws desert,
Both by precept and example
    Sinners to thy ways convert.

Rid me from this guilt's compunction,
    Lord, with healing in thy wing,

And my tongue, in sweet conjunction
  With my harp, thy truth shall sing.

With thy blessed inspiration,
  Lord, thou shalt my lips unseal,
And my mouth with exultation
  Shall thy glorious laud reveal.

Gifts for thy returning favour
  I would give, didst thou require;
But thou likest not the savour
  Which is wafted from the fire.

God's best off'ring is contrition
  From a man divinely meek;
Thou reject'st not the condition
  Of a heart at point to break.

O again be good and gracious,
  Zion's ruin'd state review;
Walls so high and streets so spacious,
  Come and build her up anew.

Thus our all-benign Creator
  We shall better please and praise;
Pray'r and gratitude are greater
  Than when loaded altars blaze.

PSALM LII

O THOU that art from God endow'd
With wealth and pow'r above the crowd,
Why is thy heart elate with pride,
If all these goods are misapplied?

Whereas benevolence divine
The mercy-beams that daily shine,
Are in proportion to the might
Of God, and gen'ral as the light.

No more let thy conception frame,
Nor tongue divulge thy neighbour's shame,
No more in keen invectives deal,
But learn to cover and conceal.

No more from virtue's precepts err,
But goodness and the Lord prefer;
Thy commerce in the world amend,
Nor truth nor decency offend.

No more let time be misemploy'd
In words which wisdom should avoid,
Whose tenour may thy neighbours hurt,
And nothing but the truth assert.

Henceforward may thy soul expect,
And find the love of God direct
To snatch thee to a better birth,
From Christians militant on earth.

The saints elect in heav'n shall see
The penitent's felicity,
And joy for such a sheep as this,
More than for ninety-nine in bliss.

Behold a man restor'd at length,
Who took not Jesus for his strength;
But put his trust in worldly store,
Behold him change to change no more.

For me—I like an olive thrive
With all my verdure still alive,

And rooted in the church I place
My trust in Christ's eternal grace.

My praises for thy mercies past,
Through all futurity shall last;
And on thy name my hope shall dwell,
For all thy servants like it well.

PSALM LIII

THE man to modes and times enslav'd,
His soul's conception is deprav'd,
  The Christian faith to blot;
And such and such alone devise
The lowest and the last of lies,
  To say that God is not.

Corrupt beyond the former times,
They are outrageous in their crimes,
  And vanities pursue;
Tho' grace alike has beam'd on all,
Tho' multitudes have heard the call,
  The chosen flock are few.

The Lord, at such a grievous cry,
Came down in person from on high,
  His creatures to restore;
And see if they would understand,
'The heav'nly kingdom is at hand,'
  And therefore sin no more.

But they are all at once astray,
And quite perverted from the way,
  Their vanities pursue;

Tho' grace alike has beam'd on all,
Tho' multitudes have heard the call,
 The chosen flock are few.

And have they understanding hearts,
These dealers in detested arts,
 My people to devour?
The faces of the poor they grind,
Nor have they to their God inclin'd,
 `Nor do they own his pow'r.

The conscious traitors stood dismay'd,
Nor knew from whence they were afraid
 For my belief to crown,
And circumventing guile to quell,
Lo! Satan to the depth of hell,
 Like lightning, is come down.

O that salvation were receiv'd,
And, Zion, all thy doom repriev'd,
 My soul is pray'r for thee!
O that the Lord would break our chains,
And where triumphant Jesus reigns,
 Would make his people free!

Then Jacob should lift up his voice,
And from his jeopardy rejoice,
 In festive garments clad;
And Israel's children to a man,
Through all our host from rear to van,
 Should be for ever glad.

PSALM LIV

O GOD, the name to which I pray,
    Of boundless love and pow'r,
O pass, if possible, away
    This bitter cup and hour.

Yet if these drops must thus be spilt,
    Thou, Father, knowest best;
And be it rather as thou wilt,
    Than to my soul's request.

Lo! strangers to thy truth arise,
    Nor put their trust in thee;
And Herod, leagu'd with Pilate, vies
    To nail me to the tree.

But God shall raise from stripes and scorn
    The Lamb betray'd and kill'd;
And on the third triumphant morn
    This temple shall rebuild.

Then thou shalt greater grace supply
    To have the worst redeem'd;
And truth shall make them free to die
    For him they once blasphem'd.

A victim patient and resign'd
    I for the cross prepare,
And bless thy name, because I find
    Such consolation there.

For he has caus'd me to respire,
    And all my vows have thriv'n;
Mine eye has seen my heart's desire
    In every foe forgiv'n.

PSALM LV

O God, with gracious ears receive
    My fervent vows in Christ addrest,
Nor take thyself away to leave
    Thy supplicant unblest.

Observe my melancholy state,
    My pangs let consolation ease,
And this vexatious grief abate
    While thus I bend my knees.

So loud opposers shout and throng,
    So near the wicked bands are seen;
For they are bent to do me wrong,
    Their malice is so keen;

My heart within me is dismay'd,
    And thoughts relating to my end,
My firmness into fear degrade,
    And all my pow'rs suspend.

A shudd'ring terror takes my limbs,
    And horrid visions fill my head;
My brain with wild confusion swims,
    And overwhelming dread.

And oh! that I had wings, I cry'd,
    To bear me ballanc'd as the dove;
Then would I to those regions glide
    Where dwells the peace I love.

Lo! then would I my course betake
    Till distance bold attempt defeat,
And to some friendly covert make
    In solitude's retreat.

514

I would my flight's direction shape,
 Myself in safety to embow'r,
Before th' imprison'd winds escape,
 And skies tempestuous low'r.

O Lord, the busy tongues confound,
 And their malevolence destroy;
For wickedness and strife abound,
 And all our streets annoy.

Idlers by day and night patrole,
 And through the worst uncleanness wade;
There dwells anxiety of soul,
 There mischief is a trade.

All love is froze within the walls
 And licens'd lust and envy burn,
And force attacks and guile enthralls
 Which way soe'er we turn.

For it was not a foe in mail
 That this extream dishonour dar'd,
To such I had been without fail
 Both patient and prepar'd.

Nor was it secret spite that wrought
 This odious deed of publick shame,
For so by pray'r I might have sought
 A cover from it's aim.

But it was even Thou, a part
 Of David, and his soul's resource;
The dear companion of his heart
 In all his painful course!

The mutual commerce of the mind
 In sweetness we were wont to share,

And at the house of God we join'd
    The work of common pray'r.

But let not sudden death surprize,
    And send them quick into the pit;
Though in their dwellings are the cries
    Of horrors they commit.

For me and for my seed I speak,
    We will to Christ our God appeal,
And he shall hear and raise the meek,
    And their salvation seal.

At morning and at evening song,
    And constant at the hour of noon,
I will my stated pray'r prolong,
    And God shall grant my boon.

'Tis God alone that has restor'd
    My peace, and my redemption won;
Nor is it numbers or the sword
    That such a deed has done.

Yea, God on his eternal throne,
    Thro' Christ shall hear me and forgive,
Whose words shall melt the hearts of stone
    That they may turn and live.

The hands of violent assault
    He laid on inoffensive folk,
From his own league he made revolt,
    His own agreement broke.

His speech as melting butter smooth
    With hostile heart the flatt'rer fram'd,
His oily words he tun'd to sooth
    Whence secret darts were aim'd.

O cast thy heavy lading down,
    And Christ himself shall give thee rest,
The proud shall not for ever frown
    Upon the poor opprest.

And as for them, the Lord shall shock
    Their pride with a tremendous blow,
When Christ, our meritorious rock,
    Shall try his friend and foe.

Short is the reign, and dread the blast
    Of bloody men by guile deprav'd,
But persevering to the last
    In Christ my soul is sav'd.

PSALM LVI

O CHRIST, have mercy on thy sheep
    From man's licentious pow'r;
Each day the foes thy fence o'erleap
    To worry and devour.

Their sweeping swarms in hostile steel
    The daily skirmish try,
I therefore to thy name appeal,
    Most holy and most high.

Whene'er I find myself dismay'd,
    Which threats at times obtain,
I will rely for instant aid
    On Christ betray'd and slain.

I will the words of Christ adore,
    Whose voice my faith confirms;
In him I trust, and dread no more
    The pow'r of dust and worms.

They daily from its true intent
    In craft my language wrest,
Thoughts misemploy'd, and time mispent,
    My ruin to suggest.

Their bands with cowardice extream
    Assemble and retreat,
And as against my life they scheme,
    They mark me by my feet.

Shall they escape the doom they dread,
    Who plan their neighbour hurt?
Yea, Jesu, from their impious head
    The final doom avert.

Thou seest the wand'rings of my pray'r
    From woes I cannot brook,
Thy phial for my tears prepare
    And note them in thy book.

Whene'er my Saviour I invoke,
    My foes the siege shall raise;
For this from heav'n I have bespoke,
    In Christ my pray'r and praise.

From Christ the word of life deriv'd,
    My joyful psalm resounds;
In Christ the word my soul reviv'd,
    Her consolation grounds.

My trust in Jesus I repose,
    And hence my hope pursue;
I will not fear my carnal foes,
    Nor what vain man can do.

To Christ my solemn vows I owe,
    My daily debt is great,

I will my mite of praise bestow,
 And at thine altar wait.

My soul from death thy merit clears,
 My feet are firm and free;
And to the public view appears
 My light renew'd in thee.

PSALM LVII

LORD, let thy mercy make me whole,
 For with a Christian's creed
I seek thy wing, until my soul
 From slavery be freed.

I will to heav'n my pray'rs detach,
 Invoking God most high,
The gracious God which shall dispatch
 The righteous cause I try.

From heav'n he shall his angel send,
 And from this foul disgrace,
The scorn of ruffian bands, defend,
 That urge the bloody chace.

The Lord shall delegate his truth,
 His mercy to display;
My soul lies open to the tooth
 Of lions in her way.

Amongst the sons of men I dwell,
 Whose guilt their conscience sears,
Whose tongues against the word rebel,
 Whose teeth are darts and spears.

Set up the standard of thy worth,
O Christ, beyond the skies,
O'er every steepl'd fane on earth
Let all thy glories rise.

To press my spirit down, a net
They have in craft prepar'd,
And in the very traps they set
They are themselves ensnar'd.

My heart is fixt, O God, my heart
Is fixt to change no more;
With all my best melodious art
I will thy praise explore.

Awake thou glorious east, and thou
Awake my lute and lyre,
Myself awake, my morning vow
Right early shall aspire!

Lord, midst thy tribes with thankful mind
I will thy laud rehearse,
And 'mongst the nations of mankind
My tuneful psalms disperse.

For o'er the heav'n of heav'ns thy love
Inshrines herself in light,
And lofty is thy truth above
The clouds of highest flight.

Set up the standard of thy worth,
O Christ, beyond the skies,
O'er every steepled fane on earth
Let all thy glories rise!

PSALM LVIII

YE congregation of the tribes,
 On justice do you set your mind;
And are ye free from guile and bribes
 Ye judges of mankind?

Nay, ye of frail and mortal mould
 Imagine mischief in your heart;
Your suffrages and selves are sold
 Unto the gen'ral mart.

Men of unrighteous seed betray
 Perverseness from their mother's womb;
As soon as they can run astray,
 Against the truth presume.

They are with foul infection stain'd,
 Ev'n with the serpent's taint impure;
Their ears to blest persuasion chain'd,
 And lock'd against her lure.

Tho' Christ himself the pipe should tune,
 They will not to the measure tread,
Nor will they with his grief commune
 Tho' tears of blood he shed.

Lord, humanize their scoff and scorn,
 And their malevolence defeat;
Of water and the spirit born
 Let grace their change compleat.

Let them with pious ardour burn,
 And make thy holy church their choice;
To thee with all their passions turn,
 And in thy light rejoice.

As quick as lightning to its mark,
    So let thy gracious angel speed;
And take their spirits in thine ark
    To their eternal mead.

The righteous shall exult the more
    As he such pow'rful mercy sees,
Such wrecks and ruins safe on shore,
    Such tortur'd souls at ease.

So that a man shall say, no doubt,
    The penitent has his reward;
There is a God to bear him out,
    And he is Christ our Lord.

PSALM LIX

O RESCUE me, thou God of all,
    As foes against my life conspire,
That follow the command of Saul
    For hatred and for hire.

Preserve me from the bands expert
    In vice and vengeance from the first,
That still procure their neighbour's hurt,
    As for their blood they thirst.

For lo! with treach'rous sword and spear
    Their lawless bands my soul assault;
A mighty force—while I am clear
    Of all offence or fault.

Without my fault themselves they arm,
    From post to post they pitch their tents;
Arise and shield my steps from harm,
    Thou Lord of all events.

O God of all the hosts above,
　　Stand up thou Lord of Jacob's might;
Let not the ballance of thy love
　　Be for the sons of spite.

These fugitives from God to sin,
　　At ev'ning's dubious light one meets,
As dogs without a master grin,
　　And quest along the streets.

Behold! their fawning lips abound
　　With oil, and yet conceal a dart;
For 'who is he whose skill can found
　　The language of our heart?'

But thou, Lord Jesus, shall deride,
　　And keep them from the depths they seek;
By winning souls from worldly pride,
　　And making boasters meek.

The strength by which such ills I bear,
　　O God, I will ascribe to thee;
For to thy succour I repair,
　　And for my refuge flee.

To me his grace the Lord bestows
　　In measure, and shall make me blest,
By his converting of my foes,
　　Which is my soul's request.

Lord, slay them not amidst their crimes,
　　But as examples of remorse
To vicious manners, evil times,
　　Their alter'd lives enforce.

For now their lips shall not offend
　　With words indecent and uncouth;

523

Their pride they shall by pray'r amend,
    And preach of peace and truth.

Let them be spar'd till fury cools,
    Whene'er thy vengeful bolts are hurl'd;
And know that 'tis the Lord that rules,
    All Israel and the world.

Returning then to God from sin,
    They'll haunt no more their usual beats,
As dogs without a master grin,
    And quest along the streets.

No more they will their neighbours judge,
    And seek for craving malice food,
Nor in their conversation grudge,
    If Christian love intrude.

For me, I will my praise commence
    To bless thy love at morning's dawn,
And pow'r, which has been my defence
    When other help was gone.

To thee, O God, I sing, the goal
    And blest supporter of my race;
Thou art the bosom of my soul,
    And refuge from disgrace.

PSALM LX

O GOD, thy flock thou hast dispers'd
    In every clime and shore;
O let our sentence be revers'd
    And be displeas'd no more.

524

Thou sent'st an earthquake to convulse,
 And rend the land in twain;
Heal thou the shock of that repulse
 Whose terrors still remain.

Our heavy hearts despond and shrink
 At such an awful sign,
And thou hast made thy people drink
 Of wrath's unmingled wine.

Thou didst a gracious signal make
 For such as own'd thy fear;
That they might triumph for the sake
 Of truth, whose voice they hear.

Hence good men have not undergone,
 Nor felt the gen'ral dread;
O save us from the gulphs that yawn,
 And let our pray'r be sped.

God in his holiness profess'd
 My mercy shall regale,
And canton Sichem to be bless'd,
 And measure Succoth's vale.

Mine is all Gilead's balmy realm,
 Manasses is my own;
Let Ephraim be salvation's helm,
 And Judah grace the throne.

Moab's a purifying vase,
 And Edom shall be shod,
With gospel-peace—Philistia's race,
 Rejoice yourselves in God.

What harbinger shall shew the way
 To Edom's forts and tow'rs,

That they may see Christ's streamers play,
 And join their pray'rs with ours.

Has God deserted then our coast,
 And will he not employ,
His angel to conduct our host
 To such a work of joy?

O send thy succour from on high
 When woes or wealth increase;
For man is but a poor ally
 In trouble or in peace.

Thro' Christ our Saviour we shall do
 Beyond our strength or skill,
And he shall all our foes subdue
 To his most blessed will.

PSALM LXI

O God, thy gracious ear apply,
 And keep me from despair,
Look down upon my streaming eye,
Give audience to the bursting sigh,
 Which interrupts my plaintive pray'r.

Where'er on earth I pitch my tent,
 I will thy name invoke,
To sooth me when my strength is spent,
And toilsome heaviness has bent
 My heart and members to her yoke.

O land me on some rocky shore
 Above my helpless height;

Thou art my hope from long before,
The fortress that mine eyes explore,
  As spoilers for my shipwreck wait.

I will within thy temple dwell
  And there for ever sing;
There likewise all the choir compell,
For mine infirmities are well
  Beneath the shadow of thy wing.

For thou, O righteous Lord, hast heard
  My soul's supreme desires;
And hast in covenant appear'd
To those that have thy name rever'd,
  And act as thy blest word inspires.

Thou shalt unto thy king extend
  The number of his days,
So that his reign shall have no end,
And to his years thou shalt commend
  The lot of everlasting praise.

He shall before God's face abide
  In sempiternal youth,
O thou whose hosts in heav'n reside,
For his reception there provide
  Thy loving mercy—and thy truth.

So shall I never cease to bless
  The glory of thy name,
To that in penitence confess,
To that in gratitude address,
  By goodly pride and honest shame.

PSALM LXII

TRULY all my soul's reliance
    Is the patient hope, she pleads;
And in Christ she rests affiance
    For from him her health proceeds.

This is faithful—my salvation
    And my strength is Christ alone;
From that rock of exaltation
    By no blast shall I be blown.

Ever shall your tongues dissemble,
    And your hearts your neighbours wound;
Frail and like the walls that tremble,
    Hanging o'er a broken mound.

Their device is to diminish
    Him whom God has made so great:
Flatt'ring they begin, and finish
    In deception, lies and hate.

Thou my spirit, notwithstanding,
    Still expect the Lord's release;
For I trust at thy commanding
    That she shall be sped to peace.

That is faithful—my salvation
    And my strength is Christ alone,
From that rock of exaltation
    By no blast shall I be blown.

Help and hope, and strength are Jesus,
    And the glories, as they glow;
To that height from whence he sees us,
    At the last I trust to go.

O confide with meek subjection
 In the Lord, ye faithful flock,
Kneeling with sincere affection,
 For Christ Jesus is our rock.

Men, without his grace attending,
 Are but emptiness and lies,
Lighter in the scale ascending
 Than the vanities they prize.

Keep from theft, nor be injurious,
 Quit the scenes of pomp and pride;
Be not in your wealth penurious,
 Nor in worldly goods confide.

God himself in glory seated
 Spake amidst seraphic throngs;
Twice I've heard the same repeated,
 'That the pow'r to God belongs.'

And that thou, O Lord, delightest
 Grace and mercy to diffuse;
And the sons of men requitest
 Ev'n as they their talents use.

PSALM LXIII

ABBA, Father, my dependence
 Is on thee, thou most benign,
Early will I pay attendance,
 O my God, before thy shrine.

Hear I languish for thy blessing,
 Spirits faint and wearied out;
Thirst and grievous heat oppressing
 In a land of dearth and drought.

Thus in pray'r I have expected
  That thou wouldst thy mercy show'r,
And mine eyes might be directed
  Where thy glory comes in pow'r.

For thy charity is better
  Than the life that is thy loan,
I profess myself thy debtor,
  And my lips thy praise shall own.

Long as I that life inherit
  I will give thee laud, to thee,
In the flesh and in the spirit,
  Lifted hands and bended knee.

In this dreary situation,
  As with dainties I shall fare,
While my lips in exultation
  Bless the sure effects of pray'r.

When I to my rest surrender,
  Are not thoughts of thee my dream?
Do I not, when waking, tender
  Homage to thy pow'r supreme?

For secure of thy protection,
  In the shadow of thy wings,
With due rev'rence and affection
  My delighted spirit clings.

Thy benignities embolden
  Souls that to thy truth adhere;
And thy right hand has upholden
  Mine infirmities and fear.

These that seek my soul to wound her,
  In th' unhospitable waste,

That deserve to sink around her,
    And the pangs of terror taste;

Threaten'd with the sword's perdition,
    Destin'd to the beasts for food—
Give them, Christ, to true contrition,
    Let them be with grace renew'd.

Thus the king shall be victorious
    In the Lord's thrice-honour'd name;
While the wicked and vain-glorious
    Shall be put to silent shame.

PSALM LXIV

HEAR, O my God, my voice accept
My wailings, and the tears I wept
    In agony of pray'r,
Preserve my soul from those that deal
In death, who have not sense to feel,
    Nor pity to forbear.

Prevent me from the secret mines,
And rescue from the dark designs
    Of guilt combin'd with rage;
From those who rising in a band
To do the work that Satan plann'd,
    By mutual ties engage.

Their tongues exasperate with spite,
Like falchions whetted for the fight,
    Are eager to defame;
They bend their bows, and strain their strings,
And give their poison'd arrows wings,
    E'en bitter words of shame.

That they may from an ambush shoot
At those that yield abundant fruit,
    The godly and the just;
And swift the desp'rate archers dart
The pointed mischief to the heart
    Of men without mistrust.

To wickedness they plight their troth,
And work each other up to wrath,
    And in their crimes agree;
They privily by stealth convene,
And sneak to lay their snares unseen,
    Blaspheming 'who shall see!'

In malice mischief they conceive,
And then to murder and to thieve,
    Their several bands they file;
Each on his fellow's guilt relies,
And all their practices disguise
    In subtlety and guile.

But God, their treason to detect,
Against the traitors shall direct
    His arrows swift as thought;
And terror shall their conscience wound,
And all the schemes that they propound
    Be to confusion brought.

Yea, they their dealings shall impeach
With their own tongues, and make a breach
    Upon the webs they spun;
And they that their event behold,
And those that hear their story told,
    Their deeds shall scorn and shun.

And they that their event behold,
And those that hear their story told

Shall praise the Lord alone;—
'It is the Lord's resistless pow'r,
That sav'd us in the dreadful hour,
    The people and the throne.'

Inspir'd with mercies so profuse,
The wise and good shall give a loose
    To transport and delight;
And every man, whose heart is whole
From treason, shall with all his soul
    This song of joy recite.

PSALM LXV

To thee, O God, on Zion's hill,
    Shall praise and adoration bow,
And Salem's dome thy saints shall fill
    To pay their daily vow.

Thou, whose paternal ears receive
    The contrite sinners as they kneel,
In thee shall all mankind believe,
    And to thy love appeal.

Thro' rooted vice my spirits fail,
    Which o'er my heart an empire wins,
O let thy mercy countervail
    To cover all our sins.

The man is blest thou hast ordain'd,
    Which from the pulpit feeds thy sheep;
In sweet serenity sustain'd
    Thy treasures he shall keep.

The Lord our Saviour shall disclose,
    His wond'rous truths till all applaud;

Thou hope of utmost earth and those
    That plough the briny broad.

The mighty mountains of the earth
    His hands upon their bases found;
For unresisted pow'r's the girth
    With which his loins are bound.

At his command the waves asswage,
    The roaring seas are peace enjoin'd,
And clamours of the crowd, that rage
    With every shifting wind.

To those that dwell in climes afar,
    Thy dispensations dread excite,
Which mak'st the morn and evening star
    To praise thy purer light.

Thy gracious visitation cheers,
    And blesses all the genial soil;
The rising wealth of fruitful years
    Repays the workman's toil.

The stream by God's direction glides,
    To yield abundance in its course;
Thro' thee the season'd corn provides
    An annual due resource.

Each ridge and furrow of the field
    Is water'd by the dew of God;
The blessed rains their nurture yield
    In every soften'd clod.

The years, by thy good hand renew'd,
    Are to their consummation led;
Thy clouds etherial richness brood,
    And from their chambers shed.

They shall in mild profusion show'r
    Their drops upon the tented green,
The little hills, which trees embow'r,
    Shall gladden all the scene.

The thriving sheep the folds shall throng,
    Rank ears the golden valley grace;
To call forth laughter and a song
    From nature's voice and face.

PSALM LXVI

THE honours of the pow'r supreme,
    All earth with joy rehearse;
O make his praise the glorious theme
    Of everlasting verse.

Confess with wonder and delight,
    O God, thy works abound;
How thy magnificence and might
    Thine enemies confound!

For ev'ry nation, tongue and clime
    Shall adoration pay,
And raise to thee the strains sublime
    Thy glories to display.

O come ye, to his church repair,
    And from his wonders trace;
How vast his providential care
    From all the human race.

The floods were dried at his decree,
    On foot through waves we went;
And in the middle of the sea
    We sung the great event.

For ever o'er the realms, he rules,
    He casts a father's eyes;
But harden'd unbelieving fools
    Shall to no honour rise.

Our God, ye realms, with praises crown,
    And bless his righteous reign,
And make the voice of his renown
    Sweet, audible and plain.

In him we live, we move and breathe,
    And all our beings hold;
And lest we slip by guile beneath,
    The tempter is controul'd.

For we, O God, thy test abide,
    In love's kind ballance weigh'd;
Thou also hast our spirits try'd
    As silver is essay'd.

In hostile snares our bands were caught
    Forsaken of our God;
And thou upon our loins has brought
    The terrors of thy rod.

Thou suffer'dst men to bruise our head,
    And our fair fame to brand;
At length thro' fire and seas we sped
    Into this wealthy land.

I will before thy holy shrine
    With precious odours wait,
And pay that solemn vow of mine
    When I was in a strait.

The rams and goats that us'd to burn,
    The Saviour Christ reprieves,

And hymns and anthems serve the turn
    Of kidlings and of beeves.

O come, ye guests, whom God has bid
    Within his church to bless,
And I will shew you what he did
    For David in distress.

To God, who has my organs tun'd,
    I with my mouth have sung,
And with him in my heart commun'd,
    Which harmoniz'd my tongue.

Should I to wickedness desert,
    Who such conviction feel,
The Lord will not my cause assert,
    Nor bless me when I kneel.

But now my pray'r his pity moves,
    As on my knees I bend;
And he considers and approves
    My sighs as they ascend.

Blest be the Lord, which gives me fruit,
    As thus I pray and fast;
Nor turns his mercy from my suit,
    But loves me to the last.

PSALM LXVII

O God, indulge us with thy grace,
    And bless with evangelic light,
And shew the lustre of that face
    Which mercy makes so bright.

That Christ his gospel may be known,
    Where lands extend or oceans roll,

And all the scatter'd nations own
  That health which saves the soul.

The glory and the praise be thine,
  O God, from every heart and tongue;
Yea, let all congregations join
  When such a song is sung.

O let the nations far and wide
  Speak forth triumphant joy and mirth,
For righteous shalt thou reign and guide
  The nations upon earth.

The glory and the praise be thine,
  O God, from every heart and tongue;
Yea, let all congregations join
  When such a song is sung.

Then shall the riches of increase
  Upon earth's fertile glebe attend;
And God, the God of Israel's peace,
  His daily blessing send!

God shall his faithful people bless,
  And all the nations of mankind
Shall by our commerce have access
  His saving grace to find.

PSALM LXVIII

AROUSE—and let thy foes disperse
Thou master of the universe,
  Arouse thee from on high;
Take up the trumpet and alarm,
And at the terror of thine arm
  Let those that hate thee fly.

Like as afflicting smoke's dispell'd,
Let them be driv'n away and quell'd,
    As wax before the fire,
Let fraud at thine effulgence fail,
And let the multitudes in mail
    Before my God retire.

But let the men of righteous seed,
Accepted in their father's deed,
    Rejoice before the shrine;
Yea, let them shout till heav'n resounds,
There is no need of end or bounds
    To joyfulness divine.

Give praise—with songs your praises blend,
And as your thoughts to heav'n ascend,
    And leave the world beneath,
Extol his universal name,
Who rides on the celestial flame,
    In IAH, which all things breathe.

The father of the friendless child,
To keep the damsel undefil'd,
    And judge the widow's cause,
Is God upon his righteous throne,
Whence he the hands to rapine prone
    O'ersees and overawes.

Thy Lord domestick peace creates,
And those his Mercy congregates,
    Who solitary dwell;
The slave delivers from his chain,
But rebels in dry wastes remain,
    And where no waters well.

When thou Jehovah led the way,
Before thy people in array,
    From Egypt's barb'rous cost;

Thro' boundless wilds exposed and parch'd,
In pillar'd majesty thou march'd
    The captain of the host.

The earth in ecstasy gave place,
With vast vibrations on her base
    The present God she found;
Ev'n Israel's God—the heav'ns dissolv'd,
And Sinai's mount in clouds involv'd,
    Felt all his rocks rebound.

O God, thou bad'st the heav'ns dispense
The bread of thy benevolence,
    Down with the daily dew;
And fixt the people of thy pow'r,
Amidst their doubtings by a show'r
    Miraculous and new.

Therein thy congregation dwelt,
E'en midst the manna, which thou dealt
    So plentiful and pure;
Thy goodness to confirm the weak,
Thy charity to bless and break,
    The largess for the poor.

God, in stupendous glory deck'd,
His gracious covenant direct,
    Came down from heav'n to teach;
Great was the trembling and the fear
Of crouds, that rush'd that word to hear,
    They were enjoin'd to preach.

Each talking tyrant at the head
Of thousands and ten thousands fled,
    They fled with all their might;
And all Judea's blooming pride,
The spouse, the damsel and the bride,
    Dispos'd the spoil at night.

Though ye the bitter bondage wept,
And midst Rhamnesian tripods slept,
    Hereafter is your own;
Ye shall as turtle-doves unfold,
The silver plumage wing'd with gold,
    And make melodious moan.

When kings were scatter'd for our sake,
And God alarm'd his host to take
    His vengeance on the foe;
On Israel's countenance benign
He made his radiant grace to shine
    As bright as Salmon's snow.

Jehovah's hill's a noble heap,
And ev'n as Bashan's spiry steep,
    From which the cedars nod;
And Zion's mount herself sublimes,
And swells her goodly crest and climbs
    To meet descending God.

Ye haughty hills that leap so high,
What is th' exertion that ye try?
    This is God's hallow'd mount,
On whose blest top the glories play,
And where the Lord desires to stay
    While we his praise recount.

The chariots of the Lord are made
Of angels in a cavalcade
    Ev'n twenty thousand strong,
Those thousands of the first degree,
O'er Sinai—in the midst is HE,
    And bears the pomp along.

God is gone up from whence he rose
With gifts accepted for his foes,
    His loaded altars smoke;

Captivity, from chains repriev'd,
Is made his captive, and receiv'd
    To thy most blessed yoke.

God is our help from every ill,
And gives to every want its fill,
    For us and all our race;
By him we're every hour review'd,
To him the daily pray'r's renew'd
    For daily bread and grace.

God, that great God whom we profess,
Is all-benevolent to bless,
    Omnipotent to save;
In God alone is our escape,
From death and all the gulphs that gape,
    From terror and the grave.

God shall not send his blessing down
To rest upon the hoary crown
    Of those which grace resist;
But shall afflict the heads of all,
That after his repeated call
    To penitence, persist.

From Bashan, which they pass'd of yore,
Said God, I will my tribes restore,
    And bring them back again;
Where Abr'ham worshipp'd and was bless'd,
Of Canaan they shall be possess'd,
    Emerging from the main.

That thy baptized foot may tread,
Where proud blasphemers laid their head,
    By judgments unreclaim'd;
And that thy shepherd's dogs may chace
Thy flocks into their pleasant place,
    Who made the earth asham'd.

They've seen their errors to disprove
My God in blest procession move,
    The pomp of God my king;
Accordant to the train below,
The dances rise, the streamers flow,
    And holy flow'rs they fling.

The goodly shew the singers lead,
The minstrels next in place proceed,
    With musick sweet and loud;
The damsels, that with wild delight,
The brisk-resounding timbrels smite,
    Are in the mid-most crowd.

O thou Jeshurun, yield thy thanks,
All ages, sexes, tribes and ranks,
    In congregated bands;
To God united thanks restore,
Brought from the heart its inmost core,
    And with protesting hands.

There Benjamin in triumph goes,
Least but in love the Lord of those
    That dwell in tents and bow'rs;
And Judah next to the most high,
With Zebulon and Naphtali
    Their princedoms and their powr's.

God to the sires of all the tribes
Some great peculiar gift ascribes,
    To each his talents told;
The loan with such long-suff'ring lent,
Do thou establish and augment
    Ten thousand thousand fold.

From this thy temple which we lay,
To thee the homage they shall pay,
    To thee the praise impute;

Kings shall their annual gifts renew,
And give Melchisedec his due,
   The glory and the fruit.

Rebuke the spearmen with thy word,
Those calves and bulls of Bashan's herd,
   Which from our ways abhor;
Let them pay toll, and hue the wood,
Which are at enmity with good,
   And love the voice of war.

The nobles from the sons of Ham,
Shall bring the bullock and the ram,
   Idolatrous no more;
The Morians soon shall offer alms,
And bow their heads, and spread their palms,
   God's mercy to implore.

Ye blessed angels of the Lord,
Of nations and of kings the ward,
   That further thanks and pray'r,
To Jesus Christ your praise resound,
Collected from the regions round
   Your tutelary care.

In other days before the sev'n,
Upon that ante-mundane heav'n,
   In glorious pomp he rode—
He sends a voice, which voice is might,
In inconceivable delight
   Th' acknowledg'd word of God.

Ye heroes foremost in the field
That couch the spear, or bear the shield,
   Bless God that ye prevail;
His splendour is on Israel's brow,
He stands all-pow'rful on the prow
   Midst all the clouds that sail.

O God, all miracle thou art,
Ev'n thou the God of Israel's heart
    Within thy holy shrine,
Thou shalt with strength and pow'r protect,
Thy people in the Lord elect,
    Praise, endless praise be thine.

PSALM LXIX

O SAVE me, thou supremely blest,
    These floods of tears controul,
For inward weeping clogs my breast,
    And overwhelms my soul.

I am bemir'd in filth so deep,
    And where no bottom lies;
Mine enemies in torrents sweep
    My remnant, as they rise.

I am fatigu'd, as thus I wail,
    My throat is hoarse and dry;
Mine eyes with looking upward fail,
    As to the Lord I cry.

More than my hairs the sons of strife
    In causeless hate unite,
And foes against my guiltless life
    Have muster'd all their might.

I paid extortioners their price
    For what they yet detain;
Thou know'st my simpleness, my vice,
    O God, is but too plain.

Let not thy sons, O Lord of hosts
    Be for my follies blam'd,

Nor let thy servants quit their posts
    Thro' my default asham'd.

And why! I suffer for thy sake,
    Dishearten'd and reprov'd;
And of this foul disgrace partake
    From thy defence remov'd.

I am become to all my kin
    As foreign to their care;
My mothers children from within
    Refuse me entrance there.

For zeal relating to thy cause
    Upon my spirit preys;
And, who blasphemes thy church and laws,
    Against my heart inveighs.

I wept and mortify'd my flesh
    With fasting and with tears;
On that my foes came on afresh
    With obloquy and sneers.

The sackcloth too in grief I wore,
    And threw me on the dust,
Which meekness but provok'd the more
    Their jesting and disgust.

The mob that sit without the gate
    Are pleasant on my wrongs,
And drunkards make mine abject state
    The subject of their songs.

But Lord, I will my pray'r submit
    To thy most righteous pow'r,
And of my vow myself acquit
    In this propitious hour.

Hear me, O Lord, in thine excess
    Of goodness to my need,
According to thy truth express,
    In which my sins are freed.

Take me from out the sinking slough,
    And set me on the ground;
And from the scorner's angry brow,
    And from the gulph profound.

Let not the water flood of woes
    Above my level swell,
Nor let the deep it's jaws disclose
    To shew the pit of hell.

Thy cordial clemency extend,
    And hear me as I pray;
And as it knows nor bounds nor end,
    Again thy love display.

Do not thy radiant face withdraw
    For trouble presses hard;
And as the pangs vexatious gnaw,
    With speed my groans regard.

Draw nigh, my soul in mercy save
    With pregnant anguish big,
O come and rescue from the grave
    Which spite and treach'ry dig.

This shame, reproof, and foul disgrace
    So justly made my own,
Thou know'st, and seest the coward race
    Which prostrate mis'ry stone.

Thine anger touches me so nigh
    That care disturbs my mind;
547

I look'd, but not a pitying eye
    No comfort cou'd I find.

They for my morsel gave me gall
    Their sinking souls to plunge,
And to my poignant thirst withal
    They minister'd the spunge.

Yet let them not the less receive
    The lot of plenteous wealth,
And their condemn'd estate reprieve
    With thine eternal health.

Ope thou their eyes, that they may see
    Thy glory's heav'nly tracks,
And lay, while they submit their knee,
    Thy burden on their backs.

In love account thèm of thy fold,
    And on thy bread subsist;
Give them thy presence to behold,
    And of thy saints inlist.

With children let their house be fill'd
    And of misfortunes void,
And let their fertile lands be till'd,
    And granaries employ'd.

Do this for them, who yet awhile
    Embarrass'd grief perplex,
And who, as Satan's snares beguile,
    Thy wounded servant vex.

Let them emerge from strength to strength,
    And rise as they repent;
And their converted souls at length
    To final peace be sent.

Let them escape the hand that wipes
    The recreant from thy page,
And live in those eternal types
    Which write the saint and sage.

Me, while these agonies I feel,
    In such dejection sunk,
O God, thy help shall ease and heal
    The sinews which have shrunk.

O God, I will extoll thy name
    In ever-grateful verse,
And records of thy glorious fame
    Throughout the world disperse.

These God had rather I should give,
    Love's unpolluted proofs,
Than beasts, which he has made to live,
    And fenc'd with horns and hoofs.

The humble shall consider this,
    And be for ever glad;
Seek ye the Lord, and heav'nly bliss
    He to your souls shall add.

For there is audience to the poor
    With their all-gracious Lord,
Who scorns not those whom bars immure,
    And keepers have in ward.

Let earth adore, as from the spring
    Her choicest flow'rs she straws;
Let heav'n and ocean have their swing
    Of infinite applause.

For Jesus shall repair the road
    To Zion's heav'nly courts,

That men may settle their abode
    Where endless joy transports.

And there the race of his elect
    Shall hold their souls in peace;
And all that his dear name affect,
    Its lustre shall increase.

PSALM LXX

HASTE, haste to do me right.
    And give my suff'rings ease,
Lord Jesus, speed thy flight
    To David on his knees.

Let all this bloody chace
    In shame and sorrow cease,
And grant the traitors grace
    That plot against my peace.

With speed their spirits break
    To heart-afflicting sighs,
That thus insult the meek,
    'There, there the grov'ler lies.'

But endless joy reward
    The saints of Christ the king,
And all that love the Lord
    Their hallelujah sing.

The pangs of pinching need
    My pow'r of patience tire;
Redouble, Lord, thy speed,
    And aid me to respire.

Thou art, O Christ, alone
   My Saviour, God, and friend,
No longer then postpone,
   But on my pray'rs attend.

PSALM LXXI

In thy name my faith is rooted,
   Save me, Jesu, from dismay;
Have me rescu'd and recruited,
   And, All-righteous, hear me pray.

Be my bulwark to secure me,
   And the promis'd help fulfil;
In thy strongest fort immure me,
   For thou art my Saviour still.

From the godless and licentious,
   Lord, thy supplicant release;
From the cruel and contentious,
   Joining hands against my peace.

For with ardour heav'nly minded
   Thee, Lord Jesus, I embrace;
Nor by carnal pleasures blinded,
   Ev'n from youth I court thy grace.

From my birth thou hast sustain'd me,
   From the womb hast set me free,
And the praises thou ordain'd me
   Shall for ever flow to thee.

In the vulgar estimation
   As a monster am I thought,
Yet I hope for thy salvation,
   Which by Jesus Christ was bought.

551

Give me gracious elocution
　　Day by day thy laud to tell,
That with grateful retribution
　　On thy glory I may dwell.

Leave me not with age declining,
　　As increasing years prevail,
When my lamp no longer shining,
　　Strength and wonted spirits fail.

For my sland'rous foes have taken
　　Ev'ry step to have it said,
'Grind him, of his God forsaken;
　　Seize him, destitute of aid.'

Go not far from my petition,
　　O my God, when life's at stake;
Haste with gracious expedition,
　　O my God, for Christ his sake.

Yet for all their deeds despiteful,
　　Keep them from eternal shame;
And disgrace and pain so rightful
　　Let them 'scape in Christ his name.

As for me, I will endeavour
　　Patience to support by pray'r,
And thy glorious laud for ever
　　More and more will I declare.

Daily shall my mouth make mention
　　Of the Christian faith and hope,
Though 'tis not in man's invention
　　To define their boundless scope.

Made in Christ another creature,
　　And through grace to fulness grown,

I will sing in holy metre
  Of thy righteousness alone.

Lord, thou taught the first noviciate
  Of my grace-directed youth,
Therefore shall mine age officiate
  To promulge thy wond'rous truth.

Spare me, Lord, so weak and hoary,
  As the vital heat decays,
Till I shew the pow'r and glory
  Of thy reign to future days.

Far above revenge and rigour
  Tow'rs thy truth sublimely bright,
What comparison or figure
  Shall describe thy matchless might?

In what floods of grief immersing
  Hast thou prov'd me! in what pain!
Yet my bitter lot reversing,
  Thou hast brought me up again.

Thou hast rais'd me to promotion,
  These imperial reins to guide,
And encourag'd my devotion
  To thy name on ev'ry side.

Wherefore with my verse harmonious
  I thy faithfulness will sing,
Striking from the harp symphonious
  Praise to Christ the spotless king.

With my lips by zeal impassion'd,
  And the heart thou hast restor'd;
To the thought the numbers fashion'd,
  Thee I sing, O most ador'd.

And thy truth shall be refounded
Daily in my speech and song;
For the wretches are confounded
That conspir'd to do me wrong.

PSALM LXXII

FROM thine everlasting tables,
O my God, the king endue,
While thy grace his son enables
Thy just judgments to pursue.

Then shall he preside, directing
After thy behoof his reign,
And defend the poor, respecting
Those that in distress complain.

With rich harvests on the mountains
Peace her garners shall amass,
And the hills shall play their fountains
To bring righteousness to pass.

By his upright jurisdiction
Widows, orphans he shall feed,
And the cause of their affliction
He the spoilers shall implead.

Each succeeding generation
They thy justice shall revere,
Long as the prescrib'd rotation
Of the lights that rule the year.

He shall come on earth, descending,
Like the rain, on Gideon's fleece,
As the genial dew commending
Everlasting joy and peace.

554

In his time the saints shall flourish,
   And benevolence divine,
And sweet peace abundance nourish,
   Long as sun and moon shall shine.

His domain shall be stupendous,
   Spreading wide from pole to pole;
And the pow'r that shall defend us
   Reach the world's extreamest goal.

In the wild the sons of error
   Shall kneel down before his feet,
And his foes, abash'd with terror,
   Fall to earth, and grace intreat.

They of Tharsis gifts shall offer,
   Sheba's kings, and isles remote,
Sages from th' Arabian coffer,
   Myrrh and frankincense devote.

Ev'ry king shall fall before him
   In humiliation meek;
All the subject world adore him,
   And to his redemption seek.

For the poor, the sick, the stranger,
   Halt, and dumb, and deaf, and blind,
To his triumph from his manger,
   In thy love their help shall find.

To the simple folk and needy
   He the gospel light shall show,
Ever gracious, ever speedy
   To relieve the souls in woe.

From the Herods and the Neros
   He his martyrs shall requite,

And the blood of Christian heroes
 Shall be precious in his sight.

He shall live for everlasting,
 High above all empire rais'd,
And with off'rings, pray'r, and fasting
 Daily shall his name be prais'd.

Fill'd by his angelic legions,
 Crops and vintages shall teem,
And all cultivated regions
 Fresh as Lebanon shall seem.

Fame is his through all the stages
 Of posterities and times;
Blest through him, the better ages
 Shall adorn converted climes.

Blessed be the Lord, indulging
 To his people grace anew,
By his precious words promulging
 What his matchless wonders shew.

To his glorious name all orders,
 Men and angels, bend your knee,
Preach'd through earth's remotest borders,
 YEA—for Christ his merit—YEA.

PSALM LXXIII

GOD is in very truth benign
 To Jacob, and his seed,
To such as heartily decline
 From filth in word and deed.

And yet my feet had well nigh lost
 The conduct of their guide,
And my firm treadings, to my cost,
 Were on the point to slide.

For wherefore? I was griev'd to see
 Ungodly men so great,
And wealth and pow'r to that degree
 On Satan's servants wait.

For they themselves of age assure,
 As though excus'd to die,
And lustily they live secure,
 And Christ in strength deny.

The tides of trouble, that confound
 Their betters, they can stem;
And crosses, which their neighbours wound,
 Are far enough from them.

Hence pride has bound their stiffen'd neck
 As with a gorgeous chain,
And as in robes themselves they deck
 In wrath and high disdain.

Their wanton eyes with fatness swell,
 As in themselves they trust,
And in proud palaces they dwell,
 To do whate'er they lust.

Their commerce is contagious too,
 As loudly they blaspheme;
Their conversation they renew,
 Against the great *Supreme*.

For with their clamour they invade,
 Where heav'n its vault sublimes,

And their untoward talk is made
    The fashion of the times.

Therefore to them the people crave
    For profit and for ease;
And from each voluntary slave
    No trivial tax they squeeze.

Shall God (the scorners say) perceive,
    Who dwells in heavens unknown,
And what we dare and disbelieve,
    Be laid before his throne?

Lo! these are what religion brands,
    Yet make the world their mart,
If so, in vain I've wash'd my hands,
    I cry'd, and purg'd my heart.

I have been mortify'd all day,
    And griev'd such men were born,
And chasten'd with the rising ray
    For many an irksome morn.

Yea, I had almost join'd the fools—
    But then I shou'd have blam'd
The wholesome discipline, which schools
    Thy sons that are reclaim'd.

Then labour'd I to comprehend
    This mystery of thine,
But could not its immediate end
    With all my skill divine.

Until I went into thy fane
    To recommend my plea,
And there thou mad'st it very plain
    Why these events should be.

To wit, how all their pride they prop
    Upon a tott'ring base,
Whence at thy bidding down they drop,
    And sink into disgrace.

How instantaneous one and all
    Are blasted and consume,
And perish at thy wrath, and fall
    Upon a dreadful doom.

Like as a dream, when men awake,
    And from their fright are freed;
So from the city shalt thou make
    Their image to recede.

Thus in my heart was discontent,
    And gall within me flow'd,
And thro' my loins vexation went,
    And in my reins abode.

So foolish in my vain dispute
    Was I before my God,
And void of wisdom as the brute,
    By which the corn is trod.

And yet I keep within thy courts
    One constant strain of pray'r,
And my right hand thy pow'r supports,
    While I thy surplice wear.

My road thy counsel shall direct,
    And thro' all straits convoy,
And thou shalt welcome thine elect
    To glory and to joy.

Whom have I in the heav'ns above
    Like thee my hope to raise,

Nor is there ought on earth I love,
    In measure as thy praise?

My spirits have forsook my heart,
    My vigour fails my flesh;
But God, in whom I have a part,
    Shall with new strength refresh.

For they that from thy banner run,
    Shall find an hasty grave,
Nor ought but thine all-righteous Son
    Can such adult'rers save.

But it is good for me to hold
    My service and my song,
And God—the works of God unfold,
    Where Zion's daughters throng.

PSALM LXXIV

Lord Jesus, why dost thou retard
    The grace thou lov'st to send,
And all thy pastoral regard
    In kindling wrath suspend?

O think upon thy chosen seed,
    Reproach'd and disesteem'd,
Which, as thy holy word decreed,
    Thy precious blood redeem'd.

O think upon Jehudah's race,
    The tribe so much thine own,
And on fair Zion's special place,
    Where thou hast fixt thy throne.

Prepare thy blessed feet, and come
    With peace angelic shod,
And purge away the dross and scum,
    That stain the house of God.

Thy foes display their flags and boast,
    That they thy battles fight,
And schismatics maintain their post
    Amongst the sons of light.

The servile hand that hew'd the wood
    From out the stately trees,
Was, in his place, ordain'd to good,
    And shap'd his work to please.

But now these artizans untune
    The musick that they made,
The carvers break each fair festoon,
    And counteract their trade.

Nay more, they've carried force and fire
    Against each shrine around;
And levell'd, in their godless ire,
    Thy temple with the ground.

Yea, in their wishes they combine
    That not a church should stand,
And thus incendiaries mine
    The faith of all the land.

No signs the wonted grace attest—
    The services unsung;
And few to prophesy the best,
    And learn each sacred tongue.

O God, how long shall traitor's sting,
    And hiss with spite and guile,

And with th' establish'd church and king
    Their Saviour Christ revile?

Why dost thou our defence withdraw
    At this so great alarm,
Nor keepest Antichrist in awe
    By thine almighty arm?

For Christ, my king from long ago,
    Is with me to this hour;
All hope above, and help below,
    Are solely from his pow'r.

That pow'r astonish'd floods avow'd,
    Dividing heap from heap;
Thou smote the dragons as they plough'd
    The waters of the deep.

The huge Leviathan was stunn'd
    At that stupendous roar
Of billows, breaking to refund
    The fishes on the shore.

The living springs and streams profuse
    Thy people to supply,
Thy mandate could from rocks educe,
    And made the river dry.

The day is subject to thy rule,
    The night to thy decree,
The blessed sunshine and the cool
    Are made and chang'd by thee.

Thou by thy wisdom hast ordain'd
    The borders of the world,
And summer's genial heat maintain'd,
    And wintry winds unfurl'd.

Consider, Lord, how men blaspheme
    The honour of thy name,
And fools, in their ambitious dream,
    Have lost the sense of shame.

Let not thy turtle-dove be sold,
    To crowds and ruffian rage,
Nor from the prostrate poor withhold
    Thy love for such an age!

Thy gracious covenant review,
    For in this earth beneath
The worldlings dark designs pursue,
    And fell revenge they breathe.

Let not the simple man depart
    Abash'd at fruitless pray'r;
But give the poor a joyful heart
    Thy glory to declare.

Arise, O God, thy cause support,
    Thine own eternal cause,
Reclaim the folly that in sport
    Contemns thy name and laws.

O let thy words of comfort drown
    The voice of rank excess,
And bring their gross presumption down
    To worship and to bless.

PSALM LXXV

To thee Jeshurun, of all ranks,
    In thankful pray'r agree,
—Yea, Lord, we yield the thanks
    To mercy, love and Thee.

Thy blessed word is also nigh
 Each day and every hour,
And that thy works imply
 In spirit and in pow'r.

What time th' assembly shall attend
 On my judicial chair,
I will the truth defend,
 Deciding right and fair.

Earth totters on her lowest base,
 And all her tenants shrink;
But Jesus shall replace
 Her pillars, ere she sink.

I said unto the fools, eschew
 Your pride and senseless scorn,
And to the godless crew,
 No more exalt your horn.

No more exalt your horn in vain,
 But your ambition check,
Nor for your speeches strain
 With such a stiffen'd neck.

For tho' promotion plumes your crest,
 And fills with pomp your mouth,
'Tis not from east or west,
 Nor is it from the south.

And why the Lord is judge supreme,
 And one man he degrades,
And one from want extreme
 He raises up and aids.

For in his hand the Lord presents
 A cup of vinous juice,

Full mixt with red contents,
    And pours it out profuse:

The dregs thereof the men of pride,
    From out th' inverted cup
Shall drink as they subside,
    And wholly suck them up.

But I will fashion my discourse
    Of Jacob's God to sing,
And evermore inforce
    The praise of Zion's king.

Recall thy servants, that revolt,
    Again to pay their vows,
And righteous men exalt,
    And crown their honour'd brows.

PSALM LXXVI

In Jury is the Lord renown'd
    The nation that he chose,
His name Jeshurun's songs resound,
    And to his glory close.

At Salem his pavilions stand
    Amidst celestial fires,
His seat is in the Holy Land,
    Where Zion's hill aspires.

And there he brake the bowman's shaft,
    The javeline and the shield,
The sword and the proud warriour's craft,
    And all th' embattled field.

Thy matchless might, which knows no change,
    More lustre has assum'd,

Than yonder everlasting range
    Of hills, where clouds are plum'd.

Contending tyrants now are friends,
    All dreams of empire cease,
As his own olivet ascends
    The prince of endless peace,

At thy rebuke, O Lord, alarm
    Upon the mighty came;
Thy host both horse and car disarm,
    And put the chiefs to shame.

Thou, Lord, ev'n thou by trembling fear
    Art worthily ador'd,
Nor wrath nor rapine persevere
    When thou hast sheath'd the sword.

Christ his own oracle declares
    Supremely just and wise,
And silenc'd Satan now forbears
    His dark ambiguous lies.

When Shilo shall his meek embrace,
    And wolves with lambkins play,
Where flourish in the bramble's place
    The myrtle and the bay.

The fierceness of the men of war
    Thou shalt to praise convert,
And those that from thy peace abhor,
    Thy gospel shall assert.

To God engage and keep your vow,
    Your vassalage renew,
Bring presents, and by pray'r allow
    That rev'rence is his due.

He by his wonders shall refrain
    The spirit of the prince,
And of his everlasting reign
    Usurping man convince.

PSALM LXXVII

To God I will my voice direct,
    A voice of love and fear,
And it shall have the due effect
    With his paternal ear.

To Christ my Saviour I complain
    Midst sores and raging smart;
When tedious night increases pain,
    Discomfort damps my heart.

When grief o'erpow'rs with its excess
    My mind, and blunts her edge,
My soul's vexation for redress
    I will to God alledge.

Mine eyes thy plagues withhold from rest,
    And on my slumbers break;
I am so feeble and oppress'd,
    That I can scarcely speak.

I have reflected on the years
    With happy seasons clast,
And strove to sooth my streaming tears
    By thinking on the past.

I call to mind my dawn and noon,
    Which were the themes of song,
And with my heart by night commune,
    To make my spirits strong.

Will God from mine incessant cries
    Eternal absence keep,
And will he send no more supplies
    To those that pray and weep?

Are all his mercies wholly gone,
    That nothing can restore,
And are his promises withdrawn
    For ever, evermore?

Has God forgotten to be kind
    When mortals are diseas'd,
And shall his goodness be confin'd,
    Because he is displeas'd?

My guilt precipitates my sand—
    I therefore will recall
The days of God's indulgent hand
    To Jacob more than all:

Thy charity to restiff souls
    Thy works and arm sublime;
And I will recognize the rolls
    Of antiquated time.

I will on that convincing force
    Of all thine actions dwell,
And in colloquial intercourse
    Thy truth and marvels tell.

Thy ways are very truth and light,
    And thee their God declare;
What pow'r in magnitude and might
    Can with our God compare?

Thou art the God, which self-aver'd
    Such wonders couldst atchieve;

And hast promulg'd thy pow'rful word,
    That mortals might believe.

The people whom thy might restor'd,
    Thy mercy shall acquit,
Redeeming Jacob from the sword,
    And Joseph from the pit.

The waters saw thee, O Most High,
    The waters were afraid,
And ocean left his bottom dry,
    His inmost depths dismay'd.

The clouds their copious rain distill'd,
    And midst the waters hot
The sounding air the thunder fill'd,
    And all thy darts were shot.

Thy thunder's voice was heard around,
    The quickning lightnings shone,
And run and flash upon the ground,
    Earth's hollow caverns groan.

Thy way is where the waters yield,
    And in the briny baths,
And there thy footsteps are conceal'd,
    Nor can one trace thy paths.

Their way, like sheep, thy people won
    Before the shepherd's rod,
Their priest was Aaron, Jethro's son
    Their chief, and Christ their God.

PSALM LXXVIII

List, O my people, to the law,
    Which grace and truth indulge,
And in your ears receive with awe
    The doctrine I promulge.

I will in high mysterious verse
    The parable unfold,
And to th' assembled tribes rehearse
    Hard sentences of old.

Ev'n such as we ourselves have heard,
    And in our mem'ries known,
Or which by filial love endear'd
    Our aged sires have shown.

That we should not such truths conceal,
    But hand directly down
To our posterity with zeal
    God's wonders and renown.

With Jacob's race a league he struck,
    A law for ev'ry tribe,
Which infants, when they ceas'd to suck,
    Might from their sires imbibe:

That thence proceeding heir from heir,
    Each other they might warn,
And a preservative prepare
    For children yet unborn;

To this intent, that when they came
    To their maturer growth,
Their issue might embrace the same
    God's solemn league and oath.

That they might their affections set
    And on their God confide.
And not his miracles forget,
    But by his laws abide.

And not be like their father's race
    Impatient and absurd
A generation far from grace
    And traitors to the word.

Like Ephraim's sons, which arm'd for blows,
    And muster'd for assault,
With their habergeons, and their bows
    Made infamous revolt.

The holy covenant of God
    Was not by them observ'd,
They left the paths of peace untrod,
    And from his ways they swerv'd;

Hence all th' atchievements that were past,
    They taught their thoughts to shun,
And those stupendous things and vast,
    Which he for them had done.

Prodigious works, THE GREAT I AM,
    Before the patriarch swains,
Accomplish'd in the land of Ham,
    And Zoan's famous plains.

He for his people's passage cleft
    The waters of the deep,
The parted billows right and left
    Ascended on an heap.

A pillar'd cloud, their guide by day,
    Forbade the sun to scorch,

And fire from heav'n to shew the way
    Was in the night their torch.

He clave the flints, which teem'd with sap
    To quench their raging drouth,
The stream descended from the gap,
    As from a torrent's mouth.

He brought out waters from the rocks
    Which other murmurs hush'd,
And for their families and flocks
    It like the rivers rush'd.

Yet for all this with eager haste
    Their congregation sinn'd
Against the Highest in the waste,
    Until their swarms he thinn'd.

They tempted goodness to defeat
    God's mercy by distrust;
With impious hearts requiring meat
    To gratify their lust.

They also blasphemously said,
    Shall God provide us food,
And shall sufficient be convey'd
    Into this desart rude?

He smote the stony rock indeed
    The thirsty to refresh,
But will the miracle succeed
    To give his people flesh?

At Israel then Jehovah's wrath
    Was kindled like a fire;
And him to whom he pledg'd his troth
    He spurn'd in grievous ire.

Because their eyes and ears they shut,
    Nor would his works believe,
Nor in his help their trust they put
    Their errors to retrieve:

So he controul'd the clouds above
    To render up their stores,
And op'd in his indulgent love
    The heav'ns exterior doors.

From heav'n itself he gave them bread,
    Their clam'rous mouths to stop,
And in due measure o'er their head
    He made the manna drop.

So man was bidden to partake
    With angels in the skies,
For to their craving maws he brake
    A plenty to suffice.

He caus'd his eastern blast to lowr
    Upon the earth beneath,
And gave the south-west wind his pow'r
    A stronger gale to breathe.

He rained flesh upon them thick
    As dust upon the ground,
And fowls he lavish'd, quill'd and quick,
    Like sand beside the sound.

Upon their camp he let them fall,
    And in their tents bestow'd;
And crouded by the rapid squall
    They came to their abode.

So they regal'd till all were fill'd,
    And their desire obtain'd;

And from their lust the fleshy-will'd
　　Were by no checks restrain'd.

But while ev'n now their meat they chew,
　　The wrath of God awoke;
And of their wealthiest princes slew,
　　And Israel's pillars broke.

And tho' this terror and alarm
　　Might better things have taught;
They sinn'd the more, nor hail'd that arm
　　Which such great works had wrought.

He therefore left their youthful bloom
　　To vain licentious ways;
Their years of travel to the doom
　　Of trouble and amaze.

When he, the Godhead to assert,
　　Destroy'd them for their crimes,
Their hearts they hasted to convert,
　　And sought the Lord betimes.

And their dead mem'ries rous'd at length,
　　Acknowledg'd that the Lord,
E'en God most highest, was their strength,
　　Their Saviour and their ward.

Yet not the less they feign'd to sooth
　　His vengeance with their tongue,
And with dissembling lips and smooth
　　Their recantation sung.

For in their heart they were not whole
　　His dictates to espouse,
Nor kept his laws with all their soul,
　　According to their vows.

Yet he was still so loving kind
 That he their sin forgave;
Nor unto death their deeds assign'd,
 But let his vengeance wave.

Yea, oft he would his wrath asswage,
 And to his love return;
Nor suffer'd all his mighty rage
 Against his tribes to burn.

For he consider'd of what stuff
 Frail mortals are begot,
And that they're like the wind—a puff
 Which passes, and is not.

Oft they conspir'd, where desarts howl,
 Their Saviour to incense;
And in the wilderness were foul
 With many a gross offence.

They turn'd them back, and chose a chief,
 God's suffering love to prove;
And by their perfidy to grief
 The holy one they move.

They thought not of his mighty hand,
 Nor of that great event,
When he the waters chang'd to land,
 And made their foes repent;

The works which he in Egypt did,
 That harden'd hearts might yield,
And all the carcasses he hid
 In Zoan's conscious field.

He turn'd their waters into blood,
 And made their rivers stink,

That in the vitiated flood
    They could not lave nor drink.

Of every sort the vermin swarm'd
    To eat them up alive;
And frogs the royal rooms deform'd,
    Too dreadful to survive.

His dread commands upon their fruit
    The locust-troops employ,
The caterpillar and the newt
    Their labours to destroy.

The hailstones batter'd down the grape
    Of so much care and cost;
Nor could the mulberries escape
    The penetrating frost.

Their cattle too with hail he smote,
    As well as verdant groves,
To death his thunderbolts devote
    Their folded flocks and droves.

His wrath and fury fierce and strict
    He sent upon their host,
And fiends he suffer'd to afflict
    And vex their trembling coast.

He let his indignation loose
    Their bodies to infest,
The blasts their forfeit lives reduce
    To perish with the pest.

And by his angel smote the prime
    Of all th' Egyptian youth;
The most exalted and sublime
    Amongst the foes of truth.

But on his chosen tribes he smil'd,
    And led them forth in peace,
And safe conducted through the wild,
    As one that tends the fleece.

He brought them from the tyrant's realm,
    And was himself their guard,
While waves prevail'd their foes to whelm,
    And all their chariots marr'd.

And as their mind his grace instructs,
    And sanctifies from vice,
To that blest mountain he conducts
    He purchas'd with the price.

His host th' idolatrous eject,
    Lest they with them should mix,
And give their land to his elect,
    His wand'ring flock to fix.

So once more they began to thwart
    The will of God most high,
And with the way his laws exhort
    They scrupl'd to comply.

Like broken bows they started back,
    Preparing to rebel,
And keeping their forefathers track
    As from the Lord they fell.

For to provoke his wrath they built
    The shrines that he forbad;
And grieving Christ, the fiends of guilt
    In human forms they clad.

These crying sins the highest reach,
    And inmost heav'n offend;

And on his tribes he makes a breach
    While vengeful bolts descend.

The tabernacle he forsook,
    And stopt the voice of mirth,
And would no longer overlook
    The tent he pitch'd on earth.

Their strength no longer reinforc'd
    He doom'd to servile toil,
And all their beauteous bloom divorc'd
    To grace a foreign soil.

He gave his people to the sword,
    Their goodly lot revers'd,
And by their pray'r no more implor'd
    His heritage amerc'd.

Their young men into flames were driv'n
    For burnings to dispatch;
So that the damsels were not giv'n
    To their connubial match.

The sword, with its remorseless edge,
    The holy priests assail'd;
Nor was there left a tender pledge
    Or widow that bewail'd.

Then up arose as from a trance
    Th' omnipotence divine,
As warriors to the field advance,
    And leave their wives and wine.

He smote his foes, their hinder parts,
    And all their boasting quash'd,
And with perpetual shame their hearts
    By his rebuke abash'd.

To Joseph's house he would not grant
    This royal rank to see,
Nor deign'd, O Ephraim, to plant
    This glorious wreath on thee.

But blessed Judah was his choice,
    The tribe of most account,
And from his heav'n he gave his voice
    For Zion's favourite mount.

There pillar'd up with molten brass,
    His temple stands secure,
Made like the earth's continual mass
    For ever to endure.

He chose out David from the ranks,
    And plac'd above the world;
From folded sheep, and from the banks
    Where silver Kidron purl'd.

From following ewes with young ones big
    The tribes his task enlarge,
To place beneath his vine and fig
    The Lord's peculiar charge.

So with a heart God's special gift,
    And love by wisdom cool'd,
And with munificence and thrift
    O'er Jacob's sons he rul'd.

PSALM LXXIX

FROM afar, O God, the nations
    Thy possessions storm and sweep,
Churches now are desolations,
    And Jerusalem an heap.

These unform'd barbarian forces
  Birds with our dead bodies feast,
And thy saints dismember'd corses
  Give they to each savage beast.

Human blood, like wasted water,
  Round about the wall is shed,
And such universal slaughter
  Leaves no burial for the dead.

Us of God's own circumcision,
  All our adversaries brand;
Scorn'd we are, the trite derision
  E'en for outcasts of the land.

Lord, how long shall thy displeasure
  Punish our perverted ways;
Fed and fann'd beyond all measure
  Shall thy jealous fury blaze?

Let the bolts of thy correction
  Those who know thee not chastise;
Realms and kings in disaffection
  Who thy glorious name despise.

For revengeful and voracious
  They have prey'd on Jacob's race,
And have laid their hands rapacious
  On his goodly dwelling place.

O remember not how grievous
  Were thy servants sins of old,
But in mercy soon relieve us
  To such fell destroyers sold.

Help us, O thou blest Redeemer,
  For the glory of thy name;

Ward the ruffian, foil the schemer,
   And have mercy on our shame.

Wherefore should the heathen scoffer
   Say with supercilious brow,
Where is he to whom they offer,
   Where is God their helper now?

O let vengeance now be sated,
   Let the blood that's shed atone,
And from those who thus have hated
   Take away the hearts of stone.

From the dungeon deep resounding
   Hear the pris'ners as they sigh;
O let grace to pow'r abounding,
   Save the poor, condemn'd to die!

For their words of foul expression,
   Which our evil neighbours urge;
Give them grace unto confession,
   With thy blood blasphemers purge.

So shall they thou chose to sever
   To thyself a special stock,
Yield thee thanks and praise for ever,
   Blessed pastor of our flock.

PSALM LXXX

O PASTOR of Jeshurun's flock,
   Whom Joseph's sons intreat,
Give audience, and the bars unlock
   Of thy cherubic seat.

While Ephraim and Manasses bow,
  By Benjamin ador'd;
Stir up thyself, thy might avow,
  And grant the help implor'd.

Turn us, O God—diffuse that light
  Which penetrates the soul,
Remove the scales that dim our sight,
  And thou shalt make us whole.

O Lord, to whom the saints resort,
  God, whom the hosts obey;
How long wilt thou thy people thwart,
  Which in contrition pray?

Their piteous souls thy throne accost,
  The bread of tears they break;
The cup of weeping they exhaust,
  As for thy grace they seek.

We are become a strife to those
  That dwell on every side;
And thou hast made our deadly foes
  Thy servants to deride.

Turn us, O God, diffuse that light,
  Which penetrates the soul,
Remove the scales that dim our sight
  And thou shalt make us whole.

From Egypt thou hast brought a vine
  Of goodly branch and bloom;
Thou mad'st thy foes the field resign,
  And set it in their room.

A place where it might spread and shoot
  Thy love dispos'd and plann'd;

And when it once had fasten'd root,
    It's clusters fill'd the land.

The hills were cover'd with the shade,
    The tendrils interwove;
The grateful bow'rs the foliage made
    Was like a cedar-grove.

Her branches to the ports she sent,
    Where wafting ocean foams,
And her strong boughs with fruit were bent
    As far as Jordan roams.

Why hast thou broken down her mound,
    And rais'd her stately tow'r;
That all the wand'ring thieves around
    Her grapes at will devour.

The furious boars with greedy tusk
    The ranges overturn,
And goats and foxes to the husk
    The luscious bunches churn.

Turn then again, O Lord of hosts,
    Thy countenance benign,
And in our provinces and coasts
    Revisit this thy vine.

And look upon the horrid waste
    Where thine own vineyard stood,
And to the wounded branches haste
    Thou made so strong and good.

Its boughs are yielded to the flame,
    Its fibres to the knife;
But let thy grace their rage reclaim,
    And they shall mend their life.

O set thine hand upon the head
    Of thine adopted heir,
And bless us, that our foes may dread
    Such savage deeds to dare.

PSALM LXXXI

To God our strength the strains repay
    With gladness and delight;
Make all the musick that you may
    To Christ's eternal might.

Take up your voice the psalm to swell,
    And strike the timbrel true;
Ye that on lute and harp excel
    The sprightly notes renew.

Blow up the trumpet, as you see
    The moon's increasing rays,
Nor bate a jot of that decree
    That bids us sing and praise.

For this was more coercive made
    By him that did no wrong,
Which met the night he was betray'd
    To hymn the parting song.

And this he likewise deign'd to teach,
    When Joseph's sons return'd
From tyrants of a foreign speech,
    With whom they had sojourn'd.

'Twas I, ev'n Christ, thy shoulders eas'd
    From weight they could not bear;
And loos'd thy hands by Pharaoh seiz'd,
    To shape the potter's ware.

I heard thee humbled and devout,
    And girt thy trembling reins;
When cataracts began to spout,
    And whirlwinds swept the plains.

I prov'd thee in the floods of strife,
    Degraded for thy sake,
The fountain and the bread of life,
    Of which ye drank and brake.

Hear, O my flock, and rest assur'd,
    Thy hope is Jesus still;
For if thou had thyself inur'd
    To my most holy will;

Thy thoughts should not have been deprav'd
    To wo ship wood and stone;
The name in which thou must be sav'd
    Is Jesus Christ alone.

I am the Lord thy God that bought
    Thy ransom on the rood;
Ope then thy mouth, thou shalt be taught
    A taste for heav'nly food.

But ah! the fools and slow of heart
    The scriptures to believe
For ever from my laws depart;
    My prophets misconceive.

So for a season they were left
    To their licentious lust,
And of the grace of God bereft,
    Their own conceits to trust.

O that my people had an ear
    To that my words expound,

For if Jeshurun's faith and fear
    Had in my ways been found;

I should have silenc'd all the boast
    Of heathens at a blow,
And turn'd the Lord's victorious host
    Against their ghostly foe.

The tongues that prophesy'd in hate
    Should have renounc'd their lies,
But deathless should have been their date,
    And their's th' immortal prize.

The shepherd had his best bestow'd
    To feed his faithful flock;
While streams of milk and honey flow'd
    From Jesus Christ thy rock.

PSALM LXXXII

WHAT time the delegates of pride
In pomp assemble to decide
    Each controverted cause;
The judge supreme of Jesse's root
Is with the doctors to dispute
    The worth of human laws.

How long (says conscience as it stings)
Will ye pronounce on men and things,
    That brib'd and bias'd sit;
The key of knowledge ye conceal,
Nor those that to her court appeal
    Your fallacies admit.

Defend the widows of the poor,
And to the fatherless secure
    The property of peace;

Do justice to th' afflicted soul,
And give the needy wretch his dole
    The pris'ner his release.

Dissembling hypocrites uncloak,
Redeem the vassal from his yoke,
    To want thine aid afford;
Restore the prodigal his pledge,
And take away the cruel edge
    Of thine avenger's sword.

They know not, neither will they mind
Blind leaders of the wilful blind,
    The sons of fraud and force;
In acts of godliness remiss,
Whence the strong springs of social bliss
    Are broke and out of course.

I called your origin divine,
And prais'd the lustre of your line,
    Ye bore your heads so high,
As sons of God, and nothing less,
Ye were so guarded of access,
    So haughty of reply.

But ye shall share the common lot
With them whose worldly goods ye got,
    The wretches you enslave;
And he, whose angel comes by stealth,
Shall take your princedom, pride and wealth,
    And sink them in the grave.

Arise, and in thine own behalf
O Christ, destroy the golden calf,
    And worshippers of gain;
Judge thou mankind, for thou shalt come,
In mercies without bound or sum,
    O'er all the worlds to reign.

PSALM LXXXIII

O GOD, no more thy word withhold,
　　Nor from our suit refrain,
But let thine oracles unfold
　　Thy gracious will again.

For lo! thy foes collect in swarms,
　　By busy murm'rers led;
And traitors in a thousand forms
　　Have lifted up their head.

For they against thy saints consult,
　　Who make the church their care;
And mine with treach'ries occult
　　The men of private pray'r.

Come let us root them out, they said,
　　By factious fury link'd,
Till tribes be desolations made,
　　And Israel's name extinct.

For they have held with one consent
　　Against the Lord's elect;
And with confed'rate discontent
　　Our infamy project.

Fierce Edomites their camp arrange,
　　And Ishmael's sons convene;
And Moabites a league exchange
　　To join the Hagarene.

Gebal with Ammon's force unites,
　　And Amalek attends;
And proud Philistia's chief invites
　　The Tyrians for his friends.

There Ashur too himself allies,
    And has his blood forgot;
And with his rebel host supplies
    The spurious seed of Lot.

But their embattl'd legions quell
    As Madian's bands of old;
As Jabin, and as Sisera fell,
    Where Kison's waters roll'd.

Who were from pompous chariots flung,
    And mixt with Endor's dust,
And their dead carcasses like dung
    Beneath the surface thrust.

As Zeb and Oreb far'd, the same
    For their attempts provide;
Yea Zeba and Zalmunna's shame
    Their chief and troops betide!

Let us with impious threats, they cry,
    Upon the temples prey,
And from the shrines of the most high
    The sacred gold convey.

Lord, back again their squadrons wheel,
    Before such deeds are done,
And light as stubble let them feel
    The changing wind and run.

As flames the woody mountain burn,
    And in themselves expire;
So on their host their fury turn,
    As they from us retire.

As thy tempestuous blasts pursue,
    And dreadful thunder sounds,

Let them be warn'd, nor more renew
    Their insults on our bounds.

O Lord, with shame's ingenuous sense
    Their listless souls awake;
That they may a new life commence
    And to thine altar make.

And all confusion in thy end,
    And terrors after death,
In thy great love do thou defend
    By thine all-pow'rful BREATH.

And they shall know, that thou whose love,
    Can from such depths redeem,
E'n thou, LORD JESUS, art above
    All thrones and pow'rs supreme.

PSALM LXXXIV

O LORD, how lovely is thy bride,
    The church thy spouse confest;
The regions where her saints reside,
    How beautiful and blest!

My soul has made thy house her choice,
    And longs thy court to see;
My heart and earning flesh rejoice,
    Thou God of life in thee.

Yea, there the sparrow takes her perch,
    And builds her house on high,
And swallows in their maker's church
    Their craving nest supply.

These freely haunt the sacred walls,
    And to thine altars cling;
O Lord of hosts, whom rapture calls,
    My Saviour and my king.

They are the blest, that in thy courts
    As in their homes remain,
And whom eternal grace supports
    Thy praises to sustain.

The man is blessed, as he prays,
    Whose reins thy strength receive,
And in whose heart thy word and ways
    A deep impression leave.

As thro' this vale of tears he goes,
    He purifies his flesh,
And washes, while the fountain flows,
    Which rain and dews refresh.

Increasing still from strength to strength,
    Such pilgrims urge their race,
And they shall see the Lord at length
    In Zion, face to face.

O Lord, thou God of hosts descend
    To these the pray'rs I make,
Thou God of Jacob's seed attend
    For Jesus Christ his sake.

O Lord, let these my sighs induce
    Thy mercy to look down
To him, on whom thou pour'd thy cruse,
    And plac'd Judea's crown.

For but a day of love and fear
    Within thy blest abode

Is better than the livelong year
    On vain pursuits bestow'd.

Me would the service better please
    God's temple-door to keep,
Than dwell, where pomp and pow'r at ease
    On gorg'ous pillows sleep.

For Christ our light and shield shall give
    An infinite reward
Of ev'ry good to them that live
    A life unto the Lord.

O Lord, thou God, whom wise and just
    The hosts of heav'n proclaim,
The man is blest, that puts his trust
    In thy thrice-hallow'd name.

OR THIS

O HOW stupendous to the sight,
What lovely mansions of delight
    Thy dwelling place displays!
O Lord, to whom the hosts belong
Of thousands, and ten thousands, strong
    In thankfulness and praise.

My heart unto thy courts aspires,
And all its longings and desires
    Are for the bliss above,
My zealous soul within me burns,
My very flesh cries out and yerns
    For Christ the life of love.

Yea there the sparrow takes her rest,
There also to her craving nest
    The swallow food may bring;
592

Ev'n at thine altar are they found,
O Thou, to whom the hosts resound,
    My Lord, my God, and king!

They are the blessed which reside,
And for eternal peace provide
    Within thy blest abodes,
With thee their spirits shall commune,
And always praising, sing and tune
    Their holy harps and odes.

The man is blest, where'er he dwells,
That in religious works excels
    With strength divine endu'd,
Whose stedfast life is to obey,
And in and from whose heart thy way
    Is graven and pursu'd.

Such, as their errors they bewail
Thro' Baca's penitential vale,
    And trust alone in him,
Refresh'd as in the well-spring's cool
Shall use it, and lo! ev'ry pool
    Is swoln above the brim.

From strength redoubl'd, as they go,
To strength increasing shall they grow,
    And to refresh and cheer
Their travail thro' the narrow gate,
The God of God's from Zion's height
    In glory shall appear.

O Lord, to whom the hosts belong
Of thousands and ten thousands strong,
    Incline thy gracious ear,
For ever and thou art the same,
The God of Jacob is thy name,
    Thou God of Jacob hear.

O ever present to defend
Let thy benevolence descend
    On this anointed head,
The face of thine elect behold,
On which, as by thy seer foretold,
    The holy cruse was shed.

For one day in thy blest abode,
O Lord, with thankfulness bestow'd
    On pray'r and praise and thee,
Better than thousands, thousand fold,
Ten thousand times ten thousand told,
    Is such a day to me.

I would with joyfulness embrace
The keeper of the temple's place,
    Whom constant care confines,
And rather there abide and bless,
Than dwell where pompous wickedness
    In sumptuous tents reclines.

For God is our defence, is light,
And with his grace he shall requite,
    With worship shall reward
Nor ought that he delights to give
Shall he withhold from them that live
    A life unto the Lord.

O God, to whom the hosts belong
Of thousands and ten thousands strong,
    That bow towards thy throne,
The man is blest, whose strength thou art
Who puts his trust with all his heart
    In thee, O Lord, alone.

PSALM LXXXV

O LORD, thy land has favour found
 And mercy speeds again,
To loosen Israel ty'd and bound
 In Satan's irksome chain.

Thy grace to Jacob's chosen seed
 With their remorse begins,
And Christ, the merit that we plead,
 Has cover'd all our sins.

With them thou deignedst to betroth
 Thou art no more displeas'd,
And God the Father's righteous wrath
 Is thro' his son appeas'd.

O Lord, the Saviour of the poor,
 Anew our hearts create,
And make the world's salvation sure
 From its abandon'd state.

When Christ his tears our sins efface,
 Can goodness ever fail,
And after this stupendous grace
 Shall vice again prevail?

Wilt thou not reconcile our souls
 To their eternal rest,
And glad our hearts, as Christ enrol's
 Our name among the blest?

O Lord thy bounteous mercy shew
 And these thy people spare,
And with thy saving health endue
 The penitents at pray'r.

I will to my supreme content
    The word of Christ explore—
'The heavenly king's at hand, repent,
    And go and sin no more.'

Whene'er a faithful two or three
    Attend the warning peal,
There Christ himself delights to be
    His glories to reveal.

Thy truth and mercy for increase
    Of love have met in bliss,
Stern righteousness and gentle peace
    Have join'd the holy kiss.

From Christ the branch fair truth shall sprout
    And bloom again on earth,
And justifying grace come out
    From heav'n at Shilo's birth.

Yea, God's benevolence shall beam
    As Satan's pow'r he stops,
And men and earth reform'd shall teem
    With grace and fruitful crops.

A gracious message shall apprize
    The world of better days;
His sermons, precepts, pray'r revise
    And regulate our ways.

PSALM LXXXVI

O Lord, thy supplicant receive
    His wishes to obtain,
With fav'ring ear indulge thy leave
    To poverty and pain.

My God for my defence prepare,
    For I am sound and pure;
And of thy providential care
    I still myself assure.

O Lord, in mercy condescend
    My fervent pray'r to meet,
For day by day my knees shall bend
    While I thy grace intreat.

O Lord, thy servant's soul refresh,
    Which heaviness dismays;
For unto thee from out my flesh
    That soul by pray'r I raise.

For thou, O Lord, art good to all,
    And gracious in excess;
And great in mercy at the call
    Of such as kneel and bless.

Attend, O Lord, while thus I pray,
    And as my voice aspires,
From humbled members hear and weigh
    The drift of my desires.

What time adversities deject,
    And anguish is severe,
I will mine orisons direct
    To thine attentive ear.

Midst angels and the thrones above,
    There is no God like thee;
Nor is there any pow'r, but love,
    That can such deeds decree.

All nations, whose stupendous sum
    Thy word came forth to frame,

O Lord, shall to thine altar come,
    And glorify thy name.

For thou art magnitude and might,
    All wonders are thine own;
In love, in omnipresent light,
    Art very God alone.

Lord, thine instructive grace impart,
    That I may keep thy law;
O to thy nature knit my heart,
    And to thine honour awe.

O Lord, my God, I will restore
    The thanks so justly due;
And from my heart for evermore
    The songs of praise renew.

For thy compassion is extream
    My sorrows to dispel,
And thou my spirit shalt redeem
    From out the depths of hell.

O God, the proud in armies rise,
    And men of guile profound,
Who have not thee before their eyes,
    Attempt my soul to wound.

But thou, O Lord our God, art fraught
    With clemency divine,
Long-suff'ring, and surpassing thought
    As faithful and benign.

O with thy mercy turn at length,
    Nor my petition shun,
And as a servant give me strength,
    And bless me as a son.

O show some token of thy grace
    My sland'rers to refute,
For all my griefs thy words solace,
    And my fatigues recruit.

PSALM LXXXVII

YEA, her foundations are sublime,
And first the holy hills we climb,
    Ere we can reach her gate;
And God fair Zion's tow'r renowns
Far more than all Judea's towns,
    And loves to make her great.

Thy beauties are a theme to raise
Encomiasts to transcendent praise,
    Illustrious as thou art;
All earth of thine alliance boasts,
Thou city of the Lord of hosts,
    And fair Judea's heart.

Rahab amongst the wonders nam'd,
And Babylon so loudly fam'd,
    Proud spires and sumptuous domes;
In these my psalms to God are known,
And they the praise of Zion own
    In all their tongues and tomes.

Behold Philistia's sons aspire,
The Morians and the Men of Tyre,
    Peculiar gifts adorn;
But Judah o'er all rivals tow'rs,
All claim and contest overpow'rs,
    There is Emanuel born.

And Zion more applause shall gain,
That there is born in her domain
 The child both God and man;
And Christ her lasting throne shall found,
From forth Beer-Sheba's utmost bound,
 Ev'n to remotest Dan.

The Lord, in everlasting verse,
In ears of angels shall rehearse
 That Jesus is his heir,
And he, by whom the tribes are seal'd
At Bethlehem—Judah is reveal'd,
 And comes incarnate there.

Then shall he marshal every row
Of Cherubs that the trumpet blow,
 And Seraphims that sing;
From Jordan purer streams shall rise,
Both Jews and Gentiles to baptize,
 And consecrated spring.

PSALM LXXXVIII

O MY Saviour, I beseech thee
 Day and night my cry to hear;
Oh! let these my breathings reach thee,
 And my calling touch thine ear.

For my soul is weak and weary,
 As the floods of grief prevail,
And my life in darkness dreary
 Is upon the point to fail.

I am of no rank accounted,
 ·Ev'n like one whom worms devour;
And consider'd as dismounted
 From all eminence and pow'r.

Free to lay me down and perish,
    Where the slaughter'd warrior moulds,
Whom no friendly mem'ries cherish,
    And thy hand no longer holds.

Thou for punishment hast laid me
    In the lowest pit to dwell,
And to outer gloom convey'd me
    In the dismal depth of hell.

Thy fierce anger has embarrass'd
    And my loaded heart depress'd;
All thy plagues at once have harrass'd,
    All thy storms have wreck'd my rest.

Thou hast broke my sweet connections,
    All my friends my wants exile;
And have turn'd their kind affections
    To malevolence and bile.

Under such severe restriction
    Am I to my bed confin'd,
That I cannot sooth affliction
    By conversing with mankind.

I am weak thro' tears habitual
    In my eyes and in my head;
Yet I daily serve thy ritual,
    And to thee my hands I spread.

Wilt thou miracles exhibit
    Wasted on the lifeless lump?
Shall the dead to pay their tribute
    Rise before the warning trump?

Wilt thou speed the gracious mission
    Of thy mercy to the pit;

And consign'd to deep perdition
    Shall thy faith the man refit?

In the dark, when dead and rotten,
    Shall the flesh thy works adore,
Where all favours are forgotten,
    And where musick is no more?

Thee, Lord Jesus, I solicit
    With my plaintive voice and lyre;
And deriv'd from faith implicit
    Early shall my pray'r aspire.

Wherefore, Lord, is this denial,
    As my spirit sues for grace?
Why at such a time of trial
    Dost thou take away thy face?

Full of pain, with terror shaken,
    Ev'n as gasping to depart,
All thy plagues I have partaken,
    Youth and age, with anxious heart.

As my faith begins to waver,
    Then the storms of wrath increase;
And the fear of thy disfavour
    Has undone my private peace.

All mine enemies combining,
    Come about me like a moat,
Harm against my life designing,
    Which they to their wrath devote.

Banish'd every friend and lover,
    Broke each link of dear delight;
And the shades of darkness hover
    O'er my desolated sight.

PSALM LXXXIX

THE loving-kindness of the Lord
    Shall grace the sacred page;
His truth the Psalmist shall record
    From age to rising age.

For I have said that mercy's reign
    Henceforward shall commence;
And fed by faithfulness maintain
    Her infinite expence.

I have renew'd with mine elect
    My covenant of peace,
And sworn to this benign effect
    To him that kept the fleece.

Thy house I will for ever build,
    And in thy seed descend;
The throne of David shall be fill'd,
    And flourish without end.

O Lord, the heav'ns with sapphire cield,
    And all the lights that blaze,
Their truth affords a beauteous field
    For social saints to praise.

For who is he to heav'n referr'd,
    Intelligence or form,
That can be nam'd with God the word,
    In whom all life is warm?

Or what is he of most account
    Amongst the pow'rs below,
That can be liken'd to the fount
    From whence all honours flow?

Amidst the synod of the blest,
    The Lord is greatly fear'd;
And with incessant pray'r addrest
    By souls of saints inspher'd.

O Lord, incomparable God,
    Thy truth around we hail,
From heav'ns first convex to the sod
    That sheathes the humble vale.

Thou rul'st the raging of the sea,
    When surges foam and chafe;
Thou bidst contending waves agree,
    To send the navy safe.

Thou hast upon th' Egyptian land
    Thy dreadful vengeance hurl'd;
And scatter'd with thy mighty hand
    Their host throughout the world.

Thine are the heav'ns, and bright array
    That in succession shine,
The earth, thy firm foundations stay,
    And all therein is thine.

Thou hast divided north and south,
    Bleak wind and genial flame;
And fragrant Hermon finds a mouth,
    And Tabor sings thy name.

Strong is thine arm in deeds of love,
    Thy hand of peerless proof;
Thy right hand brandishes above
    The heav'n's interior roof.

Justice and equity beneath
    Thy throne have placed their seat;

But truth and love thy spirit breathe,
    And thy bright presence greet.

Blest is the people, whom the voice
    Of conscience calls thine own;
Lord, in thy light they shall rejoice,
    And seek towards thy throne.

They in thy name shall take delight,
    Each consecrated hour;
And make their boast, as they recite
    Thy deeds of righteous pow'r.

Thou art the glory of our strength,
    In safeguard or assault;
And in the blessed Lamb at length
    Our horn thou shalt exalt.

For God is our redoubted fort,
    And our defence sustains,
And o'er each province, coast and port
    The Lord Jehova reigns.

Thy visionary word of late
    Thou deignedst to disclose;
A man by grace and nature great
    I have prepar'd and chose.

My servant David have I tried,
    And his good deeds allow;
My holy cruse I have applied
    To bless his honour'd brow.

My hand his sceptre shall uphold,
    And keep him in his seat;
And my right arm shall make him bold
    Opposers to defeat.

Invidious foes shall have no force
    When he his troops alarms,
The son of fraud shall have recourse
    To flight before his arms.

I will his enemies destroy
    Myself before his eyes;
And with my bitt'rest plagues annoy
    Whoe'er his worth despise.

My mercy shall be with his sword,
    My truth his acts adorn;
And by his fervent pray'r implor'd,
    I will exalt his horn.

I likewise will advance his realm
    Where distant oceans roll;
And his right hand shall hold the helm
    The billows to controul.

He shall invoke my name in pray'r,
    And in my service live;
'My God omnipotent to spare,
    My father to forgive.'

And I his pedigree will fix
    Amongst celestial things,
Whose race and rank with angels mix
    Above all earthly kings.

My mercy and mine aid shall be
    For ever on his side;
And by the grant I now decree
    I surely will abide.

Son after son he shall endure,
    His offspring will I raise;

606

And his succession will secure
  As heav'ns eternal days,

But if the shoots of such a stem
  My dictate should refuse;
And in their lives that way condemn,
  Which grace to faith foreshews;

If they should break the holy laws
  Which my commandments urge,
I will my zealous angel cause
  Their dire offence to scourge.

But yet I will not wholly take
  My kindness from his seed;
Nor void that blessed promise make
  To which my truth agreed.

I will for my own glory care,
  Nor change the word I past;
Once by my holiness I sware
  That David's house shou'd last.

The line of his descent shall run
  With deathless heroes crown'd;
Before my presence, as the sun,
  His throne shall be renown'd.

His daughters shall be sweet and fair,
  As is the lunar light;
That faithful type of heav'nly care,
  And blessing of the night.

But thou hast with abhorrence spurn'd
  And thine anointed left;
Thy love to indignation turn'd,
  And of thy grace bereft.

The covenant is of no trust,
    If thus his days he drag;
And o'er his crown, defil'd in dust,
    His foes blaspheme and brag.

Around his borders are infring'd,
    And all the tow'rs he barr'd;
The moats fill'd up, the gates unhing'd,
    The strong munitions marr'd.

All those that pass along the road,
    Upon his goods encroach;
And every neighbour comes to goad
    His conscience with reproach.

Thou liftest up the hand that throws
    The spear against his breast;
Thou hast delighted all his foes
    Which his domains infest.

No longer is his weapon edg'd
    To boast ten thousands slain,
And victory no more is fledg'd
    For his renown'd campaign.

No more his blooming honours glow
    With heav'ns effulgent beam;
His eminence is levell'd low,
    And made of none esteem.

The riper days thou hast cut off
    Of all his better age,
And giv'n his glory to the scoff
    Of obloquy and rage.

For ever, Lord, wilt thou retire
    From my submissive suit,

And shall thine anger burn like fire
    In this my disrepute?

Remember how my time is brief,
    How urgent nature's debt;
Why hast thou fashion'd man for grief,
    And unavailing sweat?

What man is he, whose strength or art
    Shall his own spirit save,
Or who, when gasping to depart,
    Can countermine the grave?

Lord, where is thine indulgent oath
    That David should despond,
And thy good truth engag'd to both
    His truncheon and his wand?

Remember how thy gallant tribes
    Are with invectives stung,
And how my loathing ear imbibes
    The taunts of many a tongue.

Wherewith thine enemies insult,
    And call our ways perverse;
And o'er thy servants faults exult,
    And their good fame asperse.

Hosanna to the throne of grace—
    Amen from all the throng;
Amen from him that holds his place
    To lead the choir in song.

PSALM XC

O LORD of everlasting praise,
Through anxious life's entangled maze,
 Our never-failing guide;
Thou art our hope from race to race,
Our refuge and the dwelling place
 In which our souls reside.

Ere on this earth were yet reliev'd
The mountains, ere this earth receiv'd
 Her being or her frame
Before all worlds supreme thy will,
From ever, and from ever still,
 Eternal is thy name.

Debas'd with error and abuse,
Thy terrors man to dust reduce,
 That penitence may grow—
Again thy love paternal cries—
Arise, ye sons of men arise,
 Return to bliss from woe.

For years thy creatures, as they flee,
Are all responsible to thee,
 The present as the past;
Ev'n thousands in thy perfect sight,
Are as the watch of yester-night
 When their account is cast.

Thou bidst them off into the deep
Of vast eternity to sleep,
 And in their peace remain;
While others like the grass succeed,
For their determin'd goal to speed,
 Nor e'er revolve again.

Grass! in the morning fresh and green,
With many a various flow'r between,
    A blessing for our eyes;
By noon to full perfection grown,
Ere evening darkens it is mown,
    And like the gath'rer dies.

For thy fierce wrath contracts our span,
And this whole edifice of man
    Is troubled and diseas'd;
And we of bitt'rest anguish taste,
And to our dissolution haste,
    When thou art once displeas'd.

The crimes, with which we are disgrac'd,
Before thy judgment seat are plac'd
    Their dreadful doom to hear;
Our lurking sins which hate the day,
All in thy sight themselves display,
    And at thy word appear.

Our days to their conclusion run,
Since wrath against thy sinful son
    Has made our frame more frail;
With pain from youth to age we climb,
And all the tenor of our time
    Is like a trav'llers tale.

Of human life th' allotted length
Is sev'nty years, uncommon strength
    Another ten survives;
Yet is that strength but toil and grief,
Whose grace of farther proof is brief,
    And soon whose end arrives.

Who knows the pow'r and blest effect
Of thy dread anger? thine elect
    Who thy just hand admire;

611

To those alone that act amiss,
And thwart their everlasting bliss,
    The Lord prolongs his ire.

So teach us, gracious, to review
The past of nature, and pursue
    The future in our mind;
To wisdom that we may apply
Our hearts, and learn like men to die,
    The task for life assign'd.

O be thou placable by pray'r,
And stand between us and despair,
    How long wilt thou postpone?
To these our off'rings as they burn,
Do thou propitiate thy return,
    And let our tears atone.

O fill us with the sweet content
Of thy free grace, as we repent;
    Thy saving health mature
For a perpetual resource
To joy and gladness, while the course
    Of nature shall endure.

Our joys according to the date
Of all our ways proportionate,
    Thou judge, immensely mild;
Let peace commence, where bondage ends,
And Canaan multiply amends
    For Egypt and the wild.

The work of thy stupendous hand,
Which leads us to the promis'd land,
    To these thy sheep compleat;
That glory may be giv'n to thee
From us and our posterity,
    Which thou in peace shalt seat.

And may the glorious rays that beam
From forth the majesty supreme,
    Each body bless and soul;
Prosper the sweat of every brow
And hand industrious—yea, do thou
    Our handy work controul.

PSALM XCI

HE that dwells beneath the cover
    Of his blessed Saviour's wings,
Shall abide where cherubs hover,
    Praising Christ, the king of kings.

I will hope for my admission,
    Thro' the Lord, amongst the just;
Thou, O God, art my munition,
    And the strength to which I trust.

For he shall thy soul deliver
    From the hunter's secret snare;
And from death's determin'd quiver
    In the pestilential air.

He beneath his wings shall hide thee,
    To his downy bosom press'd;
Faith, the shield he shall provide thee,
    Truth, the corslet of thy breast.

Thou shalt walk by night, defying
    Damp and darkness, and dismay;
And the darts of envy flying
    Thickest in the blaze of day.

Thou shalt scape the blasts contagious,
    Ambush'd in the moonless night;

And the pestilence outrageous,
    Rise in the meridian light.

Thousands, and ten thousands by thee
    At the common blow shall fall;
But the stroke shall not come nigh thee,
    Nor alarm thy life at all.

Yea, thine eyes shall see the terror
    Of th' ungodly in distress,
The reward of wilful error,
    Death and dread beyond redress.

For in Christ is expectation
    That to peace I shall go hence;
On a glorious elevation
    Stands thy fortress of defence.

No disasters shall undo thee,
    With thy house it shall be well;
Nor shall any plague pursue thee,
    But thou shalt in safety dwell.

For to guard thy life precarious,
    He th' angelic host shall send;
And thro' dangers great and various
    They thy travel shall attend.

With thy wings they shall surround thee,
    In their arms they shall sustain,
Lest a stumbling stone should wound thee,
    And delusion be thy bane.

Adders shall be void of danger,
    Lions shall their fierceness loose;
Thou the dragon in thy manger
    With thine infant heel shall bruise.

Since upon his heav'nly Father
   He has set his love divine;
I will raise his name the rather
   As he has acknowledg'd mine.

He shall call, and I will hear him,
   And be with his low estate;
From his troubles I will clear him,
   And his honour shall be great.

He shall know no dissolution,
   But shall have th' immortal prize;
And from pain and persecution
   To the joys of heav'n arise.

PSALM XCII

THE work is good, which duty claims
   To thee when praises are restor'd;
O Christ, of beings, and of names
   Most highest, most ador'd!

To tell of thy stupendous grace
   Before the rising morn betimes,
In pensive night thy truth to trace,
   When thought itself sublimes;

Upon the decachord and lute,
   Upon the musick loud and strong,
Grave tones accordant with acute,
   Upon the harp and song.

With gladness, which thy works excite,
   My soul springs upwards and expands;
And I will blazon with delight
   The wonders of thy hands.

O Lord, how glorious is that love
    Of strength such miracles to breathe;
Thy thoughts from infinite above,
    To infinite beneath!

Here he, to whom there is no beam
    Of heaven'ly wisdom, is at fault;
And his low mind to such a theme
    A fool cannot exalt.

Ev'n in their bloom and verdant years
    The godless soon shall to the grave;
But endless love thro' Christ his tears
    Shall true contrition save.

For lo! thy mischief-working foes
    Shall not continue in their guile;
Which must with death's last summons close,
    Nor more their souls defile.

But like an unicorn my crest
    Shall flourish and exalted be;
With oil anointed, newly prest,
    From God's redundant tree.

God grant it to my lifted eyes,
    To see my foes to Christ repair;
My ears to hear their contrite sighs,
    And penitential pray'r!

The righteous man shall upwards spring,
    Like palms which have with winter strove,
And spread abroad each godly wing,
    Like cedars of the grove.

Such as the Lord himself transplants
    And places in his hallow'd courts;

Their fences of protection grants,
　　And by his word supports.

In age more plenteous they shall fruit,
　　And rise beyond the temple's wall;
And from the tree-top to the root
　　Be shapely stout and tall.

That they most clearly may submit,
　　The rectitude of God to view;
That all his ways and works are fit,
　　Are holy, just and true.

PSALM XCIII

THE Lord the king himself arrays,
　　Arrays in robes of ambient light;
Around his glories as they blaze
　　He girds magnificence and might.

The earth on arches has he brac'd
　　With all the master's strength and art,
So that she may not be displac'd,
　　Nor ever from her center start.

Thou hast thy heav'nly throne of state
　　Ere since the world began decreed;
But thou from everlasting great,
　　All place and period didst precede.

O Lord, the sea tumultuous raves,
　　Contending billows foam and roar;
The floods have lifted up their waves
　　Above the rising cliffs ashore.

The sea is mighty as at will
    So dreadful mountainous he rolls;
But mightier He, whose 'peace be still',
    At once his boist'rous rage controuls.

O Christ, our faith thy pow'r supports,
    In truth thy testament excells;
And holiness in all thy courts
    With dignity for ever dwells.

PSALM XCIV

IF to God alone pertaining,
    All the pow'rs of vengeance bow,
Held in ward by love restraining,
    God of vengeance hear us now.

Judge supreme, whose righteous spirit
    Heav'n and earth pervades and tries;
Rise, and after their demerit
    Hostile pomp and pride chastise.

Lord, how long shall guilt licentious
    Take its swing and have its will;
O'er the good and conscientious
    Shall it reign and triumph still?

Hands so foul, and hearts so naughty,
    Shall they scoff and make parade;
And be arrogant and haughty
    With the parts that they degrade.

Lord, with cruel persecution,
    They transfix us to the heart;
And they damp our resolution,
    Working with vexatious art.

They the widow tear in pieces,
    And the stranger in his bed;
Nor their lust of murder ceases
    Till the fatherless has bled.

Tush they say, with scoff malicious,
    From the Lord no risque we run,
Nor is Jacob's God suspicious
    That a thing like this is done.

Be ye ware of contradiction,
    You that to your error cleave,
And amongst us brave conviction,
    When will you the truth perceive?

Shall not God—O vain derision—
    He that gave your hearing, hear,
He that form'd the orbs of vision,
    Is not his discernment clear?

Shall not he which rules the nations,
    And the heathen world sustains,
Teacher of all ranks and stations,
    Hold the scourge as well as reins?

God the human heart inspecting,
    Sees the way its workings tend;
All the plans of its projecting,
    In what vanity they end.

Blessed is a man's submission
    To his Saviour's wholesome rod;
For 'tis oft in such condition
    That we have the grace of God;

That for all the hours of sorrow
    Gifted patience may atone,

Till the terrors of to-morrow
  Frown upon the foe alone.

For they shall not be deserted,
  Which themselves of God profess;
But his pow'r is still exerted
  When his people plead distress.

Ev'n until the dread appearance
  Of the Lord to judge our race,
All true hearts with firm adherence
  Shall his blessed word embrace.

Who will join me in defiance
  Of the men that God oppose;
Where shall I obtain alliance
  To discomfit virtue's foes?

If the Lord had not befriended
  All my troops, however brave,
Doubtless this my life had ended
  In the silence of the grave.

When I found my steps had stumbled,
  Pray'r to thee was my resource—
Lord, thy mercy saw me humbled,
  And upheld me in my course.

In the cloud of sorrows pressing
  All at once upon my soul,
Thy consolatory blessing
  Shall their sad effects controul.

Shall the slaves to Mammon bowing
  Havě a part in Christ the king,
With their practice of allowing
  Mischief as a lawful thing!

While against the good convening,
   They his righteous soul afflict,
And the base and bloody skreening,
   Worth and innocence convict.

But from every vain pretender
   That conspires to pull me down,
God himself is my defender,
   And the fort of my renown.

Foes of their benign Creator,
   Would, as their own malice, fare,
Did not Christ the Mediator
   Plead his merits and his pray'r.

PSALM XCV

COME, O come with exultation,
   From your hearts your voices swell
To the strength of our salvation;
   To the Lord your transport tell.

Let us congregate before him,
   And his awful presence hail;
And with joyful psalms adore him
   As we kneel before the veil.

For the Lord our God tremendous,
   Great beyond conception tow'rs;
His dominion is stupendous
   Far o'er other thrones and pow'rs.

All the regions and recesses
   Of this earth are in his hand,
And each hill his strength confesses,
   Heap'd aloft upon the land.

Ocean is his creature, rolling
  Waves on waves which foam and roar,
And his hands, the floods controuling,
  Laid the glebe, and rais'd the shore.

Come, O come with Christian union
  Let us these our frames abase,
And approach to his communion
  Kneeling, falling on our face.

For he is our Lord and master,
  We the people of his choice;
He's a most indulgent pastor
  To the sheep that know his voice.

Rule your hearts through self-denial,
  Let my word attention win,
Nor behave as at your trial
  In the wilderness of Sin;

When your sires, my spirit grieving,
  Seeking after signs, rebell'd,
And were restiff, disbelieving
  What their very eyes beheld;

Forty years my grace was thwarted
  By this impious race I said;
From the words which I exhorted,
  From my ways their hearts have stray'd.

Unto whom I pass'd my sentence,
  That they should remain unbless'd;
Yet through faith and true repentance
  They shall come into my rest.

PSALM XCVI

O SING to Jesus Christ a song
   Of grace and novelty combin'd;
O swell an anthem sweet and strong,
   Ye nations of mankind.

O sing, your blessed Saviour's name
   With grateful blazonry display,
And let his love your breasts inflame
   Day rising upon day.

His honour to the heathen shew,
   And thence their grov'ling thoughts sublime,
And bring his wonders to the view
   Of ev'ry realm and clime.

For God is infinitely great,
   Above all praise his merit tow'rs,
Above the magnitude and height
   Of other thrones and pow'rs.

All idols are but frail and fond,
   To which the heathen pray'r's preferr'd;
But God made heav'n, and heav'n beyond,
   By his Almighty Word.

Worship and glorious pomp precede,
   Whene'er he makes his awful march,
And very pow'r and fame indeed
   His temple over-arch.

Ascribe, ye families of love,
   To God the gracious Lord of light;
Ascribe ye to the Lamb and Dove
   The worship and the might.

Ascribe ye to the Lord with zeal
   The honour which his name supports,

And with our heart's free off'ring kneel,
   And come into his courts.

With all the grace of praise and pray'r,
   And adoration's meekest bow,
O let all tongues in fear declare
   His truth, and pay their vow.

The Lord's supremacy maintain,
   And bid the heathen folk believe
On him which fixt the starry train,
   And judges to reprieve.

Rejoice ye to the FIRST and LAST,
   The heav'ns and earth, with all that breathe,
And sea voluminous and vast,
   With them that are beneath.

Let all the verdant field be glad,
   With ev'ry motion, ev'ry voice,
And trees, in blooming fragrance clad,
   Before the Lord rejoice.

For lo! he comes, he comes to try,
   And o'er the world supreme to sit,
When all that to his truth apply
   His mercy shall acquit.

PSALM XCVII

THE Lord is king, Jehovah reigns—
The hills, the valleys and the plains
   Confess their genial joys;
Hence pregnant nature blooms and smiles;
Hence gladness in unnumber'd isles
   Which ocean's bosom buoys.

In circling clouds he sits inclos'd,
Round him the darkness is dispos'd
    His radiant form to veil;
Judgment and righteousness are laid
The ground, on which his throne is made,
    Th' eternal beam and scale.

Before him of seraphic fame
Goes forward a devouring flame
    Of intellectual fire;
At which his enemies consume,
To which all peopl'd space gives room,
    All obstacles retire.

The subtle flames he fixt and sent,
And made the lightning permanent
    O'er all the world's expanse;
Earth saw and trembl'd with dismay,
And, on her pillars as she lay,
    She rous'd as from a trance.

The hills were melted at th' amaze
And fury of th' effulgent blaze,
    Like wax upon the hearth,
When he was present to dispense
The terrors of Omnipotence,
    Which sways both heav'n and earth.

The heav'ns in goodly pomp display'd,
And peerless pulchritude array'd,
    Thy perfect truth attest;
And all the earth her mingled race
Have witness'd thy descending grace,
    In shining glory drest.

Shame on the seeker after signs,
That vanity and vice enshrines,
    And serves the prince of hell;

Hear at his word, ye painted stocks,
And worship him, ye chissel'd rocks,
    And fall as Dagon fell.

Zion exulted at the stroke,
To hear, when Ashdod's god was broke,
    The tumult and the bruit,
Judah's glad damsels were alive;
Whene'er thy blessed bolts arrive,
    Love also claims its fruit.

For seated on the topmost height,
O God, thou art immensely great,
    And thine is nature's law;
Sublime above sublime he sees,
And overlooks the rocks and trees
    From whence their gods they saw.

Ye who the love of God profess,
See that no evil ye caress,
    Nor cast a look behind;
He keeps the souls of all his saints
From those whose vicious commerce taints,
    And mars both man and mind.

For Christ is justify'd alone,
Light evangelical is sown,
    And God's new day is sprung;
And from his peace he shall impart
His gladness to the sound of heart,
    And to the true of tongue.

Ye sheep of God's peculiar choice,
Whom faith has justify'd, rejoice
    That you are form'd anew;
Incessant praise, your incense heap,
By practical thanksgiving keep
    His holy name in view.

PSALM XCVIII

O FRAME the strains anew,
Your grateful natures shew
   To Christ, the source of holy song;
For passing deeds he wrought,
Until to God he brought,
   By miracle, the faithless throng.

With hands which saints revere,
And arm without compeer,
   He has the vast atchievement done,
And over death and hell,
With all the Fiends that fell,
   This day's immortal trophies won.

CHRIST JESUS has declar'd
That sinners shall be spar'd,
   And that through him salvation came;
The world could not convince
Of sin the righteous prince,
   So manifest his spotless fame.

He still has bore in mind
His mercies, loving kind,
   And truth to Jacob's house engag'd;
And all remotest earth
Have seen, in Shilo's birth,
   Salvation, as by seers presag'd.

Then, O ye peopl'd lands,
Unite in tuneful bands,
   And to the Lord your gladness tell,
For such a blest reverse
Your hymns of thanks rehearse,
   Your songs of exultation swell.

Ye jocund harpers, kneel,
As you the impulse feel,
   And to the Lord your praise intend;
Ye holy psalmists join
In harmony divine,
   And all your grateful voices blend.

The chearful trumpet sound,
And let the horns be wound,
   To yield thro' twisted brass their tone;
The choicest notes employ,
To prove your hearty joy
   In him that sits upon the throne.

Let ocean make a noise
With ev'ry isle he buoys,
   And all the life his floods contain,
The rounded world above,
And all that live and love
   Their Maker on the hills or plain.

The vast and briny broad
All hands aloft applaud,
   E'en as the mountain or the rock,
Which also have their ways,
In spirit God to praise,
   Who comes by Christ to judge his flock.

Descending from on high,
His people he shall try,
   In mercy, goodness, and in grace;
His merits we shall plead,
Till rigour must recede,
   And wrath to charity give place.

OR THIS

To the tune of the old CIV

O SING a new song, and sound an alarm
In Christ, who has done vast deeds of amaze;
With his mighty prowess, and God's holy arm
He has prov'd victorious o'er wonder and praise.

The Lord has made known his marvellous grace,
To save the whole world, submitting to view
His virtue and merits throughout the wide space
Of service and empire, to Gentile and Jew.

His mercy and truth for us has he shewn,
Remembring his oath with Abraham his friend;
Of gospel salvation good tidings have flown
From Dan to Beersheba, and to the world's end.

O make yourselves glad in God, all ye lands,
Ye nations and tongues your Saviour proclaim,
With sweet exultation, and palms in your hands,
Present your thanksgiving, and dwell on his name.

His goodness extol with hand on the lyre,
And as the strings vie in songs of delight;
In joy to Jehovah, ye psalmists aspire,
As gratitude dictates, his praises recite.

With soul-soothing in tune to the wings
    shawms,
Of breezes serene O temper your mirth,
And with the shrill trumpet sound, hail King of kings,
Thy creatures adore thee their Saviour on earth.

Let sea make a noise, his legions and shoals,
Which glide on his wave, or love the still deep,
And let the round convex exult on his poles,
With all that beneath it God's benefits reap.

629

Resound ye proud floods with glorious applause,
And soar as the hills which range on the shore;
Let both bless together the Lord and his laws,
For he comes in judgment the world to restore.

'Tis he comes to judge in mercy supream
The just for unjust, to live and to die,
When his sinful people his love shall redeem,
And to the lost myriads his merits apply.

PSALM XCIX

THE Lord is king, the world submits
    And trembles to his sway;
'Twixt cherubims he sits,
    Let utmost earth obey.

On Zion's hill the Lord is great,
    Sublime upon sublime,
And of exalted state
    O'er ev'ry realm and clime.

They shall give thanks, and bless his name
    From ev'ry peopl'd land,
Which is of hallow'd fame,
    And wonderful and grand.

The pow'r of Christ is righteous love,
    Whose ways thou hast prepar'd;
Thy word from heav'n above
    To Jacob's tents declar'd.

O magnify the Lord your God,
    And on your face remain,
Meek hearts, and feet unshod,
    For holy is his reign.

Moses and Aaron of his priests,
　And Samuel of his seers,
These worship'd in the east,
　And God, when blest, appears.

He spake from out the pillar'd cloud,
　Their faithfulness to try,
And they his laws avow'd,
　As publish'd from on high.

O Lord, our God, thy mercy sav'd
　Their sinking souls from hell;
From them thy wrath was wav'd,
　And on their idols fell.

O magnify the Lord our God,
　Upon his mount remain,
Meek hearts, and feet unshod,
　For holy is his reign.

PSALM C

HOSANNA! let the choir be mann'd,
　To God ye distant regions throng,
In one melodious service band,
　And glad his presence with a song.

Know Christ is God, the human frame
　Is not of mortal will or deed;
His creatures from his hands we came,
　His flock upon his pasture feed.

O go your way into his gates,
　Approach with thankful heart the veil,
As gratitude his laud relates,
　His name with loud applauses hail.

For endless grace the Lord supplies,
    And boundless love his word contains;
His truth with his duration vies,
    And still from race to race remains.

ANOTHER OF THE C

HOSANNA! people of all lands
Unite your voices, lift your hands,
    And to the Lord repair,
And thankful fall upon your face,
And hail with songs the throne of grace,
    And shew your gladness there.

Yourselves in this belief confirm,
That man his talent and his term
    Are God's, and not his own;
We are the flock he folds and feeds
With milk and honey in his meads,
    The Lord is God alone.

O go, but send your song before,
Into his courts, his temple door,
    His name in anthems raise—
Give thanks the soul's immortal food,
And speak him great, and speak him good,
    Your hearts with rapture blaze.

For race by race he is renown'd
In mercies which to peace abound,
    In truth reveal'd and taught;
And gracious is the Lord of love,
Above all estimate, above
    The flight of time and thought.

PSALM CI

My song shall be of mercy's reign,
 And of the great tremendous day;
And I will consecrate the strain
 To Christ's triumphant sway.

O make my notions strong and clear
 Of ev'ry word thy laws promulge,
And that I may thy truth revere,
 Her brightest rays indulge.

With thine illuminations blest,
 When thou thy Spirit shalt impart,
I will prepare for such a guest
 An open honest heart.

I basely will not undertake
 To act injustice, or deceive;
I hate the vices of the snake,
 To such I will not cleave.

Whoe'er defrauds, or goes beyond
 His brother, him I will expel;
With churls I will not correspond,
 Or with the wicked dwell.

Whoe'er with private caution smite
 Behind their backs their neighbour's fame,
Their folly and their dastard spite
 I from my soul disclaim.

Whose heart is hard, and stomach high,
 And looks disdainful on the poor,
I will not to his word reply,
 Nor his discourse endure.

By search industrious in my mind,
   I cast about, and with my eyes
To find the good and well-inclin'd
   For friends and for allies.

Whoe'er is studious to deserve,
   And lives in innocence and pray'r,
O'er all my servants he shall serve,
   And in my substance share.

But treachery, disguise, and fraud,
   Shall not be seen beneath my roof,
And he that carries lies abroad,
   Shall keep himself aloof.

I soon shall banish with the rod
   Of justice all the worthless crew;
But I with meekness pray to God
   That threats alone may do.

PSALM CII

To my pray'r, O Lord, applying
   Thine indulgent ear, give heed,
Let the voice of hardship crying
   In its orisons succeed.

In the tedious hours of trouble,
   As for pity thus I pine,
And my soul's complaint redouble,
   Quickly to my vows incline.

For my days in pain revolving,
   Like the wreathed smoke expire,
And my wasted bones dissolving,
   Are like billets in the fire.

In my heart I am dejected,
  Wither'd like the garner'd hay,
And through dread I have neglected
  The refreshment of the day.

For with thine afflicting arrow
  I reiterate my groans,
There's no nurture in my marrow,
  Nor consistence in my bones.

In this dreary situation,
  Like a pelican I seem,
Or an owl, that takes her station
  Where the moons on deserts gleam.

I have labour'd my researches,
  Pond'ring on my lonely state,
Watching as the sparrow perches
  On the house without his mate.

For their malice advantageous
  This my case my foes deride;
All day long they are outrageous,
  That against me are ally'd.

For with tears these ashes steeping,
  I have eaten them for bread;
And my cup with bitter weeping
  I have mingled on my bed.

This proceeds from thy resentment,
  Which afflicts me more than all;
And the days of my contentment
  Now exasperate my fall.

Vain and void of satisfaction,
  All my days like shadows pass;

And through illness and inaction,
   I am wither'd as the grass.

But thy Spirit by transfusion,
   Height and depth eternal sounds,
And in glorious revolution
   Thy memorial has no bounds.

Rise, and with thy gracious blessing,
   Visit Zion in her woe;
For necessity is pressing
   That thy mercy-beams should flow.

For her fabricks firm and stately
   Are thy servant's grief and care,
And the rubbish, which was lately
   Tow'rs and Spires aloft in air.

As thy truth their doubt convinces,
   Heathen realms thy name shall fear,
And the world's remotest princes
   Shall thy majesty revere.

When the Lord his domes rebuilding,
   Shall again fair Zion raise,
And her roofs from Ophir gilding,
   When again his glories blaze.

When he to the poor aspiring,
   Shall vouchsafe his pray'rs their fruit,
And to sorrow deep-desiring
   His blest Comforter depute.

This a memorable chapter
   In the chronicles shall stand;
And posterity with rapture
   Shall adore their Saviour's hand.

For the holiest heav'ns unfolding,
 In the Spirit he descends,
And terrestrial things beholding,
 On our wants his love attends.

To decide the pris'ners causes,
 And their bondage to unseal,
That, as human vengeance pauses,
 He their sentence may repeal.

That with joy they may expatiate
 On thy name at Zion's hill,
And their souls they may ingratiate,
 As thy worship they fulfil.

When the multitude assemble
 Their thanksgiving to unite,
And presented kingdoms tremble
 At his throne, who judges right.—

He my youthful strength afflicted,
 As my pilgrimage I made,
And my progress interdicted,
 Cutting off his blessed aid.

But my soul besought assistance,
 O my Saviour, spare my prime;
As for thy divine existence,
 It is not of space or time.

Thou, O Lord, this earth hast founded,
 And her hills and valleys deckt,
And the lucid heav'ns were rounded
 By thy hands of blest effect.

They shall perish—but the splendor
 Of thy glory shall endure,

They like garments must surrender
　　All their gloss, and be obscure.

They shall change at thy direction,
　　And be folded like a scroll,
But in permanent perfection
　　All thy years eternal roll.

Our good offspring shall continue
　　Through our faith in Christ his name,
And with arms of genuine sinew
　　Shall support their father's fame.

PSALM CIII

THE praises, O my soul, restore
　　To God, as thus I kneel,
And all mine inward man adore
　　His holy name with zeal.

The praises, O my soul, repeat
　　To Christ, which paid thy debt,
Nor ever to remembrance sweet
　　His benefits forget;

Which all thy fault and frailty spares,
　　As his high merits plead,
And thine infirmity repairs
　　With succour in thy need.

Which suffer'd from the gulf profound
　　Thy spirit to redeem,
And has thy life with mercy crown'd,
　　And tenderness extreme.

638

Which makes a plenteous fare thine own,
    And all thy nerves has strung;
E'en like an eagle newly flown,
    So lusty and so young.

The Lord in righteousness decrees
    The judgment of the poor,
And from the foul oppressor frees
    All those that wrong endure.

His way to Moses he disclos'd
    On Horeb's hallow'd rock;
His works stupendous interpos'd
    To save his chosen flock.

The Lord, with boundless love and grace,
    Has mercy on our state;
And long he bears the headstrong race,
    His goodness is so great.

His spirit will not always strive
    With guilt abash'd by fear,
Nor can his utmost wrath survive
    One penitential tear.

He has not with our vices dealt
    According to their cry;
Nor have our sins his anger felt,
    Like their most grievous dye.

For look how high the heav'n is made
    Above the verdant sod,
So great his mercy is display'd
    To all that fear their God.

And see how wide yon eastern ray
    Is from its western course,

So far from us that weep and pray
    He shall our sins divorce.

Yea, as a tender father's love
    Is to his child inclin'd,
E'en with such pity—far above
    Such pity—God is kind.

For well the Maker knows the mould,
    And gives allowance just;
And he remembers that we hold
    A frame of mortal dust.

The days of man are as the hour
    Of verdure on the lawn—
He thrives as flourishes the flow'r
    That opens to the dawn.

For chives and stem to death are doom'd
    By passing winds that blow,
And that gay place on which they bloom'd
    No more their sweets shall know.

But God the Word has ever stood
    By all his faithful sons,
And in the blood benign and good,
    The certain blessing runs

For such as with attention deep
    Reflect upon his will,
And all his laws with spirit keep,
    And chearfully fulfil.

God on his right has rais'd a seat
    To place the spotless Lamb;
Thrones, Pow'rs, Dominions kiss the feet
    Of Jesus Christ 'I AM'.

O praise the Lord, angelic band,
    In excellency strong;
Ye that obey his dread command,
    Or hearken to his song.

O praise the Lord, all ye his hosts,
    Upon his will intent;
Ye servants that maintain your posts
    In highest heav'n's ascent.

O all ye works, your Maker bless,
    The good and gracious Lord;
And with all energy and stress
    Do thou, my soul, accord.

OR THIS

O PRAISE the Lord, my soul endu'd
With all the grace of gratitude,
    And zeal's divinest flame:
And all that is within me bless
The merits of his holiness,
    And honour of his name.

O praise the Lord, my soul—excite
Thy heart's free pow'rs do him right,
    Which has such comfort sent;
His mercies present and behind
Remember, and maintain a mind
    Upon his love intent.

Which thee of all thy crime acquits,
And thine iniquity remits
    By his most precious cross;

Which earns thy troubles to appease,
And to remove thy sore disease,
    And purify thy dross.

Which, by his tenderness extreme,
Could from the gulph of death redeem
    Thy soul to vengeance bound;
And with his everlasting care,
His benediction on thy pray'r,
    Thy forfeit life has crown'd.

Which has thine appetite restor'd
From pining sickness, and thy board
    With plenteous bounty blest;
And has renew'd thy lusty strength,
Like some young eagle fledg'd at length,
    And tow'ring from his nest.

The Lord his righteousness asserts,
And his avenging pow'r exerts
    Against the tyrant's pride;
He hears the cries of saints oppress'd,
And sees their grievances redress'd,
    And all their wants supply'd.

His holy ways himself he taught
To Moses, and the tribes he brought
    To Horeb's hallow'd mount;
And deign'd in person, as they pray'd,
And were in meek prostration laid,
    His wonders to recount.

The Lord is infinitely great
In mercy for our weak estate,
    And gracious to endear;
His indignation he retards,
And all-beneficent regards
    The penitential tear.

He will not long with Israel strive,
Nor let his chastisement survive
    One pang of due remorse;
His wrath upon the rebel race
Is but a momentary space,
    And not of endless force.

We have not his resentment felt
In measure, like as we have dealt
    By his divine decrees;
Nor will he our misdoings try,
According to that heinous dye
    Which in his truth he sees.

As that vast interval between,
Yon azure cloud and forests green,
    Heav'ns vault o'er earth's expanse;
So marvellously great and clear,
For all the servants of his fear
    His mercy-beams advance.

And as the womb of early day
Is distant from the setting ray
    Which cheques the western shade;
So far from our afflicted sight
Into the realms of endless night
    He has our sins convey'd.

Yea, as the father to his child
With fervent haste is reconcil'd,
    And pities to forgive;
So shall the Lord of love receive
The children which on him believe,
    And in his service live.

Because he knows our feeble frame,
Both what we are, and whence we came,
    And where we loath or lust;

And he remembers well our terms,
How shortly must we to the worms
    Resign our sinful dust.

The days of human life recede
Like grass, that's gather'd from the mead,
    And which the cattle crops;
And all its pride, and all its pow'r,
Is but the triumph of a flow'r,
    That buds, and blooms, and drops.

For soon as on the fragrant beds
The tempest blows, its chives it sheds,
    And all its balmy store;
And that gay place on which it grew,
No more shall boast its beauteous hue,
    And taste its sweets no more.

But God his mercies to his fold
From ever and for ever hold,
    And his most righteous sway
From race to race is still maintain'd,
And childrens children unprofan'd,
    His holy laws obey.

Such as his covenant peruse
With zealous diligence, and chuse
    The paths of endless bliss;
Such as his testaments respect,
And in the truths his laws direct
    Are never found remiss.

For one accepted Son alone
God has prepar'd an endless throne
    In heav'ns stupendous height;
His irresistible domain
He shall o'er all the world retain,
    Each region, realm, and state.

O bless the Lord, ye sons of light,
Ye that are excellent in might
    To do his dread command;
Which in his presence are preferr'd,
And to the thunder of his word
    In transport understand.

O bless the Lord, and make your boast
Of his perfection, all the host
    Of Jesus and his spouse;
Ye his good pleasure who fulfill,
And act in all things as his will
    Permits or disallows.

O bless the Lord in every part,
Ye works of his consummate art,
    Where'er his wisdom guides;
From pole to sympathetic pole,
And thou too bless him, O my soul,
    Which in my heart presides.

PSALM CIV

BLESS thou the Lord, my soul—how great,
O Lord, what a stupendous weight
    Of honours crown thy name;
Thou'rt cloath'd with majesty and might,
And glories how exceeding bright
    Come clust'ring on thy fame!

With light, which thou hast purer made,
As with a robe thou art array'd,
    Whose pow'r the world upholds;
And hang'st the skies in beauteous blue,
Wav'd like a curtain to the view,
    Down heav'n's high dome in folds.

His chamber-beams in floods he shrouds,
His chariots are the rolling clouds
    Upon th' etherial arch;
And on the rapid winds their wings
Majestical, the king of kings
    Walks in his awful march.

The guardian spirits know their post,
His heralds are th' angelic host
    Obedient to his will;
The delegated lightnings fly,
And flames are sent on embassy
    His mandates to fulfill.

Fair and full-finished at her birth,
Firm at the first he fixt the earth,
    And wrought her bases fast;
Her deep foundations has he girt,
That as the lively springs exert,
    Her state of rest might last.

Upon the surface deep and wide
Thou pouredst out the flowing tide,
    Like some loose garment spread;
The rising waters stood around,
And swoln above the level ground,
    O'ertop the mountain's head.

But at the thunder of thy word
Their inundations were deterr'd,
    And thy rebuke obey'd;
And to the centre from the top,
Th' unfathom'd ocean to a drop
    Was pacify'd and laid.

Then up into the hills they go,
And down upon the vales below
    Again their way they find;

Till at such places they abide,
And in those due directions glide
   Thy wisdom has assign'd.

Thou over-rul'st the liquid mass,
And in the bounds they may not pass
   Thou shalt their floods restrain;
The way that is prescrib'd they learn
For ever, nor shall they return
   To cover earth again.

The living springs at his command
Are sent a succour to the land,
   For rivers the resource;
Which as by stooping woods they curve
'Mongst intermingl'd hills preserve
   Their interrupted course.

All beasts that haunt the distant groves,
Frequent the lucid stream in droves,
   As need and nature rule,
And asses of the wild, assuage
Their thirst, and the meridian age
   Of sultry sun-beams cool.

Near them thro' blossoms bursting ripe
The birds upon the perches pipe,
   As boughs the herbage shield;
And while each other they salute,
The trees from every quiv'ring shoot,
   Melodious musick yield.

He from his chambers dew distills,
And waters with his rain the hills
   Where'er their summits soar;
The vales, with sweet luxuriance clad,
Make all the face of nature glad
   With never-failing store.

He laid the verdant turf to graze,
That earth the due supplies might raise
    Of annual food and wealth;
And fragrant herbs and flow'rs profuse
The seasons on the field produce
    For pleasure and for health.

He planted on the rock the vine,
To glad the heart of man with wine,
  . And crown the thankful bowl;
And to exhilarate the face,
He gave the cruise, and broke in grace
    His bread sustains the soul.

The trees with precious balsam sweat,
Which GRACE in seemly rows has set
    By her almighty pow'r;
And Lebanon, which God perfumes,
His crest with stately cedar plumes,
    Whose tufted tops embow'r.

The feather'd families of air
Contrive their cunning fabricks there,
    What time the sexes mix;
The storks for elevation seek
To loftier firs with bolder beak
    Their pensile house to fix.

The kid that brouses on the thyme,
Looks from the precipice sublime,
    And every peril braves;
The skulking connies dwell secure,
And for defence their young immure
    In quarries and in caves.

He taught the silver moon her way,
Her monthly and nocturnal sway,
    Where'er she wanes or grows;

The glorious globe that gilds the skies
Is conscious of his early rise,
  And his descent he knows.

The lines of light and shade to mark
Is thine, thou bidst the night be dark,
  Beneath whose solemn gloom
The forest-beasts forsake their den,
And all that shun the walks of men,
  Their wonted haunts resume.

The lions rouse to fill the scene,
With eyes of baleful lightning keen
  Upon the desart rude;
And as in surly-sounding tone
They make the hollow caverns groan,
  From God require their food.

But at the glancing of the dawn,
Ere yet the sun-beams o'er the lawn
  The burnish'd orb unveil;
Alarm'd they flee their nightly round,
And in their place with peace profound
  Their weary'd limbs regale.

While man, frail nature to sustain,
Awakes to labour and to pain,
  Till from the wish'd-for west
Th' approaches of the dusky eve
Give to his toil a short reprieve,
  And send him home to rest.

How manifold thy works are made,
O Lord—by thankful man survey'd,
  What an exhaustless theme!
In wisdom didst thou all dispense,
How with thy vast munificence
  Heav'n, earth, air, all things teem!

So does the sea, whose shelvy rocks
And depths with numberless he stocks
    From life's eternal fount;
Some in the nether crannies skulk,
And some of huge enormous bulk
    The swelling floods surmount.

There go the ships from shore to shore,
Of distant climes the diff'rent store
    To take and to discharge;
There that Leviathan resorts,
Which at thy blessed bidding sports
    At leisure and at large.

All these upon thy love depend,
And on thy providence attend
    Their daily wants to urge;
And as the stated hour revolves,
The bread is broke, the dew dissolves
    Upon the rising surge.

They gather that which is diffus'd,
Nor ought is wasted or abus'd,
    So has thy wisdom will'd;
Thy bounteous hand prepares a feast,
And all from greatest to the least
    Thou fillest, and they're fill'd.

Thou hid'st thy face—however brief
Thy absence, it is instant grief
    Of infinite degree;
'Tis thine to give, and to withdraw
Their breath, and by a stablish'd law
    They are, or cease to be.

But by succession they survive,
And sense and pow'r to move derive,
    As from thy spirit sent;

Anew their moulded dust is warm'd—
Ev'n earth herself by thee reform'd,
    Shall other scenes present.

The glorious majesty and love
Of God shall have no bounds, above
    All mortal change and chance;
The Lord shall heav'ns whole choir employ
In anthems of exceeding joy
    To see his works advance.

Abash'd at his tremendous look,
The earth with strong commotions shook,
    Which all her awe bespoke;
He touch'd the hills, their summits nod,
And at the weighty hand of God
    They totter, and they smoke.

That goodness which these years prolongs,
Shall give new spirit to my songs
    As measure to my span;
While I my life and limbs possess,
The bounteous author will I bless
    With all the might of man.

As in the spirit I repeat
His praise, my musings shall be sweet,
    To just refinement wrought;
Yea, while I yet suppress my voice,
To thee, O Lord, will I rejoice
    In melody of thought.

The men, by carnal sins entic'd,
Must fall before the rod of Christ,
    Confounded and amaz'd;—
Praise thou the Lord, my soul apart—
Praise ye, who hear with voice and heart—
    The Lord our God be prais'd.

PSALM CV

O TO the Lord restore your thanks,
    Invoke his name in pray'r;
And to the people of all ranks
    His wond'rous works declare.

O let your holy songs ascend
    In ecstasy of praise,
And let your conversation tend
    His miracles to blaze.

With joy his hallow'd name revere,
    And let your mirth aspire;
And let their hearts be of good cheer
    Which after him enquire.

Seek ye the Lord, and pay your court
    For ever to his might;
Your bodies and your souls deport
    Toward his heav'nly light.

Remember his stupendous hand
    The blessings it conferr'd;
His visitations dreadful grand,
    And judgments of his word.

O ye that from his servant rose
    The fruit of Abraham's loins;
Ye sons of Jacob, whom he chose,
    And from the world disjoins.

He is the Lord our God alone,
    And from our faithful tribes
His truth o'er all the world is sown,
    And laws which he prescribes.

He has been mindful of the deed
    Where love and truth engage;
To bless and raise the patriarch's seed,
    Ev'n to the thousandth age.

The grant at first for Abraham made,
    Which still his oath confirms,
And then to Isaac was convey'd
    Upon as easy terms.

And therewith Jacob in his turn
    Was order'd to comply;
A law of infinite concern
    And everlasting tie.

Importing 'I will give to thee
    A land of wine and oil,
And thou shalt peace and plenty see
    In Canaan's pleasant soil.'

And this high grace he deign'd to shew
    To pilgrims on the road,
When Israel was yet but few,
    And of no fixt abode.

What time they with their flocks and kine
    Thro' various nations rang'd;
And led by providence divine
    So many climes they chang'd.

No man could hurt their goods or lives
    As they their tents remov'd,
And for the virtue of their wives
    He mighty kings reprov'd.

'Touch not mine elders, on whose head
    I've pour'd my hallow'd cruse,

And save my prophets from the dread
    Of insult and abuse.'

Moreover, he the famine sent,
    Which in their coasts prevail'd;
Till all their corn and bread was spent,
    And their provision fail'd.

But still extremities to stave
    He sped a man before;
E'n Joseph, who was made a slave
    The plenty to restore.

Whose feet they in the stocks enthrall'd,
    And to the soul they pierc'd;
For in the spirit he was gall'd
    To find himself amerc'd.

Until his hardship in his youth
    Was weigh'd, and cause was heard;
And by the Lord's prophetic truth
    His innocence appear'd.

His words of peace the king convince—
    Who straight his bounds enlarg'd,
And Egypt's fierce despotic prince
    His jeopardy discharg'd.

And as he took him from his ward
    Proceeded to console,
By making him a mighty lord
    All Egypt to controul.

To teach their princes to conduct
    Themselves by virtue's rule,
And all their senators instruct
    In wisdom's godly school.

And Israel drove his herds and flocks
 Where he was Pharaoh's guest,
And Jacob with his silver locks
 Th' Egyptian monarch blest.

And by his grace his people rose
 To be a mighty host;
And they were stronger than their foes
 In their wide-peopl'd coast.

Whose heart was chang'd to black deceit
 From friendship and good will;
The men with cruelty to treat,
 And put in chains and kill.

Then Moses his command appoints
 To succour their complaint,
And by the Holy Ghost anoints
 Great Aaron for his saint.

And these applied his vengeful rod
 Against their hate and guile,
And shew'd the miracles of God
 In all the coasts of Nile.

He sent the dark till it was felt,
 And grievous was the gloom;
Nor yet their hearts with pity melt,
 But stiffly still presume.

He turn'd their waters into blood
 As they rebell'd the more,
And fishes choak'd in such a flood
 Were thrown upon the shore.

The pools o'erflow'd with frogs unclean
 Which on the land were heap'd,

And were in royal chambers seen,
    And on the couches leap'd.

He spake—and of a thousand forms
    Came flies of deadly sting,
And filthy lice in swarms on swarms
    On pompous garments cling.

The hail in massy stones he shot
    The trees and herbs to wound;
And 'midst the show'r the lightnings hot
    Came flashing on the ground.

He smote their vines and fig-trees void
    Of blossom, leaf, and fruit;
And all their woods and groves destroy'd,
    By breaking branch and root.

He spoke—the caterpillars came,
    And locust with his pow'rs,
A numerous troop, to mar and maim
    The tender grass and flow'rs.

The first born of the land he smote,
    And caus'd a gen'ral grief,
Their youths of most especial note,
    And of their strength the chief.

He brought them forth with gems and gold,
    And led himself the van;
Nor could they in their tribes behold
    One feeble child or man.

Egypt was glad when all their force
    From their domains decamp'd,
Such terror added to remorse
    Had their oppressors dampt.

A cloud its milder light reflects
 Their rout by day to guide;
And fire their nightly march directs
 From heav'n itself supply'd.

While to his name with cries they sought,
 As life had been at stake,
Innumerable quails he brought,
 The bread of heav'n he brake.

He call'd forth water from the veins
 Of marble to their thirst,
So much, that on the desart plains
 A new-form'd river burst.

For wherefore? he remember'd well
 His covenant of grace,
When faithful Abraham meekly fell
 Before him on his face.

Thus he his people to release
 Kept angels in employ,
And led his heritage in peace,
 His chosen flock with joy.

And he transferr'd into their hands
 The heathen's vine to dress;
And all their labours and their lands
 To people and possess;

That they might worship him, and serve
 For more abundant cause,
And with fidelity observe
 The dictates of his laws.

PSALM CVI

O RENDER thanks to God unfeign'd
    For his exceeding grace,
Because his mercy is maintain'd
    From race to rising race.

Who can his noble acts express
    By which the world he sways,
Or with sufficient ardour bless
    In all the modes of praise?

They are the blest to whom is giv'n
    A deep judicious mind,
And who have in their dealings thriv'n
    By being just and kind.

Regard my suit in that degree,
    Thou blest our herds and fleece,
And made thy people fat and free—
    O visit me with peace.

That I may see, and seeing share
    The bliss of thine elect,
And join their gen'ral thanks and pray'r
    Whom heav'nly pow'rs protect.

But maugre all we've seen and felt
    Of gratify'd desires,
We have in base injustice dealt,
    Offending like our sires.

Our fathers learnt not to regard
    Thy pow'r and love display'd
In Egypt, but their hearts were hard,
    When seas, ev'n seas obey'd.

Yet still the helpless he supplyd,
    Weak heads with heart of stone,
That he might make his pow'r to pride
    And heathen baseness known.

He gave the sea a reprimand—
    It cleft itself in two;
And there, as on the desert land,
    He led his people through.

And from their enemies he sav'd
    And every servile fear,
And that stupendous gulph they brav'd
    With armies in their rear;

Which as they harrass'd their retreat,
    Returning waters drown'd,
And total was the strange defeat,
    Not one a refuge found.

Then gave they credence to his word
    Which freed their souls from wrong,
And praise upon the march preferr'd,
    And sang the pilgrim's song.

But soon they hasted to forget
    His wonders, and were naught;
Nor would their vain affections set
    Upon the word he taught,

Their minds abandoning to lust
    While they were in the wild,
And still provoking God's disgust
    As they themselves defil'd.

And to their murmurs he bestow'd
    Their bodies to regale,

While conscience ply'd his inward goad,
    And made their spirits fail.

And Moses too, the man of God,
    They in their tents inflam'd,
And Aaron—till the budding rod
    The priest of God proclaim'd.

So yawning earth took Dathan in,
    And all his sect devour'd,
And bold Abiram and his kin
    The terror overpow'r'd.

From hell the fiery torrents rush'd
    The rebels to consume,
And all th' ungodly crew were crush'd
    In this tremendous doom.

At Horeb's mount they dar'd rebel,
    When Aaron they controul'd,
And in absurd prostration fell
    Before a calf of gold.

And thus they danc'd and made a feast
    Their glory to estrange
Into the likeness of a beast,
    That feeds upon the grange.

And God no longer was esteem'd,
    Which from their woes and toils
And Egypt's grievous chains redeem'd
    In triumph and with spoils.

Which did such wonders in the coast
    Of them that disbeliev'd,
And in the sea o'er Pharaoh's host
    Such fearful things atchiev'd.

So that the fatal hour was fixt
    For lust and discontent,
If Moses had not stood betwixt
    Perdition to prevent.

Yea, with misdoubtings and in scorn
    That pleasant land they view'd,
The honey, milk, the wine and corn,
    Which by his word he shew'd.

And murmur'd loudly in their camp
    Against their Saviour's choice,
His goodness in conceit to cramp—
    Nor hearken'd to his voice.

Then on their clamours and distaste
    He rous'd his arm to lift,
And overthrew them in the waste,
    And sent their souls adrift.

Their seed amidst their foes to cast
    Upon a distant shore;
And whirl them with an adverse blast
    Where comfort is no more.

To Baal-Peor in crowds they swarm'd
    With folly at their head,
And ate, as they the rites perform'd,
    Their off'rings of the dead.

Thus reprobate, and idly vague
    From his indulgent yoke,
The tribes he visits with a plague
    Determin'd to provoke.

Then Phineas had the grace to kneel,
    And to the Lord he pray'd;

And as he whirl'd the missive steel
    The plague at once was stay'd.

And this was plac'd to his account
    As righteous and sublime,
By which his glory shall surmount
    The force of death and time.

They also anger'd him by doubt
    At Marah's floods of gall;
So that he let his fury out
    On one to rescue all.

Because they wou'd their chief incense
    By clamours in their drowth,
So that he fell upon offence
    Incautious with his mouth:

Nor were th' idolatrous destroy'd
    According to their charge,
But with their wiles were they decoy'd,
    And let them live at large;

And mingled with the spurious foe
    The genuine seed of Seth,
Which now into their customs grow,
    And learn their deeds of death.

In such, that to a hammer'd stock
    Their souls from God they wean'd,
And offer'd, human ears to shock,
    Their children to the fiend.

Yea, their own tender babes themselves
    They nipp'd in early bud,
Devoting them to Canaan's elves
    Till earth was whelm'd with blood.

Thus with their works they went astray,
    Their bodies to pollute
With acts of shame that shun the day,
    From,which there is no fruit.

Wherefore a dread consuming wrath
    Was kindled from the Lord;
That those to whom he pledg'd his troth
    He from his heart abhorr'd.

And into strangers hand he gave
    Their liberties and lives,
Who schem'd their manners to deprave,
    And put their limbs in gyves.

The barb'rous foe oppress'd their loins
    Their morals to infect;
What God from his good grace disjoins,
    The tyrant can subject.

Yea, many a time their ransom cost
    A most stupendous price;
His patience they the more exhaust
    With crimes of black device.

But when their cries began to pierce
    Thro' hardship and constraint,
He gave their terrors a reverse,
    And favour'd their complaint.

Himself in boundless love he binds
    His mercy to maintain;
Nay more, he humaniz'd the minds
    Of those that held their chain.

From heathen realms and gross revolt
    To rank thy tribes restore,

And thee, O God! we will exalt,
    And in thy praises soar.

Give endless praise to Christ the king
    From ev'ry tongue and pen,
And let all congregations sing
    Hosanna and Amen.

PSALM CVII

Your thanks return,
O ye that burn
    With zeal's immortal blaze;
For mercies beam
From God supream
    To claim perpetual praise.

Let them repay
Their thanks to-day,
    Who find themselves enlarg'd;
Whose galling yoke
The Lord has broke,
    And from their foes discharg'd.

And call'd their bands
From distant lands
    By mandate of his mouth;
From toil to rest
From east and west,
    Cold north, and scorching south.

They took their rout,
And round about
    Far from the ready road

In wilds remain'd,
Till they obtain'd
  To settle their abode.

In desarts rude,
For lack of food,
  And waters of the brook,
A gen'ral damp
Throughout the camp
  For thirst their spirits took.

So through distress
The Lord they press
  By force of fervent pray'r,
And to their need
His angels speed
  To save them from despair.

He led them right
By day and night,
  His influence they felt,
Until they came
To build and name
  The cities where they dwelt.

O that our race
Had sense and grace
  To bear a thankful mind,
And joyful own
His wonders shown
  In goodness to mankind!

For in his courts
His word supports
  All weakness, want and woe;
And for the poor
He will procure
  What bounty can bestow.

Whom men commit,
Disgrac'd to sit
   In misery and bonds;
Whom cares consume,
And in the gloom
   Of death whose heart desponds.

And for this cause—
Against the laws
   Of Jesus they rebell'd,
And set no price
On God's advice,
   When he the council held.

He therefore brought
Their pride to nought,
   And dash'd with gall their cup;
Which when they drunk,
In grief they sunk,
   And none would help them up.

So through distress
The Lord they press,
   By force of fervent pray'r,
And to their need
His angels speed
   To save them from despair.

From horror's wing,
And from the sting
   Of death they gat release;
He broke their gyves,
And sav'd their lives
   For plenty and for peace.

O that our race
Had sense and grace
   To bear a thankful mind,

And joyful own
His wonders shown
  In goodness to mankind!

For gates of brass,
That we might pass,
  He threw into the moat;
Embattl'd cars
Drove o'er the bars
  Of steel in sunder smote.

His vengeance schools
The heart of fools
  To purge them of offence;
And from their sins
By grace he wins
  To thought and sober sense.

Left by the Lord,
Their souls abhorr'd
  To take a crumb or drop,
As throes convulse,
The vital pulse
  Was at the point to stop.

So through distress
The Lord they press
  By force of fervent pray'r,
And to their need
His angels speed
  To save them from despair.

He sent his word,
And though they err'd,
  Their grievances he heal'd;
Perdition stav'd,
Their souls he sav'd,
  And sentences repeal'd.

O that our race
Had sense and grace
   To bear a thankful mind,
And joyful own
His wonders shown
   In goodness to mankind!

That all and each
Would heart and speech
   To blaze his works employ,
And praise prefer,
With spice and myrrh,
   To Christ in thanks and joy.

They that go down
To seek renown,
   Which ships of war maintain,
Or ply their trade,
By winds convey'd
   Upon the mighty main;

These men behold
The sea controul'd,
   And in observance keep
Each day and hour
God's work of pow'r,
   And wonders in the deep.

For as he speaks,
All ocean reeks,
   The stormy winds arise,
And boist'rous blow
The tides that flow
   In billows to the skies.

Then up as high
As heav'n they fly,
   And down again they drive

To gulphs beneath;
They scarce can breathe
   To keep their souls alive.

With frequent shocks
The vessel rocks,
   They stagger as in drink;
And as they toss,
Are at a loss
   For pow'r to act or think.

So through distress
The Lord they press,
   By force of fervent pray'r,
And to their need
His angels speed
   To save them from despair.

For when he chides,
The storm subsides,
   Submissive to his will;
And all the rage
Of winds assuage,
   When he says 'PEACE, BE STILL!'

Then they rejoice,
Because his voice
   Has still'd the meek profound,
And as they sail,
A fav'ring gale
   Conveys them where they're bound.

O that our race
Had sense and grace
   To bear a thankful mind,
And joyful own
His wonders shown
   In goodness to mankind!

That when they throng
To pray'r and song
　　They would exalt his laud,
And at the seat
Where senates meet
　　His glorious arm applaud!

His word can make
The spacious lake
　　A verdant lawn and wood;
And sent by him,
Whole navies swim
　　Where hilly desarts stood.

A fruitful soil
Of wine and oil
　　He turns to thorns and weeds;
And this event
From discontent
　　Of thankless lords proceeds.

Again he pours
The floods in show'rs
　　To make the wild a pool,
And gives the heath
A turfy sheath
　　Midst fountains fresh and cool.

And there prescribes
His hungry tribes
　　To set them down and feast,
And build and plan
High tow'rs for man,
　　And humble folds for beast.

There by his grant
They vineyards plant,
　　And sow their fields with corn,

And trees, whose fruit
And climbing shoot
   The shaded land adorn.

His peace he sends
Which blessing tends
   To multiply them all;
Nor lets their flock,
Or horned stock,
   By rot or murrain fall.

If, on reverse,
The Lord amerse,
   And all their wealth reduce;
The tyrant's rod,
Or plague from God,
   Upon them be let loose;

Though for a while
He cease to smile,
   Nor usual grace perform,
And lets them roam,
Remote from home,
   In desarts, wind, and storm;

Yet is he seen
To stand between
   The poor and utmost grief;
From caves and dens
His fold he pens
   Their shepherd and their chief.

On things like these
Upon their knees
   The righteous shall reflect,
And clam'rous foes,
That truth oppose,
   Shall finally be checkt.

A man whose ways
True wisdom sways
  Such wonders will observe,
And thence shall find
How good and kind
  Is God to whom we serve.

PSALM CVIII

My heart, Lord Jesus, is resign'd,
And fix'd to ev'ry point injoin'd
  By thy divine decree;
I praise thee with my lips, the best
Of all my members, for they're blest
  In magnifying thee.

Awake, and be thy strains renew'd,
Thou glory of my gratitude,
  Awake, my harp, and play—
Awake, my lute—myself shall rise,
As soon as these uplifted eyes
  Can catch a glance of day.

O Lord, with thankful voice and hand
Amongst the natives of the land
  I will thy mercies blaze;
To strangers I will sing thy worth,
And make my progress through the earth,
  To propagate thy praise.

That mercy which prevails in thee
Is greater than eternity,
  Which nothing bounds or ends;
Thy truth illustrious and renown'd
Is from beneath the vast profound,
  And o'er the heav'n ascends.

O God, arise, thyself exalt
Beyond the heav'n's stupendous vault
　　From whence thy glories flow,
Thy royal majesty assert,
And thy magnificence exert
　　O'er all the world below.

That thy belov'd, howe'er dispers'd,
Their banishment may be revers'd
　　By thy paternal care;
And that they may be sav'd from harm,
Lift thou thy mighty stretcht-out arm,
　　And expedite my pray'r.

My joy in Christ shall never cease,
The Word which God has sent in peace
　　To canton Sechem out,
And measure Succoth with my reed,
That there I may recall and feed
　　The sons of sin and doubt.

All Gilead's incense shall be mine,
Manasses of the blessed line
　　Shall yet be more my own;
Ephraim, who from the standard fled,
Shall be the strengthner of my head,
　　And Judah grace my throne.

Lot's devious children shall return,
And for a purifying urn
　　E'en Moab shall be spar'd;
Proud Palestine I will subdue,
O'er Edom I will cast my shoe
　　With gospel peace prepar'd.

Who leads me up to yonder tow'rs,
Whose local strength and active powers
　　Embattl'd troops deride;

Who spears against so grand a mark,
And on the ramparts sets our ark
    Where Edom's dukes reside.

Shall it not be our watch and ward,
Can help be other than the Lord
    To whom our pray'rs apply,
And wilt thou not our cause maintain,
And shall not in thy name again
    Judea's streamers fly?

Lord, in the hour of doubt and chance
Thine efficacious aid advance,
    Do thou direct our swords;
Our thoughts and deeds are of no price,
And vain the help and weak th' advice
    That feeble man affords.

Through God our valour shall be proof
To make each adverse hand and hoof
    Before our walls retreat,
With palm his champions he shall crown,
And finally beat Satan down
    Beneath his servants feet.

PSALM CIX

O GOD, to whom I make my suit,
Let not thine oracles be mute,
· For vice, yea violence and fraud
Have spread their specious lies abroad.

And from their tongues with falshood fraught
They have their accusation brought,
And come about me with abuse,
Without a motive to induce.

But for the very love I bore,
Behold, they are my friends no more;
Mean while I practise to forbear,
Resign'd to patience and to pray'r.

Thus in my progress have they stood,
And thus rewarded bad for good,
Devising and committing ill
For turns of kindness and good-will.

Set thou a man of virtuous fame
My foe to rule and to reclaim,
And let thy holy angel stand
To guide the motions of his hand.

Whene'er his cause is heard and try'd,
Give thou the sentence on his side,
And let his pray'r thy favour win,
Refin'd from gross conceits and sin.

As he repents his former ways,
Add length unto his better days,
And grant him thine especial grace
To keep and to adorn his place.

To many children let him be
A sire, and live their sons to see,
And let him cherish in his wife
A help-meet to a godly life.

And let his rising race be fed
With freedom's best ingenuous bread;
To their own garners let them go,
Nor dearth nor desolation know.

Let God's good blessing of increase
Be on his cattle and his fleece,

Nor let the foreigner approach
Upon his labours to incroach.

Let him be register'd and clast
'Mongst neighbours of the Christian cast,
And for his heirs lay up the fort
And treasure of a good report.

Let his posterities extend
The honours that from him descend,
And when his years he has fulfil'd,
His name to greater credit build.

Let what his fathers did amiss
Be sunk in such a change as this,
And let him, as his praise exalts,
Atone for all his mother's faults.

And let the total sum of all,
His race recover'd from their fall,
Be shewn for mercy to behold,
And be by Christ himself enroll'd.

And this the more, as at the first
His mind was fashion'd for the worst,
And in vexatious actions dealt,
With soul unsympathiz'd to melt.

In unbelief he took delight,
In deeds of obloquy and spite;
But now he shall his tongue employ
In benediction, love, and joy.

From habits of invet'rate root
He had no grace, and bore no fruit;
But now through Christ his heart is new,
He shall another course pursue.

Let him by faith his sins uncloke,
And God through penitence invoke,
And let the Lord's most holy word
His loins with purity begird.

Let such returns as these dispose
To quick conversion all my foes,
And thus in love may I controul
The persecutors of my soul.

But thou, O Lord, benignly deal
With me, who thus for sinners feel,
According to thy name intreat
Thy servant, for thy love is sweet.

O let my charity procure
Thy speedy help, for I am poor,
And as mine enemies afflict,
My heart within my breast is prickt.

I haste this fleshly veil to quit,
Reduc'd like shadowy forms that flit,
And hurry'd from my vernal day,
Am driv'n like grashoppers away.

As with such rigour I abstain,
My knees are feeble and in pain;
For want of their nutricious sap
My lips and all my body chap.

Moreover I became the jest
Of those that knew me at the best,
And as they saw my alter'd look,
Their heads with shrewd remarks they shook.

O Lord, my Saviour, whom I serve,
From these calamities preserve,

And as with meekness I behave,
According to thy mercy save.

And they shall know that this degree
Of goodness is alone from thee,
That thou thyself to pray'r reveal'd,
All my infirmities hast heal'd.

Though they with ceaseless wrath malign,
Be thou the more and more benign,
And baffle those that bear me down,
With joys my fervent vows to crown.

Let all my foes to grace be sped,
By shame to true contrition led,
And find in a propitious hour
The Lord's regenerating pow'r.

To God I will my duty shew
With all that gratitude can do,
And where the multitude resort
By songs to lively praise exhort.

For Jesus shall the poor assist
The flesh and mammon to resist,
Who saves the soul from Satan's sieve,
And judges not but to forgive.

PSALM CX

THE Lord unto my Lord declar'd,
At my right hand I have prepar'd
    Thine everlasting seat;
The subject universe is ours,
Kingdoms, dominions, thrones and pow'rs
    All plac'd beneath thy feet.

The wand of thy pacific reign,
Behold, I give thee to sustain
        From Zion's hallow'd shrine;
Be thou the Saviour of the soul,
And all thine enemies controul
        By clemency divine.

The day thou art install'd the king,
From far shall pious easterns bring
        Their off'rings of perfume;
The benediction on thy birth
Is as the dew-drops fresh on earth
        From morning's pregnant womb.

He sware, nor shall the Lord repent,
For ever on the man I sent
        My priesthood I transferr'd;
I know thee without blame or speck,
Thy order is Melchisedeck,
        E'en God, th' incarnate Word.

The Lord of hosts upon thy right
Shall kings in indignation smite
        With many a grievous wound;
But in thy stripes they shall be heal'd,
And all vindictive laws repeal'd,
        When CHARITY is crown'd.

His judgment shall be to forgive,
And by his pow'r the dead shall live,
        And issue from their grave;
The heads of all the various realms,
Whom vice enormous overwhelms,
        His precious blood shall save.

Where the breeze sigh'd and Cedron purl'd,
There drank the Saviour of the world,
        Without an home or friend;

For which his name above all names
Is glorious, and his meekness claims
   All honour without end.

PSALM CXI

Tune of the old CXIII

MY hearty thanks I will renew
To Christ amidst a faithful few
   In private and domestic song,
And with the public worship close,
Where pious churchmen fill the rows,
   And congregated angels throng.

The works of God are good and great,
And in the mind of man create
   A zeal for infinite applause;
And all that take sublime delight,
The scholars of the word unite
   Their studies in their truth and laws.

The works of God's consummate art
To laud and rev'rence warm the heart,
   Where might and merit are supreme;
His justice o'er the foe prevails,
Suspending her impartial scales
   Upon an everlasting beam.

The miracles of God the Son
In such stupendous grace are done,
   And mercy to the race restor'd,
That their memorial should be kept,
And he that bled, and he that wept,
   By ceaseless thanks and pray'rs ador'd.

By him his faithful flock is fed
With drink indeed and living bread,
 Thro' which their grievous wounds are heal'd;
And happy they that take the crumbs
When now the promis'd Shiloh comes,
 When now the testament is seal'd.

His goodness and his pow'r divine
He shew'd unto the patriarch's line,
 The people which he nam'd his own,
That thence Emanuel's wondrous birth,
Salvation to remotest earth,
 From Israel's learning might be known.

His works are very truth, and wrought
To full perfection of his thought,
 Dispos'd in Christ the master's skill;
The angels of his word are just,
Which keep the records of his trust,
 And all his prophecies fulfil.

His everlasting types display
Those truths which never can decay,
 Tho' worlds consume and language cease;
Their doctrine's infinitely sound,
Their dispensations all abound
 With matchless equity and peace.

He sent his Christ with joyful news
To foil the fiend and disabuse
 The sinners, for whose sake he came;
He fixt his covenant of grace
Upon a sempiternal base;
 August and holy is his name.

The fear of God begins the man—
'Tis our first wisdom and the plan
 All hopeful edifice to raise;

Obedience God's applause obtains,
Where Christ our resurrection reigns
   In everlasting pow'r and praise.

PSALM CXII

THE man of reverence to God
   Is blessed in the highest class;
His ready feet with joy are shod,
   To bring the word to pass.

His seed shall mighty pow'r invest,
   And gain on earth the first repute,
And all the branches shall be blest
   Of such a faithful root.

His soul shall have her full repast
   Of wealth and earth's redundant store,
And his integrity shall last
   In heav'n for evermore.

The good midst Satan's dark domain
   The day-spring has before his view,
Such are benevolent in grain,
   And loving, kind and true.

A good man is a common friend,
   And in all characters complete,
He will be merciful to lend,
   And in his words discreet.

For he shall never change his side,
   But still keep stedfast and the same,
And God the honest man shall guide
   To sempiternal fame.

His spirit shall not be dismay'd
   At evil tidings unawares,
And his firm heart to Christ his aid
   Submits his soul's affairs.

His heart none alteration knows,
   Nor is from God to Belial wav'd;
And his desire upon his foes
   Is that they should be sav'd.

His worldly goods unto the poor
   He hath distributed around;
His worth for ever shall endure
   In exaltation crown'd.

The wicked shall behold his rise,
   And learn and imitate his ways,
Till all their envy, all their vice
   Subside in pray'r and praise.

PSALM CXIII

Tune of old C

ATTEND, ye ministers of song,
   And bless your ever-gracious Lord,
The praises of his name prolong
   Upon the full-resounding chord.

In ceaseless blessing be he nam'd,
   As by the fathers heretofore,
And in all tongues and times proclaim'd
   From henceforth and for evermore.

All flesh his glorious MAKER hails,
   Avow'd the GREATEST and the BEST,

683

From whence the sun the morn unveils
    To his department in the WEST.

The Lord is high above the kings
    Of all the scatter'd regions round,
The radiance of his glory springs,
    And leaves the topmost heav'n aground.

Whence can comparison be made,
    The God above sublime to shew,
Which deigns his glory to degrade,
    The kings in heav'n and earth to view?

He takes the simple from the dust,
    As down he meekly kneels to bless,
And all the poor that put their trust
    In him, he succours from distress.

That he may raise their low degree,
    And give them with the princes place,
And let presumptuous rulers see
    Their virtue rescu'd from disgrace.

He makes the barren woman big,
    If she beseech the Lord for seed;
And blest beneath her vine and fig
    The prattling innocents to feed.

PSALM CXIV

WHEN Israel came from Egypt's coast,
    And Goshen's marshy plains,
And Jacob with his joyful host
    From servitude and chains;

Then was it seen how much the Jews
    Were holy in his sight,
And God did Israel's kingdom chuse
    To manifest his might.

The sea beheld it, and with dread
    Retreated to make way;
And Jordan to his fountain head
    Ran backwards in dismay.

The mountains, like the rams that bound,
    Exulted on their base;
Like lambs the little hills around
    Skipt lightly from their place.

What is the cause, thou mighty sea,
    That thou thyself shou'd shun;
And Jordan, what is come to thee,
    That thou shou'd backward run?

Ye mountains that ye leap'd so high
    From off the solid rock,
Ye hills that ye should gambols try,
    Like firstlings of the flock?

EARTH, from the centre to the sod
    His fearful presence hail,
The presence of Jeshurun's God,
    In whom our arms prevail.

Who beds of rocks in pools to stand
    Can by his word compell,
And from the veiny flint command
    The fountain and the well.

PSALM CXV

NOT to ourselves the praise we take,
　　O Lord, but to thy name
Ascribe for truth and mercy's sake
　　The merit of the claim.

Why should the heathen, who this hour
　　Have felt thy chast'ning rod,
Make impious question of thy pow'r
　　With 'where is now their God?'

Our God, which has the battle won,
　　O'er heav'n and mortals reigns,
Whate'er his wisdom wills is done,
　　And what is done remains.

The stocks to which the pagan fools
　　Their sighs and incense waft,
Are gold and silver form'd by tools
　　Of mean mechanic craft.

Their mouths are fashion'd, but from thence,
　　Nor voice nor accent falls;
Their eyes are grav'd, but have no sense
　　Of vision in their balls;

Their ears are hollow'd, which to hear
　　No clamour can compell;
The noses of their busts appear
　　With which they cannot smell.

Their hands are form'd, but not to feel
　　Their feet, but not to move;
Nor thro' their throats, while madmen kneel,
　　Comes breath their life to prove.

The stupid maker's like the bust,
    And so are all degrees
Of impious slaves that put their trust,
    And bow to gods like these.

But thou, Jeshurun, in the Lord
    Alone your trust repose;
He is their saving-health to ward
    The swords of all their foes.

And you, ye priests of Aaron's stock,
    With faithfulness devout,
Trust in the Lord, he is their rock,
    And unapproach'd redoubt.

And ye whose heart thro' fear repents,
    Who meek obeisance yield,
Trust in the Lord—in all events
    He is their help and shield.

The Lord regards us in success,
    And in our day of need;
And Israel's children he shall bless,
    And bless all Aaron's seed.

He blesses all that fear, and thank
    Their Saviour for his grace;
As well the men of meaner rank
    As those of wealth and place.

The Lord shall bless you more and more
    In all you take in hand,
And prosper your increase and store,
    Your children and your land.

Ye are thro' grace the Lord's elect,
    And he can keep you free,

Which could th' etherial vault erect
 O'er continent and sea.

The heav'ns are God's imperial throne
 Beyond all mortal ken;
Earth to be travers'd, till'd and sown
 He has bestow'd on men.

The barren grave affords no fruit,
 O God, to praise or pray'r;
And mirth and melody are mute
 In darkness and despair.

But we with all our zeal and force
 Will in thy praises rise,
Praise ye the Lord thro' nature's course,
 And for th' immortal prize.

PSALM CXVI

Joy has taken full possession
 Of my heart and triumphs there;
Since, thro' Christ his intercession,
 God has hearken'd to my pray'r.

Since, his gracious ear inclining,
 He has met my fervent vow,
To his name the praise assigning,
 All my life my knees shall bow.

Long and painful did I languish,
 Death his snares began to spread;
Horror and despair and anguish
 Brought their terrors to my bed.

Grief and trouble are conditions,
 And the colour of my state;

688

Hence my soul the Lord petitions
  'Save thou blessed UNCREATE!'

For the Lord our God is gracious
  And omnipotently true,
And his mercies efficacious
  Weeping sinners to renew.

God receives to his protection
  Simple folk when they repent;
I was in the last dejection
  And his comforter he sent.

Turn again unto thy Saviour,
  O my soul, and take thy rest;
God has weigh'd thy meek behaviour,
  And with recompence hath blest.

For, my soul from death redeeming,
  Thou thy servant hast solac'd;
Wip'd his eyes with sorrow streaming,
  And his falling feet replac'd.

I shall therefore walk before thee,
  And in God direct my ways,
Open in the light adore thee
  For example and for praise.

My belief was firmly founded,
  Therefore I with freedom spoke
From an heart with anguish wounded,
  'All our race their meaning cloak.'

For his mercies great and tender,
  For his benefits benign,
Is their recompence to render,
  Is their honour to assign?

Mine infirmities uncloaking
  I will my confession make,
At thy shrine thy grace invoking,
  As thine eucharist I take.

In thy holy church with fervour
  Now I will my vows direct;
Dear to their divine preserver
  Are the lives of his elect.

See, O Lord, that I am under
  The dominion of thy name,
Thou hast broke my bonds in sunder,
  And I from thy handmaid came.

I will sacrifice thanksgiving,
  Swelling voice and sounding chord;
In the fragance of good living
  I will worship to the Lord.

In thy holy church with fervour
  Now my soul her pray'r shall frame;
Salem bless thy great preserver,
  Priests and people praise his name.

PSALM CXVII

PRAISE the Lord with awful mirth
  Every nation, tribe and tongue;
Christians militant on earth,
  Let your Saviour's praise be sung.

For his ministers of grace
  Ever more and more impart;
Truth is his from race to race,
  Hallelujah from the heart!

690

OR THIS

O ALL ye nations of the peopl'd earth,
   Whatever clime ye fill, whatever zone;
Praise God with hallow'd mirth,
   Make Christ his merits known.

Because the current of his mercy flows
   For evermore abundant, good and great;
His truth no period knows;
   Hosanna in the height.

PSALM CXVIII

O COME ye to the holy place,
And pay to God's exceeding grace
   What grateful natures owe;
For due descending day by day,
His mercy-beams themselves display,
   Nor pause nor period know.

Let thankful Israel now confess
That he is gracious in excess,
   To wrath and anger sow;
And that descending day by day,
His mercy-beams themselves display,
   Nor pause nor period know.

Let Aaron's houshold now confess
That he is bountiful to bless,
   From whom all mercies flow;
And that descending day by day,
His mercy-beams themselves display,
   Nor pause nor period know.

Yea, let the congregation, here
Assembled in religious fear
    In many a goodly row,
Confess with joy that day by day,
His mercy-beams themselves display,
    Nor pause nor period know.

In sorrows bitt'rest depths immerg'd,
To God of heav'n my suit I urg'd
    His vengeance to forbear;
And he my evil case review'd,
And in its utmost latitude
    He granted all my pray'r.

Almighty God, which knows my heart,
Is always first to take my part
    For love and mercy's sake;
I will not fear a fleshy arm,
Nor any terror or alarm
    That mortal men can make.

The Lord, which my distress defends,
Is with all those that are my friends,
    And in my band inlist;
So shall I have my heart's desire
To see mine enemies retire,
    And their attempts desist.

'Tis better in the Lord to trust,
And all your actions to adjust
    By what his laws explain,
Than on the son of man to lean,
Too weak an aid, a prop too mean
    To succour or sustain.

'Tis better in the Lord to trust,
And to a holy God and just
    With zeal to pay your court,

Than any confidence to ground
In princes, by the world renown'd
    For honour or support.

All nations compass'd me about,
And strove my faithful troops to rout;
    My courage to appall;
With multitudes their leaders came,
But in the Lord's tremendous name
    I will defy them all.

On every side with black intent
My stedfast few to circumvent,
    And work at once my fall,
They kept me in on every side,
But in the name of God my guide
    I will defy them all.

Like swarms of hornets they came on,
Like fire extinguish'd they are gone
    Through him on whom I call;
For in the name and matchless might
Of God my everlasting light
    I will defy them all.

His steel the desp'rate swordsman drew,
And made a pass to run me thro'
    With his determin'd blade;
But God in a propitious hour
Against the foe and all his pow'r
    Came instant to my aid.

'Tis God alone that makes me strong,
And is the spirit of my song,
    Which to my harp I chant;
He shall my name in heav'n enroll,
And sure salvation to my soul
    Hereafter he shall grant.

The bloom of health and pleasure's voice
Dwell in their tents, whose wiser choice
    Is virtue and the Lord;
The right hand of the King of kings
Atchieves sublime and glorious things
    To punish and reward.

That right hand which can death dispense,
Or life—and hath pre-eminence,
    O'er earth, and heav'n and hell,
Stupendous miracles has wrought,
Which all the pow'r of word and thought
    By infinites excell!

DAVID, there is no death for thee,
Thy name is immortality,
    And thou wert born to live,
God's wond'rous mercy to declare,
Which is omnipotent to spare,
    To pity, to forgive.

The Lord his servant has chastis'd,
But hath not utterly despis'd,
    Nor all his grace withdrawn;
And his compassion intervenes
'Twixt death and all the gloomy scenes
    Where vaults sepulchral yawn.

As in the faith of God I knock,
The gates of righteousness unlock,
    That I may enter first;
And there the fragrant odours burn,
And there demonstrate and return
    The thanks with which I burst!

This is the gate the Lord has made,
And they that have his will obey'd,
    The righteous, here may pass;

Who scorning Mammon and his leavn,
High in the treasuries of heav'n
   Immortal wealth amass.

I will my hearty thanks restore,
That thou hast set so wide a door
   To speed the pray'r I form'd;
And in salvation art so rich,
Which blessing to the highest pitch
   My gratitude has warm'd.

That rock neglected and unknown
Is now become the corner stone
   Ev'n of the house of God;
Which all the builders to a man
Refus'd, from him that drew the plan,
   To him that bore the hod.

It is the work of God direct,
For he himself is architect,
   So beautiful and bold;
'Tis elevated to surprize,
Beyond our thought, before our eyes,
   Believe ye, and behold.

This is the day, whose livelier beams
The Lord has glorified, and teems
   With thankfulness and praise;
In pleasure's whiter vestments clad,
We will be joyful, gay and glad,
   And brighten to the blaze.

Now is the happy season, now,
O Lord, attend to hear my vow,
   And further my pursuits;
Propitiate all thy people's toil,
And bless their corn, their wine and oil,
   Their pastures and their fruits.

Blessed be he, or ere he came
On such a work, in such a name,
    The Son of God indeed!
All ye that reckon to his fold,
Or in his church your office hold,
    We wish you to succeed.

Christ Jesus is that light, the word
Above all thrones and pow'rs preferr'd,
    Who brought the day-spring down;
Let loose the lambs for blood design'd,
And all the chains of death unbind—
    With flow'rs his altar crown.

Thou art the God which I adore,
To thee the praise I will restore
    As holden by thy laws;
Thou art the God in whom I live,
The glory and my life I give
    To thee, and for thy cause.

O come ye to the holy place,
And pay to God's exceeding grace
    What grateful natures owe;
For due descending day by day,
His mercy-beams themselves display,
    Nor pause nor period know.

PSALM CXIX

א

THEY are the blest, whom free from guile
No carnal appetites defile,
    As they their way pursue;

Who by God's mandates walk direct,
And keep, severely circumspect;
 His holy will in view.

They are the blest, the which abide,
Nor to the right or left aside
 From his commandments start;
Who worship with observance meek,
And to their Lord and Saviour seek
 With all their mind and heart.

For he who wisely shuns the snares
Of sin and Satan, and forbears,
 To lead his life amiss,
Nor with his conscience holds debate,
Walks in the way, he makes so straight,
 For everlasting bliss.

Thou hast with wondrous love enlarg'd
Upon our filial fear, and charg'd
 With thy paternal care,
That we the laws thy church dispense,
Should keep with anxious diligence,
 Nor pains nor patience spare.

O that my ways were made so clean,
And that I could myself demean
 So regular and right,
That to thy temple when I speed,
I to thy statutes may give heed,
 And in thy words delight!

So shall I never dread the lash
Of censure, nor shall shame abash
 My spirit or my face,
While I thy holy word obey,
And an impartial reverence pay
 To all thy laws by grace.

I will the debt of love restore,
And bless thy bounty more and more
    With gratitude unfeign'd,
When I by Christ shall have access
To knowledge and true holiness,
    I have through him attain'd.

I will to all thy rites adhere,
That order, decency revere,
    Thy holy church adorn;
O never leave me to my foes,
Nor thy communicant expose
    To malice and to scorn.

ב

How shall a young man shun the lure
Of pleasures, and his way secure,
    Thro' purity to peace?
Ev'n in conforming to thy word,
By which the devil is deterr'd,
    And fleshly cravings cease.

With all my heart's desire, the tide
Of passions sway'd by God their guide,
    I have thy presence sought;
O let me not from truth decline,
Nor deviate from the blest design
    Of what thy voice has taught.

Thy wholesome dictates are imprest,
And treasur'd up within my breast,
    As pearls of passing price,
That I may not the haunts repeat
Of fell temptation and deceit,
    And turn from thee to vice.

O Lord, thy blessedness is great,
And is avow'd by those that wait
    Upon thy righteous will;
To me thy blameless doctrine shew,
With wisdom and with grace endue
    To know and to fulfill.

My lips are practis'd to recite
Those venerable rules of right,
    God gave the tribes he chose;
Also the new command he sent,
That christian charity cement
    All parties, sects and foes.

I have delight in that great end
To which thy testimonies tend,
    Immortal life and fame,
More than in all the mighty mass
Of hoarded riches, which surpass
    Their owner's pow'r to name.

My conversation shall abound
To good improvement, and confound
    What profligates object;
And to the tenor of thy ways,
Thy glory and eternal praise,
    I will have due respect.

Thy statutes shall be mine employ,
My private and sequester'd joy,
    And to the world my boast;
I will confess thy wise decrees,
And those, when most myself I please,
    I shall remember most.

ב

O to thy servant be thou kind,
Nor from the motions of my mind
    Thine influence withdraw;
My need supply, my sin forgive,
My strength confirm, that I may live,
    And live up to thy law.

Dispel each obstacle that lies
'Twixt truth and me, and to mine eyes
    Thy mysteries unfold;
That when I to thy shrine advance
The wonders of thine ordinance
    I clearly may behold.

I am a stranger upon earth,
And to my burial from my birth
    Is all a pilgrim's task;
O let thy temple open wide,
Nor from me thy commandments hide
    When I for guidance ask.

My soul from out my flesh escapes,
And up to thee her flight she shapes
    With fervour of desire;
Which, at all times, and every place,
She has thy judgments to embrace,
    And nearer home admire.

Thou hast rebuk'd and disallow'd
The pompous speeches of the proud,
    Who talk'd so fierce and fast;
The one thing needful to defer,
And from thy dread commandments err,
    Is fatal at the last.

700

O from foul shame my lot remove,
Nor let contemptuous fools reprove
    The servant of thine hand;
Because I for thy tables care,
And with solicitude and pray'r
    Obey what they command.

The princes of this world convene
Their vile dependents, and their spleen
    Against thy servant vent;
But he is happily bely'd,
That in thy truth is occupy'd,
    And on thy bus'ness bent.

For I with joy to Christ repair,
His sermons, parables and pray'r
    Which all conceptions hit;
And for instructions, on my march
As soldier of the Lord, I search
    The rules of holy writ.

ד

My soul adheres to lowth and dust,
And worldly cares and carnal lust
    Her excellence degrade:
O with thy quick'ning spirit warm
My breast, and graciously perform
    The promise thou hast made!

I have with meek contrition own'd
My ways, and for the past aton'd
    With all my best amends;
Thou condescended to my suit—
O in thy precepts institute,
    On which my peace depends,

Make me to comprehend thy way,
That I thy precepts may convey
    In all their genuine force;
So shall the works of the supreme,
And all his wonders be the theme
    I chuse for my discourse.

My soul, which daily care involves,
In its vexatious feuds dissolves
    Thro' burthensome fatigue;
Let thou thine holy word refresh
My spirit from the world and flesh,
    That make up Satan's league.

The liars and their ways expel
From my communion, and repel
    The babbler and his tale;
Cause me the sland'rers to despise,
Thy laws to cherish and to prize,
    Which o'er their spite prevail.

From my first hope in early youth
The way of thine eternal truth
    I have preferr'd and trac'd;
As life is perilous and short,
Thy judgments, which from sin dehort,
    I have before me plac'd.

I have on thy behalf believ'd,
And to thy testimonies cleav'd
    As constant in thy cause;
O Lord, let no foul stain confuse,
Nor scoffers of the world amuse
    My labour from thy laws!

Thy way, by grace so well begun,
I shall have farther strength to run
    Until I reach the goal;

When, Jesus, from this low degree,
And bondage of mortality,
    Thou hast enlarged my soul.

ה

Thy statutes in my heart inscribe,
And teach me, that I may imbibe
    Thy salutary lore;
O Lord, do thou the text explain,
And in my mind I shall retain
    The sermon evermore!

Disperse and quell the guilt and gloom
Of baleful prejudice, illume
    My heart with wisdom's dow'r;
So from thy laws I shall not swerve,
But their remonstrances observe
    With all my strength and pow'r.

By thy benign assistance lead,
That in thy path I may proceed,
    And to thy truth aspire;
For there I long with love intense,
And change the world's concupiscence
    With that divine desire.

Endue me with the special gift
To keep thy statutes, and the thrift
    Which heaps eternal hoards;
And let me not myself beguile
With perishable things and vile,
    That earth beneath affords.

O from the pomp and pride below,
And this vain world's external show
    To thee mine eyes avert;

That I may scorn the carnal leav'n,
And expedite my way to heav'n
   Thy quick'ning grace exert!

O in my heart thy dictates root,
That I may bear such blessed fruit
   As year by year improves;
And meekly worship at thy feet,
As for a sinner it is meet,
   And servant it behoves!

Strike hellish defamation dumb,
Lest an offence thro' me should come,
   Which is a shame I dread;
For all thy judgments love include,
And therefore let no man obtrude
   His sentence in thy stead.

Behold I in thy words rejoice,
And pay obedience to thy voice,
   O with thy quick'ning ray
Be with me, that I may not want
Religious courage to comfront
   The foes of truth and day!

ך

Moreover for the cross I bear,
Let Christ thy promis'd word declare,
   Thy righteous wrath appeas'd;
Since now the Dove's command is done
Hear this, my Son, my darling Son,
   In whom I rest well pleas'd.

So shall I check the sland'rous fool,
And tutor'd in the christian school,
   Benevolence retort

For all his mockery and wrath,
Since I believe and give my troth
    To what thy words exhort.

O let no superstition shut
The volume of thy truth, nor put
    To silence pray'r and song;
For to thy judgments I submit,
And trust thy mercy will acquit
    Thy holy church of wrong!

Thus in thine house betimes and late,
I shall observe and cultivate
    The laws thy finger wrote;
Yea, to thy blessed word and will
For ever and for ever still
    My services devote.

And free from tyranny and strife
I walk the pilgrimage of life,
    And 'scape both floods and flame;
For those commandments in thine ark
Are what I seek for, and the mark
    Where I direct my aim.

I likewise will myself present,
And speak upon thy Testament
    Before the face of kings;
Nor shall a blush my cheeks invest,
'Tis God's ambassador profest
    The sov'reign mandate brings.

This also to my peace shall add
A new delight, and make me glad
    To think on things above;
And with just fear for all and each
Proceed to practise and to preach
    Thy precepts which I love.

My hands I also will address
Thy precepts which I love to bless,
    And lift them up on high;
And thy commandments to peruse,
And on their gracious import muse,
    With studious care apply.

ז

O to thy servant have respect,
And all thy goodness recollect
    For this mine humbled dust;
According to thy word of pow'r,
In which mine expectations tow'r,
    And where I ground my trust!

The same is in the hour of woe
My consolation, when I go
    About my soul's affairs;
For 'tis thy word, of cordial taste,
Which nature's weariness and waste
    Requickens and repairs.

The proud, whose vanity is fed
By fools and flatt'rers, on my head
    Their taunts unceasing heap;
They scoff, they menace, and they boast,
But yet I shrink not from my post,
    Which is thy law to keep.

For when I to this truth attend,
That thy just judgments know not end,
    Nor thy compassion bounds,
And that the term of life is brief,
The thought administers relief
    And balm into my wounds.

Terror and fearful tremblings chill
My members, and, foreboding ill,
    My soul within me shakes,
When I behold how folly thrives,
And with what peril of their lives
    The world thy law forsakes.

The precepts which thy words endear
To mine affections and mine ear,
    And in my heart implant,
All my anxieties assuage,
And in this toilsome pilgrimage
    They are the songs I chant.

At night, when contemplation broods,
Nor business of the world intrudes,
    My meditations soar,
And on thy name in rapture think;
While others on their couches sink,
    My pray'rs thy word adore.

To this degree of grace I grew
As to my loud professions true
    I kept my ways from guilt;
Prompt at all seasons to maintain
Allegiance to thy laws and reign,
    In which my hopes are built.

ת

Thou art my portion, the reward
And end of all my pains, O Lord;
    I stand engag'd and bound
Before thy mercy-seat to pray,
And with a filial love obey
    The truth thy laws propound.

Thy loving favour I besought,
When to sincere repentance brought
    I at thine altar knelt;
O let thy work and word agree,
And to my heart's impassion'd plea
    With tender mercy melt!

The failings of the former times,
And all my abdicated crimes
    I have with tears review'd;
The loathsome filth of vice I spurn'd,
And to thy testimonies turn'd
    With all the man renew'd.

I hasted from the paths impure
My soul's obedience to mature,
    And consecrate my bloom;
Nor left what thy command appoints
For wither'd hands and feeble joints,
    Which years and cares consume.

Tho' thieves into a gang unite,
And to despoil me of my right,
    By dark my doors beset;
I keep my catechism still,
'Thou shalt not steal, thou shalt not kill,'
    I well remember yet.

At midnight I will musick make,
And keep my gratitude awake
    Before the blazing lamp;
Because the laws thou didst enact
Are righteous, to the truth exact,
    And bear thine heav'nly stamp.

I my most cordial love attach
To godly men, and such as match
    Their manly fear with mine;

My neighbours are the good and great,
And who from excellence innate
    Unto thy laws incline.

This earth, O Lord, is heap'd and press'd,
And with thy benefits is bless'd,
    Which day by day descend;
In thy New Testament instruct
My heart, and to my peace conduct,
    As I by that shall mend.

ב

O Lord, thy favour is extream,
And on my head thy mercies beam
    Inestimably kind!
And to thy promise thou hast stood,
Beyond my hopes immensely good
    Thy work of love I find.

O give me wisdom to discern,
And lively diligence to learn,
    And relish what I read;
For thy commands I have believ'd,
With gladness thy report receiv'd,
    And to its truth accede!

I went astray, and far from God
I wander'd, till thy vengeful rod
    My grievous fault chastis'd;
But now, to vice no more a slave,
I with sobriety behave,
    As by thy word advis'd.

Thy goodness glories to refresh
Thy creatures, and towards all flesh
    Thy bounties are diffus'd;

O to my heart thy statutes teach
That I may keep them free from breach,
    By conscience unaccus'd!

The proud, who thy decrees disdain,
Against thy servant falshoods feign,
    And in them persevere;
But to thy laws I will ally
My heart with every pow'rful tye,
    And with regard sincere.

While wealth abounds, and flatt'rers fawn,
With luxury as fat as brawn
    Their carnal hearts they choak;
But I my consolation build
In that thy word I have fulfill'd,
    And yield me to thy yoke.

'Tis good that with a hand so strict
And frequent stripes thou didst afflict
    My youth to pain inur'd;
That I thy statutes thus might know,
And all my trials undergo
    Undaunted and assur'd.

The law, which for thy mercies sake
Thy mouth amidst the thund'rings spake
    To Jacob's sons of old,
Is in my sight of greater worth
Than all the treasuries of earth
    In silver and in gold.

From thy creative hands I came
Compleat, and in a goodly frame
    Thou hast my soul enwrapt;

My feeble faculties endow,
And to thy precepts as I bow,
　　By grace my thoughts adapt.

They that in fear thy name confess,
And on whose countenance express
　　Thy radiant blessing glows,
My glory will rejoice to see,
Since in thy holy word and thee
　　I still my trust repose.

I know, O Lord, thou judgest right,
And pains my gross misdeeds requite
　　Their filthiness to purge;
Thou shalt thy faithfulness exalt,
In that thou visitest my fault
　　With thy terrific scourge.

O send thy comforter to sooth
My bitter agonies, and smooth
　　My way thro' toil and care;
According to thy word of truth,
Where, in thy servant's early youth,
　　Acceptance bless'd his pray'r!

O show'r thy loving mercies down
At once my rising hopes to crown,
　　And to prolong my days;
For in thy law my life is spent,
Hence pleasure and serene content
　　My face in smiles arrays!

The scoffers and their pride abash,
And all their deep devices quash
　　With which they would destroy
And with contempt thy servant brand,
For in the word of thy command
　　I will myself employ.

711

Let such as in thy grace are grown,
And have thy testimonies known,
    With all their precious terms,
Be turn'd to me—example warms
The penitent, yet more reforms
    And ev'n the strong confirms.

O in my heart thy statutes ground,
Work it regenerate and sound,
    That nothing may estrange
My soul from her eternal rest,
Or raise a terror in my breast,
    Or make my colour change!

כ

Cloy'd with the dull delights of sense,
For thy divine benevolence
    With all my soul I long;
And I for that translation look,
As in the sanction of thy book
    My tow'ring hope is strong.

Mine eyes, which to thy throne above
I lift in extacy of love,
    Thy saving word beseech;
O when wilt thou refresh my soul,
I cry, while tears incessant roll,
    Their sympathetic speech?

For tears and sobs mine utt'rance choke,
Like bottles season'd in the smoke
    Mine organs are become;
Yet still upon thy word I wait,
Nor sin hath made me an ingrate,
    Tho' sorrow strikes me dumb.

How many of my days remain,
When from this state of pray'r and pain
    Shall I to thee remove?
When shall the wretches, who debase
Their souls by malice, have thy grace,
    And by thy word improve?

The proud, who see me thus forlorn,
Increase their malice and their scorn,
    They dig their pits by stealth,
Invoking all the pow'rs of hell,
And thus against thy laws rebel,
    Thy peace and saving health.

All thy divine commands are true,
Which from my heart I keep and do,
    O to mine aid attend,
And drive my furious foes aloof,
Who would condemn me without proof,
    And punish without end!

I well nigh perish'd by the force
Of ruffian hands without remorse,
    In wounds and death expert;
Yet was I never overaw'd
With open violence and fraud
    Thy dictates to desert.

O with thy love my heart revive,
And to those truths I shall arrive
    Thy blessed lips instill'd,
And in thy laws my life enjoy,
Which Jesus came not to destroy,
    But for us all fulfill'd!

ל

O Lord, of everlasting pow'r,
Whose throne immortal palms embow'r,
   Where cherubims are heard,
And angels kneel—thy glorious word
For ever is in heav'n preferr'd,
   Exalted and inspher'd.

Thy truth from race to race consists,
And from eternities exists;
   The far-extended sweep
Of stedfast earth thou hast display'd,
And on the pillar'd arches laid
   The waters of the deep.

Thy works continue to this day,
Both those that on their bases stay
   And they which are revolv'd;
For all things at thy word began,
And serving to thy wondrous plan
   Are into thee resolv'd.

Had I not valu'd from my birth
Thy laws for their internal worth,
   And took delight therein,
My strength could not have been supply'd,
But in my trouble I had dy'd
   In sorrow and in sin.

I keep my mind, while life permits,
Retentive of thy benefits,
   Nor shall my tongue be mute
Upon the lessons of thy charge,
For my conceptions they are large,
   And quicken my pursuit.

From baptism my god-childhood vow,
From confirmation until now
    I am inlisted thine;
Save me, who with the price am bought,
For I with diligence have sought
    The way thy laws injoin.

Ungodly men in numbers swarm'd,
And their conspiracy they form'd
    To slay me with the sword;
But I will search for my relief
The words which to Jeshurun's chief
    Thy gracious hand restor'd.

I see that all things have their doom,
And all the vanities consume
    On which the world is bent;
But greater far than death and time
Thy word is simple and sublime,
    And of immense extent.

מ

Lord, how my study and delight
Is all the livelong day and night
    To turn thy sacred page,
From whose clear mirror I derive
Ensamples for my youth and hive,
    Resources for mine age.

I through thy spirit am discreet
Beyond my foes and their deceit,
    Beyond my rivals wise;
For I thy word about me bear,
As bracelets on my wrist I wear,
    And frontlets on my eyes.

715

Mine understanding comprehends
More than my regulating friends,
    Or anxious teachers know;
For with shrewd questions unperplext,
My studies are the genuine text
    Whence all good morals flow.

My prudence is beyond my years,
And elders, hoary priests and seers
    Are of inferior skill,
Because, by special grace sustain'd,
I keep those precepts unprofan'd
    Which thy commands instill.

My cautious feet from folly's maze
I have refrain'd, and all the ways
    Of subtlety and craft,
That fruit thy covenant may yield,
Which is upon my forehead seal'd,
    And on my heart ingraft.

I will not from thy banner run,
Or leave thy holy will undone
    Whate'er the tempter threats;
For thou art with me to controul,
And the preceptor of my soul
    A blessed pattern sets.

O thou hast sent my soul to sooth
Thy words, how musically smooth,
    And elegantly chaste;
Yea sweeter they their sounds endear
To my conception and mine ear
    Than honey to my taste!

Through thy monitions I explore
The depts of intellectual store,
    And thence my steps adjust;

Therefore the ways that I suspect,
And all things base and indirect,
    I from my soul disgust.

ב

Thy word, as through the dang'rous road
Of life I bear a cumb'rous load,
    Like lamps upon a fort,
Directs my path o'er treach'rous tides,
And by that light my vessel glides
    Safe to the destin'd port.

I've sworn, and will observe the terms
While thine assistant grace confirms
    The sanction of mine oath,
To keep with stedfast faith, and bless
The judgments of thy righteousness
    From actual sin and sloth.

Incroaching grief by fits devours
My strength, nor can my weaken'd pow'rs
    With such afflictions cope;
O Lord, my faculties renew,
That mercy to thy servant shew,
    Thy word inspires to hope.

Let the free tribute of my tongue,
In hymns before mine altar sung,
    Which love and faith suggest,
Be pleasing in thy sight, O Lord,
And all thy dread decrees record
    Upon thy servant's breast.

In daily jeopardy I stand,
My soul is always in my hand,
    And trembles in suspense;

Yet will I not forget a clause
Of what is written in thy laws
    Through error or offence.

To traps and snares the traitors stoop,
Nor have they courage in their troop
    To make a bold assault;
But I revere what thou hast taught,
Nor shall thy servant, e'en in thought,
    From thy commands revolt.

With hopes of heav'nly bliss inflam'd,
I've in thy testimonies claim'd
    An everlasting part;
And why? to be with thine and thee
Is the supreme felicity
    Of my transported heart.

My heart I have with care revis'd,
And in thy statutes exercis'd,
    Which also to perform
I will persist while that shall beat,
And while the bloomy vital heat
    My swelling veins shall warm.

ᴅ

I hate the wretches that invert
God's order, and imagine hurt
    Against the souls of men;
But I thy law in love receive,
And thence for all the best believe
    Within conception's ken.

Where'er I rest, where'er I roam,
Thou art my sure defence at home,
    And buckler for the fight;

And trusting in thy pow'r to save,
I fear that word beyond the grave,
    Evangelists indite.

Away, ye ministers of hell,
Whose hearts against the light rebel,
    And start as conscience stings;
For o'er God's charge I pray and fast,
And my true loyalty shall last
    To Christ the King of kings.

O stablish me, which by thy word
Thou to thy servant hast averr'd,
    That I in peace may live;
All my misgiving fears remove,
Nor let that hope abortive prove,
    Which thou hast deign'd to give.

I shall emerge, if thou sustain,
And in security remain
    By thy compassion buoy'd;
Yea, and as faith and hope compute
Thy statutes their eternal fruit,
    Be with delight employ'd.

Thou hast rejected, and shalt crush
All them that to perdition rush
    From thine eternal truth;
For they're deceitful in their souls,
Their artful tongue with flatt'ry trowls,
    And poison in their tooth.

Thou from thy presence shalt divorce
The men who take an evil course,
    Like dross from purer ore,
Who hug the snake, and spurn the Dove,
Therefore thy covenant I love
    The mightier and the more.

From head to foot the tremblings seize
My body, while with bended knees
    I think on my misdeeds,
And on thy great tribunal-day;
But still thy judgments to delay
    Prevailing mercy pleads.

י

In truth and equity I deal,
And to thy righteous laws appeal
    To justify my fame;
O save me from the pow'r of those
That on my back at once impose
    The burden and the blame.

By thy compulsive grace instill
An inclination to thy will,
    And to delight in good,
That wheresoe'er the proud and strong
Conspire to do thy servant wrong,
    Their force may be withstood.

Mine eyes with watchfulness and tears
Are wasting, till thy mercy clears
    The clouds that intervene,
And till thy righteous word be sent
To make a warning world repent,
    And close the bloody scene.

O estimate my soul's offence
By thy divine benevolence,
    Not from its grievous dye;
And on my heart thy laws impress,
That I in thankful faithfulness
    All others may outvie!

I serve as teacher to thy fold,
The blessed doctrine which I hold,
   O give me strength to scan!
And on the sacred text descant,
And urge the gracious covenant
   Thou hast reveal'd to man.

'Tis time, O Lord, the flames to slack
With which the schismatics attack
   Thine house, nor brook restraint,
And thy just judgments they deride,
Polluting all things sanctify'd,
   And trampling every saint.

For thy commandments, which assist
The meek, whose words dispel the mist,
   And raging torrent stems,
I prize in love's eternal bond
Beyond all pleasure, and beyond
   Fine gold and polish'd gems.

Wherefore with firmness I conclude
That all thy laws are rectitude;
   And all false ways that war
Against the welfare of mankind,
And in base chains the conscience bind,
   I from my soul abhor.

פ

Thy sacred oracles are great,
Above all wonder, and elate
   The soul to glorious laud;
Therefore, where'er I set my staff,
I keep them in my own behalf,
   And spread their use abroad.

Whene'er thy mighty word is shown,
And rolls in thunder from thy throne
    Amidst celestial fires,
It cleanses that which is impure,
And lightens those that are obscure,
    And simple folk inspires.

Thou, Lord and Master of my heart,
And well I say, for so thou art
    In thine own words exprest;
My mouth I open'd, or had burst,
And hunger after thee, and thirst
    For thy divine behest.

O on my bondage look and loose,
And with the rays of love transfuse
    In pity to my case;
As thou art ever wont to do
To that select and blessed few,
    Which thy dread name embrace!

Dispose me that my steps I take,
And act in all things for thy sake,
    And as thy word appoints;
So shall no traitor over-reach,
Nor Satan with his crimes impeach
    The man whom Christ anoints.

O shield me from the lewd reproach
Of loose companions, that incroach
    Upon thy servant's bounds,
That I, nor broken nor beguil'd,
May keep thy doctrine undefil'd,
    Whose light itself expounds.

Against this world of change and chance
Pour down thy radiant countenance,
    And bless me to be brave;

The words that God pronounc'd from heav'n,
And Jesus gave his own eleven,
    Upon my heart ingrave.

Mine eyes with tears of anguish gush,
And for the gen'ral guilt I blush,
    With sobs my bosom heaves,
Because thy laws they will not fear,
But still with troubl'd minds we hear
    Of murd'rers and of thieves.

ב

The fair perfection of thy reign
Is endless justice without stain,
    O sovereign Lord of Lords!
Thy judgments are exceeding wise,
The threaten'd death, the proffer'd prize,
    Thy terrors and rewards!

The words of thy divine command,
Which high above thine altar stand,
    That all may kneel and read,
Their truth and righteousness unblam'd,
All laws and rules that e'er were fram'd,
    In worth and weight exceed.

My zeal upon my vitals preys,
Because of those perverted ways,
    Which all my foes espouse;
Who, while thy statutes they forget,
And with thy goodness run in debt,
    Mine indignation rouse.

Thy word in all extremes is try'd,
And can their ordeal flames abide,
    More glorious from the proof;

And I, as join'd to thine elect,
With all my soul's desire affect
    Its beauty and behoof.

I am but small and of no class,
The meanest of thy saints surpass
    My utmost in desert;
Yet will I not thy precept slight,
But with all vehemence and might
    Their excellence assert.

Thou art our righteousness declar'd,
And all things are, with thee compar'd,
    Ungracious and uncouth,
And thine is the transcendent sway,
Which shall its eminence display
    In sempiternal truth.

All bliss and comfort here below,
Thro' sad inquietude and woe,
    Upon my spirit pall;
Yet have I joys which never fail,
When to thy word before the veil
    With prostrate face I fall.

Thy testimonies are reveal'd
In justice not to be repeal'd,
    And to retrench or add
Is not for mortals: O increase
My knowledge, and with endless peace
    To transport make me glad.

פ

O Lord, for strength to bear thy yoke,
Thee from my closet I invoke,
    Thee, likewise, from my couch;

As from my heart my pray'rs ascend,
Thine ear to my devotions lend,
    For I thy laws avouch!

Yea, thee will I invoke for aid,
And pray thy pity to persuade
    To these my vows aspire,
And by thy help thou shalt enlarge
My mind her duty to discharge,
    As thy decrees require.

To thee my soul herself sublimes,
And utt'ring her complaint betimes,
    She must her griefs alledge;
For to the word thou deign'd to shew,
When thy tremendous trumpet blew,
    My stedfast troth I pledge.

Mine eyes, upon thy word intent,
The watches of the night prevent,
    Thy volumes I unroll,
And from all worldly cares detach
My spirit, that I may dispatch
    The bus'ness of my soul.

O Lord, as I thy throne accost,
Let not my humble suit be lost,
    But hearken to my plea;
According to thine usual grace,
Assist and animate my race
    To heav'nly bliss and thee!

The rebels, by thy laws untaught,
And with malicious vengeance fraught,
    My very doors besiege,
And by their wickedness evince,
How far they are from peace her prince,
    And only sovereign liege.

Be thou, my Saviour, also nigh,
And to my need thy help apply,
    Against this hostile rage;
For in thy truth thou hast decreed
A blessing on the righteous seed
    Like to the thousandth age.

Thy holy laws, which Jesus crown'd
By sinless piety, redound,
    To gen'ral joy and use,
And e'en by children understood,
Are fashion'd for eternal good,
    To which they all conduce.

ר

O with a fatherly regard
Consider my distress, how hard
    Amongst thy sons my lot;
Attend and patronize my cause,
For mine allegiance to thy laws
    I never have forgot.

For me and for my foes decide,
Against their virulence and pride,
    And all their weapons ward;
Encourage me my woes to bear,
By praise, by patience, and by pray'r,
    And to thy word accord.

Health is from wicked men remote,
Which on the pomp of Mammon glote,
    And court the dust and moth;
Which, in all offices remiss,
Heed not the hopes of heavenly bliss,
    Nor hazard of thy wrath.

Great is thy goodness in its fruits,
Of all thy blessed attributes
  The nearest to thy heart;
My listless faculties arouse,
O Lord, and to my daily vows
  Thy wonted grace impart!

I am oppress'd with foes and feuds,
And by combining multitudes
  In tumult overborne;
Yet will I not in thought despise
Thy statutes, or apostatize
  From that which I have sworn.

It grieves my heart when I behold
The world so careless and so cold
  In what their soul concerns,
Because they will not be resolv'd,
But each, in carnal cares involv'd,
  From church to vice returns.

Consider, ev'n in deep distress,
With what affection I caress
  The Gospel Jesus spake.
O Lord, as thou art loving-kind,
Of all thy mercies in my mind
  A lively sense awake!

Thy words are everlasting life,
And can their purpose in the strife
  Of elements maintain;
And though the Lord predicts a day,
When heav'n and earth must pass away,
  His Gospel shall remain.

ש

Proud potentates, on no pretence,
And with unbounded insolence,
 Against me have inveigh'd;
But with thy word my heart I arm,
And all their terror and alarm
 Is clamour and parade.

When from thy word of light supreme
Some new illuminations beam,
 I with the prize am pleas'd,
As one, that after blood and toil,
Upon some rich and gorgeous spoil
 With eager hand has seiz'd.

All lies, and wretches who suborn
Their brethren to deceit, I scorn,
 Of thought and speech the shame;
But I have fix'd my heart's delight
Upon those blessed rules of right,
 Which bear our Saviour's name.

Each day, at sev'n appointed hours,
My soul to thee in fervour tow'rs
 To bless thy pow'r divine;
Because thy gifts for homage call
And thy blest dispensations all
 Are righteous and benign.

All those that keep themselves from sin,
Have great tranquillity within,
 As they thy name adore,
Nor are offended at the course
Of practice which thy laws inforce,
 But bless them more and more.

Lord, by a long-protracted space,
With love's impatience for thy grace,
    I have devoutly sigh'd,
And thy divine commands pursu'd,
And heav'n-conducted, self-subdu'd,
    In every point comply'd.

In all the laws of life adept,
My soul thy covenant has kept
    As of her love the test,
And tenders it exceeding dear,
The rather as she verges near
    To her eternal rest.

Thy covenant and each decree
Thou made, I keep, and bow the knee
    To thee, O Lord, alone;
For I am prov'd upon thy scale,
And all my thoughts themselves unveil
    Before thine awful throne.

ﬥ

Let my complaint, which I prefer,
That I from human weakness err,
    Thro' Christ, O Lord, be heard;
According to thy word expand
My knowledge, let the chaff be fann'd,
    And all the gloom be clear'd.

Grant to mine orisons access,
As I thy gracious throne address,
    And with acceptance greet;
True to thy word my soul reprieve
From bondage, under which I grieve,
    And all my vows compleat.

My lips, which cannot praise too much,
Shall speak as by thine hallow'd touch
   They're sanctified and tun'd,
When thou thy law hast fully taught,
And from my heart each fruitless thought,
   And vile affection prun'd.

Yea, I will take none other theme
For musick than thy word supreme,
   Upon my heart or tongue;
For thy commands in truth compriz'd,
And with such blessings harmoniz'd,
   Are worthiest to be sung.

Let thine hand save me from mischance,
That I may with my feet advance
   Where now I send my voice;
For by thy statutes I procure,
My calling and election sure,
   Because they are my choice.

I long to quit the world beneath,
And mine ejaculations breathe
   Toward my Saviour's peace;
For from thy law my gladness springs,
O Lord, and from all earthly things
   I sue for my release.

O give my soul to life and joy,
Where neither moth nor worms destroy
   My toils in triumph crown;
Amongst thy glorious saints enlist,
And still thy judgments shall assist
   While I thy name renown.

I went astray, of grace bereft,
Like some poor sheep, when he has left
   The shepherd at a loss;

Let mercy seek, if love regret,
A vagrant who could not forget
The GOSPEL of thy CROSS.

PSALM CXX

WHEN strong calamity prevail'd,
    And all my mirth was mute,
By pray'r the topmost heav'n I scal'd,
    And Jesus heard my suit.

Shield me from lips with lies replete,
    Or which their word revoke;
And from the language of the cheat
    Expert his thoughts to cloak.

O tongue, deceitful and obscene,
    What shall thy rage controul?
(Unless Christ's merits intervene)
    Sharp darts and burning coal.

How long, ye faithless crooked race,
    With you must I reside?
How long, said Christ, the prince of grace,
    Must I your ways abide?

My soul her sorrows overcharge
    Unto the last extreme,
For while I still on peace enlarge
    They question and blaspheme.

I strive to work them up to peace
    From horror and despair;
But at the word their bands increase,
    And they their cross prepare.

731

PSALM CXXI

BEYOND the mountains hoary brow
    I will my views extend,
From whence is help, and who shall now
    The needful comfort send.

My help is from the Lord of love
    In welfare or in woe,
Which arch'd the glorious heav'n above,
    And laid the land below.

Through him thy feet their ground shall keep,
    And move secure and free,
Nor shall the blessed watchman sleep,
    Which is on guard for thee.

Behold Jeshurun's ward, that draws
    The veil of thy repose,
His active nature needs no pause,
    Nor sleep nor slumber knows.

The Lord, thy keeper, is intent
    On his peculiar charge,
The Lord all dangers shall prevent,
    Thy breast-plate and thy targe;

So that the sun's meridian lamp
    Shall not thy veins inflame,
Nor shall the moon-beams, in the damp
    Of midnight, chill thy frame.

The Lord thy safety shall insure,
    All peril shall award;
Yea, and thy soul shall rest secure
    When cherish'd by the Lord.

The Lord shall for thy ways provide
    Thro' every sea and shore;
Thy travel and return to guide
    From henceforth evermore.

PSALM CXXII

My heart with gladness was elate
    To hear it thus agreed,
On Jesus let us wait,
    And to his temple speed.

Our weary foot shall rest its sole,
    No more in tents to roam,
And Salem's moat and mole
    Shall keep us safe at home.

Jerusalem's harmonious plan
    Of building well describes
Our order man by man,
    And union of our tribes.

For there the tribes, howe'er remote,
    Upon the Lord attend,
Their off'rings to devote
    And gratitude commend.

There is the mercy-seat, the place
    For Israel to appeal,
For David and his race
    Impartial truth to deal.

O pray for her eternal peace,
    For Salem bend the knee;
Their welfare shall increase
    Who have a love for thee!

The peace of God within thy ports,
　　And on thy walls abide,
And in thy splendid courts
　　His plenteousness reside.

For Christ, and for the brethrens sake,
　　And those with whom I dwell,
My soul thy part shall take,
　　And ever wish thee well.

Yea, for the zeal with which I prize
　　And for the church have stood,
My heart shall still devise
　　Thy glory and thy good.

PSALM CXXIII

To thee from thy temple I lift up mine eyes,
And breathe from my heart-strings the passionate
　　sighs,
O thou that with goodness and glory replete,
Hast fixt in the holiest of holies thy seat!

The looks of a servant his master revere,
The damsel her mistress with meekness and fear,
Thus elder and matron, and all our whole race
Attend at thy footstool for strength and for grace.

O Lord, let thine angel of comfort descend,
With blessed compassion our woes to befriend,
For in this dejection and wretched estate
They make us their object of scorn and of hate.

Our souls are disgusted and loaded with care,
Whilst hardly the taunts of the wealthy we bear,
And stand all abash'd at the spiteful disdain
We daily receive from the pompous and vain.

PSALM CXXIV

If God himself, with joy and pride,
  May Israel in salvation say;
If God had not been on our side
  On that tremendous day,

The hostile swarms had overpow'r'd
  Our utmost efforts to engage,
And quick with fire and sword devour'd,
  So furious was their rage.

Yea, Rabbah's waters stain'd with blood
  Had borne our carcasses afloat,
And we had perish'd in the flood,
  That fills the circling mote.

The stream with flowing life enlarg'd,
  Had giv'n their proud revenge delight;
The deep canal, with death surcharg'd,
  Had gratify'd their spite.

But blessed be the God of peace,
  Who hath not left his chosen fold
For thieves and murderers to fleece
  With malice uncontroul'd.

As when the greedy fowler's snare
  The birds by providence elude,
Our souls are rescu'd from despair,
  And their free flight renew'd.

Our help in God's most holy name
  With perfect confidence we place,
Which made the world's harmonious frame,
  And man's unnumber'd race.

PSALM CXXV

THEY, which their faithfulness have prov'd,
   Shall, like fair Zion, spread, and soar
God's mount, that may not be remov'd,
   But stands for evermore.

Round Salem's walls the hills ascend,
   Ev'n so God's angels rank in air
His faithful people to defend,
   For evermore his care.

For godless bands, which are a scourge,
   Shall never share our blessed lot,
Lest they the righteous man should urge
   His honest fame to blot.

Lord, thy benevolence maintain,
   And kindly with thy people deal;
Thy people which are good in grain,
   And have a heart to feel.

But they whose hearts relapse to sin,
   Shall with the profligates be sped,
While peace external and within
   Shall rest on Israel's head.

PSALM CXXVI

WHEN Zion's sons, in bonds detain'd,
   God hasted to redeem,
A pleasing doubt at first remain'd
   As unto those that dream.

Then smiles bedeckt each alter'd face
   Thro' fulness of content;

And songs and anthems held the place
    Of sighs in sorrow sent.

Then said the heathen, as they freed
    Our feet from out the gyves,
God's wond'rous grace has thus decreed
    Your liberties and lives.

Yea, God has done stupendous things
    Both now and all along,
For which our grateful nation rings
    With many a joyful song.

Turn thou, O Lord, our captive state
    As southern rivers flow,
Which first foam turbid, but abate,
    And brighten as they go.

To those who mournful till the ground,
    And on the furrows weep,
Their travel shall to peace redound
    When they with pleasure reap.

He that with tears his grief relieves,
    And bears a kindly grain,
Shall in true gladness bind his sheaves
    When Christ shall come again.

PSALM CXXVII

IF the work be not direct,
    And the Lord the fabrick build,
All the plans that men project
    Are but labour idly spill'd.

If the Lord be not the guard,
  And the forts and tow'rs sustain,
All the city gates are barr'd,
  And the watchman wakes in vain.

Vainly for the bread of care
  Late and early hours ye keep,
For 'tis thus by fervent pray'r
  That he lays the blest asleep.

Lo! thy children are not thine,
  Nor the fruits of female love,
But an heritage divine,
  And a blessing from above.

Like as arrows in the grasp
  Of a valiant man of might,
Are the children that you clasp
  In some future hour of fight.

Blest! who in his quiver stows
  Darts like these, a goodly freight,
Nor shall blush when with his foes
  He shall parley in the gate.

PSALM CXXVIII

BLESSED are all that love and fear
The Lord their God, and self-severe
  Their appetites restrain,
Who follow fame, and dread dispraise,
And walk directly in the ways
  Which he has made so plain.

For thou shalt live upon thine own,
And what thine industry has sown
  Thy hand shall surely reap;

738

When thou get'st up, O well is thee,
And in serene felicity
   Securely shalt thou sleep.

Domestick sweetness shall be thine,
Thy partner like the fruitful vine
   In all its clust'ring bloom,
Which to the gard'ner's will is bent,
And spreads an useful ornament
   Round every shaded room.

The children of thy plighted vows
Shall flourish, like thine olive-boughs,
   About thy social board;
And each o'er other, as they rise,
Shall to your love-delighted eyes
   A pleasing scene afford.

Behold that blessings, great as these,
Shall rest upon the faithful knees
   Of him who fears the Lord;
And he, the father of us all,
To those that on his godhead call
   Such treasures shall award.

Reveal'd from Zion in the height,
The Lord new blessing shall create
   Alike to thine and thee,
And highly favour'd branch and stem,
The welfare of Jerusalem
   Thou all thy life shall see.

Yea, thou shalt live to see thy face
Resembled in thy children's race,
   And hail the genuine breed;
Born in good days to shear the fleece,
When God sends plenty, pow'r and peace
   To Jacob's chosen seed.

PSALM CXXIX

FULL often the barbarian host,
    May Israel urge with truth,
Arose in arms against our coast,
    To this my stablish'd reign from early youth.

Yea, many a time from youth till now
    They have our coast assail'd;
But through our valour and our vow
    They have not yet with all their force prevail'd.

With ploughs to mark their camp they came
    As on our fields they throng'd,
And harrow'd up my vital frame
    While their insulting furrows they prolong'd.

But God from fear his own exempts
    Whatever foe invade,
To quell both violent attempts,
    And foil the schemes of secret ambuscade.

Let their embattl'd lines be broke
    And turn'd to flight with shame,
Whoe'er their idols aid invoke
    Against fair Zion's fortitude and fame.

Make all the snares which they have plann'd,
    Like grass upon the wall,
Which fades without the gath'rer's hand,
    Of none effect, or benefit at all.

From whence the garner has no gain,
    Nor damsel garland weaves,
Nor can there any thing remain
    For him that whets the scythes or binds the
      sheaves.

So that the passenger beholds
    No heaps to make him bless;
The Lord increase your lands and folds,
    We wish you for the sake of Christ success.

PSALM CXXX

From out the deep with piercing strain
    My soul express'd her grief,
O Lord, let piteous cries obtain
    An audience and relief.

O ponder with paternal ears
    The voice with which I pray,
And these my penitential tears
    With melting eyes survey.

If thou, O Lord of endless bliss,
    Shouldst rigid truth assume,
To try what mortals do amiss,
    Who shall support his doom!

But pow'rful mercy is thine own
    In Christ that dy'd for all,
And therefore trembling at thy throne
    Shall adoration fall.

I look for God, and watch and fast
    To purify my dust;
My soul shall in his precepts cast
    The anchor of her trust.

My soul to God pursues her flight
    When once his aid's withdrawn,
As guards nocturnal seek the light,
    And watchmen wish for dawn.

O Israel, in the Lord your king
    A firm reliance ground,
Through him redemption's living spring
    Both grace and truth abound.

And he most surely shall redeem
    The manners and the times,
And hallow by his pow'r supreme
    All Israel from their crimes.

PSALM CXXXI

O Lord, I am not apt to deal
    In pompous thoughts and self-esteem,
Nor, with the failings that I feel,
    Upon superior greatness dream;
Nor, shew to bear my neighbour down,
A haughty supercilious frown.

I study not to train my tongue
    In subtle and abstruse disputes,
Nor is my fixt attention hung
    On him that reasons or refutes;
I am not fond to interfere
With things that soar beyond my sphere.

But grace by pray'r my soul refrains,
    And keeps it low with all her means,
As when the nurse herself constrains,
    And from the breast her infant weans;
Yea, like the suckling from the breast,
I keep my soul from food and rest.

O children of the chosen stock
    From all the nations of mankind,
Your trust repose in God your rock,

And bear his benefits in mind;
And call'd of Jesus Christ, adore
His mercies ev'n more and more.

PSALM CXXXII

REMEMBER David's care,
   O God of praise and peace,
To his complaints repair,
   And all his debts release;
Which press upon him such a load,
And his repining heart corrode.

Remember how he nam'd
   The Lord unto his vow,
And what an oath he fram'd,
   As on fair Zion's brow
His soul adjur'd the Lord of hosts,
Whose angels, Jacob, guard thy coasts.

I will not quit the sod
   From whence my pray'rs aspire,
Nor from the face of God
   To privacy retire;
Nor by temptation's hand be led
To climb and rest upon my bed.

I will not bow to yield
   Mine eyes in wonted sleep,
Nor let their lids be seal'd
   As soothing slumbers creep;
Nor these my robes of pray'r divest
To let my temples take their rest.

Until at length I trace
   For God's establish'd fane

An eligible place
  His glory to contain;
An habitation in the east
For Jacob's gracious God and priest.

Of such a blessed site
  We from the spirit learn'd,
And to our great delight
  In Ephrata discern'd;
And there we mark'd it in the wood
The temple of the GREAT and GOOD.

We will with one accord
  To his cathedral speed,
And to the blessed Lord
  Our mutual ardour feed;
With meekness there his presence greet
And fall before his altar's feet.

Arise, O God, arise,
  And to thy rest resort,
And as thy standard flies
  Thy glorious host exhort;
And to thine ark of strength come down,
The hallow'd shrine of thy renown.

Let all thy mitred seers
  With righteousness be clad,
Which rising virtue cheers
  And reprimands the bad;
And let thy saints rejoice and sing
Hosanna to the Lord their king.

Thy succour we implore,
  And that for David's sake;
Abscond thyself no more
  From these the pray'rs we make;

Nor let us breathe in vain our vows,
Nor Christ be absent from his spouse.

The Lord my seed hath sown,
    And made a faithful oath
Respecting David's throne,
    Himself and children both;
Nor will he fail his word express,
By which he bound himself to bless.

From Jesse's goodly root
    I will my BRANCH educe
Of matchless bloom and fruit,
    By giving love a loose;
I will the throne of David build
Till it shall be with Jesus fill'd.

And if thy future sons
    Shall to their Saviour earn,
The words, which he that runs
    May read, if they will learn,
Their children also in thy room
The royal sceptre shall resume.

For God has set his mind
    Upon fair Zion's mound,
The house his grace design'd
    His goodness there shall found;
And for her heart-directed songs,
And pray'rs of penitence he longs.

Upon her stately tow'rs
    My glory shall descend,
My word her height impow'rs
    To flourish without end;
All rivalry she shall excell,
And I with her will love to dwell.

745

My blessing on her food
   And on her garners sent,
Shall daily be renew'd,
   Her stores I will augment;
Her poor shall to the full be fed,
Nor ever know the want of bread.

Her priests shall glow with health,
   And strength to pray and fast,
While pleasures, thirst and wealth
   Shall to the crowd be cast;
Her saints with heav'n-assisted voice
Shall in exalted hymns rejoice.

There will I cause the horn
   Of David still to sprout,
And with those wreathes adorn
   I weave for kings devout;
I will anoint and fix him mine
In a translucent sphere to shine.

I will the tumults hush
   Which trouble his repose,
And spread a shameful blush
   Upon his noisy foes;
But in his crown the gems shall beam,
And with superior lustre stream.

PSALM CXXXIII

BEHOLD, my brethren, which around
   To these my psalms of praise attend,
How good a doctrine, and how sound,
   And in what bliss it need must end;
To dwell together in the Lord
Like-minded, and of one accord.

'Tis like the precious fragrant cruse
   When pour'd upon the hoary head,
Which ran upon the beard profuse,
   Ev'n Aaron's beard where it was shed;
And thence descending from his breast,
It reach'd the border of his vest.

'Tis like the blessed honey-dew
   Which first fair Hermon's cedars fill'd,
And thence with its etherial glue
   On Zion's mount the sweets distill'd;
So that all orders and degrees
Might take the balmy prize with ease.

For in that heav'n-directed show'r
   God deign'd a further bliss to send,
And promis'd Israel to embow'r
   In glorious mansions without end;
Eternal life—immense reward,
And that thro' Jesus Christ our Lord.

PSALM CXXXIV

ATTEND to the musick divine
   Ye people of God with the priest,
At once your Hosanna combine
   As meekly ye bow to the east.

Ye servants that look to the lights
   Which blaze in the house of the Lord,
And keep up the watch of the nights
   To bless each apartment and ward,

The holy of holies review,
   And lift up your hands with your voice,
And there sing your anthems anew,
   In praise to Jehova rejoice.

The Lord that made heav'n and earth,
   Which rules o'er the night and the day,
His blessing bestow on your mirth,
   And hear you whenever ye pray.

PSALM CXXXV

O PRAISE the Lord, and bless his name,
   Ye servants of the Lord,
To God your anthems frame
   With swelling voice and chord.

You unto whom are stated posts
   Within God's hallow'd fane,
Who serve the Lord of hosts,
   And in his courts remain,

O to the Lord address your praise,
   Which is with grace replete,
His fair perfections blaze,
   For they are passing sweet.

For Jacob claims his Saviour's care
   As God's peculiar plant,
And Israel is his heir
   Assign'd by special grant.

I know the Lord our God is great
   And infinite, above
The measure or the weight
   Of other pow'r or love.

Whatever is the Lord's command
   Beyond, beneath the sun,
In ocean or by land,
   Or in the depth, is done.

He from the world's remotest ends
   The pregnant cloud explores;
With rain he lightning sends,
   The wind is from his stores.

His plagues th' Egyptian race consume
   From greatest to the least,
The firstlings from the womb
   Of man as well as beast.

Then institutes his paschal lamb,
   And triumphs o'er the waves,
And thee, O land of Ham,
   With Pharaoh and his slaves.

He smote with his Mosaic rod
   The realms of divers climes;
And he, th' almighty God,
   Slew tyrants for their crimes.

Sihon, who dwelt at Heshbon, fell,
   And Og, the world's disgrace,
And all the tools of hell,
   In Canaan's boundless space;

And gave their regions far and wide
   Of vineyards, fruits and flow'rs,
For Israel to divide,
   Proud domes and fragrant bow'rs.

O God, thy name and word endure
   In infinite renown;
From race to race secure
   Thy fame is handed down.

For God, in our behalf arous'd,
   Will strict reprisals make;

His people thus espous'd,
  His special grace partake.

As for the gods the heathen serves
  And true religion mocks,
They're mov'd by fictious nerves,
  Cast gold and silver blocks.

Their mouths are fram'd, from whence there
    comes
  Not e'en the breath of lies;
Ecstatic death benumbs
  Their glass-constructed eyes.

Their ears are fashion'd by the mould,
  Nor can they hear a sound;
Their molten lips are cold,
  In breathless fetters bound.

The founders of such gods as these
  Resemble their own dross,
And so do all whose knees
  Are bow'd to form and gloss.

Praise ye the Lord, each branch and bud
  Of Jacob's chosen root,
And you of Aaron's blood
  The praise to God impute.

Praise ye the Lord of Levi's line
  That in the temple keep;
In fear and praises join
  Ye congregated sheep.

The Lord be praised from Zion's brow
  Which dwells in Salem's dome,
And gives his people now
  The promis'd milk and comb.

PSALM CXXXVI

O TO God your thanks repay,
For most gracious is his sway,
And his mercy, since the fall,
Is for ever and for all.

O give thanks to God, which claims
Homage from all pow'rs and names;
For his mercy, since the fall,
Is for ever and for all.

O the thanks and praise restore,
And the Lord of lords adore;
For his mercy, since the fall,
Is for ever and for all.

Which alone at once conceives,
And the wond'rous works atchieves;
For his mercy, since the fall,
Is for ever and for all.

Whose transcendent skill so high
Arch'd the cov'ring of the sky;
For his mercy, since the fall,
Is for ever and for all.

Which the pregnant earth has spread
O'er the waters purer bed;
For his mercy, since the fall,
Is for ever and for all.

Which hath fashion'd and renew'd
Lights of glorious magnitude;
For his mercy, since the fall,
Is for ever and for all.

First the sun of genial beam,
O'er laborious day supreme;
For his mercy, since the fall,
Is for ever and for all.

Then the stars and lunar light
O'er the perils of the night;
For his mercy, since the fall,
Is for ever and for all.

Egypt, that his pow'r defy'd,
He destroy'd, their prince and pride;
For his mercy, since the fall,
Is for ever and for all.

And brought Israel from his chain
In the midst of their domain;
For his mercy, since the fall,
Is for ever and for all.

With the trumpet and alarm,
Mighty hand, and stretch'd-out arm;
For his mercy, since the fall,
Is for ever and for all.

Which the Red-Sea right and left
Into wide partitions cleft;
For his mercy, since the fall,
Is for ever and for all.

And made all his people pass
Safely thro' the liquid mass;
For his mercy, since the fall,
Is for ever and for all.

But king Pharaoh and his slaves
Perish'd in the whelming waves;

For his mercy, since the fall,
Is for ever and for all.

Which in most stupendous sort
Could his tribes through wilds escort;
For his mercy, since the fall,
Is for ever and for all.

Which in indignation smote
Kings of most especial note;
For his mercy, since the fall,
Is for ever and for all.

Yea, encount'ring, overcame
Kings of memorable name;
For his mercy, since the fall
Is for ever and for all.

Sihon royally array'd,
Whom fierce Amorites obey'd;
For his mercy, since the fall,
Is for ever and for all.

With gigantic Og, the boast
And the hope of Bashan's host;
For his mercy, since the fall,
Is for ever and for all.

And their realms upon the spot
Gave for heritage by lot;
For his mercy, since the fall,
Is for ever and for all.

E'en an heritage in lands
To his own victorious bands;
For his mercy, since the fall,
Is for ever and for all.

Which remember'd us and bless'd,
When our tribes were sore oppress'd;
For his mercy, since the fall,
Is for ever and for all.

And aveng'd our righteous cause
From blasphemers of his laws;
For his mercy, since the fall,
Is for ever and for all.

Which is provident to give
Food for all that breathe and live;
For his mercy, since the fall,
Is for ever and for all.

O give thanks to God alone,
Which has made the heav'n his throne;
For his mercy, since the fall,
Is for ever and for all.

O with thankful rev'rence bow,
And the Lord of lords avow;
For his mercy, since the fall,
Is for ever and for all.

PSALM CXXXVII

PENSIVE we sat the silent hours
Where by the Babylonian tow'rs
    At large the waters stray,
Till mem'ry brought thee to our eyes,
O Zion, then the tears and sighs
    Burst out and made their way.

No matter for our harps—our care
Was not on mirth and musick there,
    All solace we declin'd;

We sate and suffer'd them in view
To hang as bended, or as blew
    The willows or the wind.

When they, that led our captive train,
Bade us our heavy hearts refrain
    From grief to joys extreme;
Thus they commanded their request,
'Sing us a song, and sing your best,
    And Zion be the theme!'

What, in a land by God abhorr'd,
Shall we profane unto the Lord
    The consecrated songs;
And Israel's harp and hands employ,
To strike up symphonies of joy
    'Mongst foreigners and wrongs?

Jerusalem! O blest in woe,
If I forget thee, or forego
    When heav'n and nature call,
May this right hand, and God's own heart
Forget his spirit, and her art
    To touch the strings at all!

May my tongue to my palate cleave
If I forget thee when I grieve;
    If to all realms on earth
I not Jerusalem prefer,
Jerusalem! and harp on her
    When most my might in mirth!

O Lord, when it shall be fulfill'd
That thou Jerusalem rebuild,
    Remember unto good,
How 'down with it, th' insulting band
Cry'd, down with it, and mar the land
    Where all that splendour stood.'

Renown'd the man! that shall reward
And serve thee as thou'st serv'd the Lord,
    Thou shalt thy turn deplore;
There's desolation too for thee,
Thou daughter of calamity,
    And Babylon no more!

But he is greatest and the best,
Who spares his enemies profest,
    And Christian mildness owns;
Who gives his captives back their lives,
Their helpless infants, weeping wives,
    And for his sin atones.

PSALM CXXXVIII

O LORD, my God, with zeal intense
I will declare the pious sense
    Which my whole bosom warms,
I will return my lively thanks,
And that before cherubic ranks,
    And glorious archangelic forms.

I will direct my face to pray
Betimes before the rising ray
    Where stands thine eastern shrine;
For truth and love, thy word and name
Are far beyond what thought can frame,
    Or utmost study can combine.

What time to thee thro' Christ I cry'd,
Thy kind attention was apply'd;
    And when my soul was faint,
In him her vigour she renew'd,
And her celestial flight pursu'd
    From grievous illness and restraint.

All kings and potentates that be,
Shall learn and give the praise to thee,
 O Lord, for Christ his sake;
For they thy gospel have perus'd,
The words which GRACE to guilt infus'd
 As humbl'd in the flesh he spake.

Yea, instituted in the ways
Which Christian verity displays,
 They shall rejoice with songs,
That Christ is magnitude and might,
That glory to the Lord of right
 And sempiternal fame belongs.

For tho' the Lord our God be high,
And tow'rs beyond the mental eye,
 He yet regards the poor;
And for the sons of pomp and scoff
He keeps them at a distance off,
 Nor can such insolence endure.

What tho' I walk along the road
Of life, while thorns of anguish goad,
 Thou shalt my way refresh;
Thy hand outstretched shall controul
The furious hunters of my soul,
 The Devil, the sinful world and flesh.

The Lord, which dy'd upon the rood,
Shall with my soul his peace conclude,
 And to his promise stand;
Thy loving kindnesses to men
Endure for ever, scorn not then
 The chosen vessels of thine hand.

PSALM CXXXIX

O LORD, my soul thy spirit tries,
Thou know'st me when I close mine eyes,
    And when my rest I leave;
My thoughts, from all deception free,
Unveil their purposes to thee
    Ere I myself conceive.

Thou art about my daily tour,
And when my respite I procure
    Thou art about my bed;
And all the complicated maze
Of truth and error in my ways
    By thee are seen and read.

For lo! there's not a word or name,
These organs of my voice can frame,
    But thou, O Lord, canst tell;
Ere yet my tongue itself prepare,
To give the measur'd accents air,
    Thou understandest well.

Thou hast adorn'd with manly grace
The features of my ruddy face
    In seemly sort agreed,
And laidst thy hand upon my loins,
Where strength with symmetry conjoins
    To bless myself and seed.

Beyond my reach such wonders tow'r,
Too excellent thy art and pow'r
    Above all height sublime;
My thoughts exalt themselves and grow,
Thy works stupendous leave them low
    How far soe'er they climb.

Where shall I then thy spirit shun,
To what extremes of distance run
    Its motions to escape;
And by what mystery or might
Shall I the bearings of my flight
    From omnipresence shape?

Should I to highest heav'n ascend,
And with superior beings blend,
    There art thou in thy reign;
Or should I in the depths immerge
Of death and hell's contiguous verge,
    And thou art there again.

If with the morning's rosy wings
Quick from her perch my spirit springs,
    And o'er the rolling tide
Her climate and her haunts she change,
And from thy house herself estrange,
    And far from home abide,

There also nothing shall obstruct
Thy careful eye, thou shalt conduct
    My wand'rings with thy hand;
And there thy right hand shall support,
And my good guard against the sport
    Of chance and malice stand.

If to the darkness I appeal,
The darkness shall at least conceal
    And quench thy piercing ray;
The thought convincing conscience checks,
And thine internal truth detects,
    And turns my night to day.

To thee the darkness is no gloom,
Alike to thee the morning's womb,
    And evening's barren shade;

Thee all created objects strike,
The dawn and the still dusk alike,
  Which their relations made.

For modell'd by thy skill divine,
The texture of my reins is thine,
  And in the female mould
When the weak embryo was inclos'd,
The forming parts thou then dispos'd,
  And didst with care infold.

To what a rapture hast thou warm'd
These limbs, for fear and trembling form'd,
  And in such wonder skill'd;
My conscious soul adores thine art,
And from the workings of my heart
  My gratitude I build.

The substance of each nerve and bone
To thee are intimately known,·
  And at my hour of birth
Thou didst thy quick'ning spirit breathe,
Though I be taken from beneath,
  And but refin'd from earth.

Thine eyes review'd th' imperfect sketch
Ere yet my limbs began to stretch
  And were for action ripe;
Before my members were of age,
For birth, thou wrote them in thy page,
  And with the fairest type.

Which day by day assay'd to live,
And as thou didst conception give,
  Were warm'd with gradual heat;
When flesh and vital moisture both
Slept in the burial of their growth,
  And none were yet compleat.

O God, to what a pitch are wrought
The councils of omniscient thought,
    How dear unto my soul,
To what an infinite of sums
Their meanest estimation comes,
    What worlds on worlds the whole!

If I should set about to count
Their number, they by far surmount
    The sand upon the shore—
When in the morning first I wake,
By pray'r towards their source I make,
    And on my face adore.

O Lord, shall not the foes to good
By thy protection be withstood,
    The reprobates repress;
Depart ye men that are the first
To violate my laws, and thirst
    For slaughter in excess?

Against thy providence they scheme,
And to thy name, which they blaspheme,
    Unrighteous things impute;
And all thine enemies avow'd
Are open, insolent and loud
    In their absurd dispute.

Are not the traitor and ingrate,
O Lord, the monsters of my hate,
    And do I not disgust
The rebels of thy holy cause,
That arm against thy church and laws,
    The fiends of wrath and lust?

Yea, from my soul I disapprove
All those dire engines that they move,
    And friends which they suborn;

And I detest them more by far
Than when my private peace they mar
　　With all their rage and scorn.

Try me, O God, and seek the ground
Of this my heart, if it be sound,
　　And worthy of a man;
Do thou unravel all the clue
Of all and every thing I do,
　　And purposes I plan.

Peruse me well, if spite or guile
My breast with inward taint defile,
　　And with my nature mix;
Reform what there thou find'st amiss,
And in the way of endless bliss
　　For Christ his merit fix.

PSALM CXL

LORD, save me from his wicked lure
　　Who for corruption strives;
And make, thro' grace, my rescue sure
　　From men of lawless lives;

From men, who mischief, for the sake
　　Of mischief, still conceive,
And keep the coals of wrath awake
　　From early day till eve.

Their tongue, by malice sharpen'd, works
　　With anger and untruth;
The venom of the viper lurks
　　Beneath their lip and tooth.

O Lord, preserve me from the hand
    Of wickedness and force,
And from the godless men, who band
    To overthrow my course.

The wealthy world's imperious lords
    Have spread abroad their net,
And aim'd to take my feet with cords,
    And traps which they have set.

Unto my Saviour I profess'd
    I have no God but Thee;
O hear me, as thy name is bless'd,
    And meekness bends my knee.

O Lord, thou shalt my health sustain,
    And art my helm and targe
Whenever in th' embattl'd plain
    I join the furious charge.

Let not the wicked have his will,
    Who wishes for the worst,
Nor his outrageous thoughts fulfill,
    Lest sin with pride should burst.

Let those that compass me around,
    Whose bitter words I feel,
Be saved themselves from every wound
    They meditate or deal.

Let not the flaming coals they blow
    The mischief-makers burn,
Nor let them to those regions go
    Whence soul nor flesh return.

A wordy man shall never reach
    The point he has in view;

The consequence of evil speech
    The babbler shall pursue.

I have a sure and certain sign
    Of comfort in my soul,
That Jesus will the helpless join,
    And with his woes condole.

The righteous also shall give thanks
    To thine eternal might,
And he shall mingle with the ranks
    Of angels in thy sight.

PSALM CXLI

LORD, I thy present help implore,
    Respect my voice, and meet
My breathings as they soar
    Towards thy holy seat.

The pray'r which I set forth receive
    As frankincense and nard,
And as a gift at eve
    My lifted hands regard.

Set thou a watch my youth to ward
    From inadvertent slips,
And lock, O gracious Lord,
    The portal of my lips.

O let my heart be clean and chaste,
    Nor let my members share
In wicked works, nor taste
    Of Mammon's tempting fare.

No, let the righteous rather thwart
  And friendly smite my cheek,
I would not then retort,
  But be resign'd and meek.

But let not what they give for balm
  Increase my raging smart;
Nay, I will pray my psalm
  Against their hand and heart.

Let such false judges as commend
  Their harsh precarious prose,
To this my song attend,
  Which in sweet measure flows.

Our bones beside the grave are straw'd
  From life's extinguish'd spark,
Like timber cast abroad,
  Which woodmen fell and bark.

But, holy Lord, and God most just,
  To thee mine eyes I turn;
In thee I put my trust,
  Nor thou my spirit spurn.

Preserve me from the cover'd mines
  That impious men have made
And from the dark designs
  Which traitors have assay'd.

Let thy deceivers be confus'd
  As they their bounds infringe;
But let my soul be loos'd
  From every net and springe.

PSALM CXLII

To thy seat, O Consolation,
    I have made my plaintive plea,
And preferr'd my supplication,
    O my Saviour God, to thee.

Tears and tender strains diffusive,
    I presented as I knelt,
And compos'd my words allusive
    To the troubles which I felt.

Thou, when all my mirth subsided,
    Saw the path I went to pray;
As to thee my steps I guided,
    Traitors laid me by the way.

To my right-hand I bestow me,
    Where my former friends were plac'd,
But I find that none will know me,
    Thus dejected and disgrac'd.

Of our refuge, not a city
    Op'd her hospitable gate,
Nor was there a man to pity
    My poor soul's abandon'd state.

To the Lord I cry'd, confessing
    His benevolence and pow'r;
Thou my hope, and thou my blessing,
    Ev'n to life's extremest hour.

O consider my condition,
    Whence arises such complaint
For, remov'd from thy tuition,
    I am quite reduc'd and faint.

From my burden disencumber,
  From my persecutors save;
For their malice, strength and number
  Are too much for me to brave.

Take me from this bondage hateful,
  Which my spirit so dismays,
That again the good and grateful
  May attend my song of praise.

PSALM CXLIII

HEAR, O Lord, and weigh the motions
  Of my spirit as I kneel,
Stoop to my sincere devotions,
  Which to love and truth appeal.

And arraign me, not demanding
  Strict account for every deed,
For at thy tribunal standing
  Sinners no excuse can plead.

For the fiend of persecution
  Has depress'd my life with those,
Whom in death and dissolution
  Darkness and the grave inclose.

Hence my spirit is tormented,
  Fretting with affliction's thorn,
And my heart is discontented,
  And within my breast forlorn.

Yet I will indulge reflexion
  As upon thy works I muse;
Yea, in thought to sooth dejection,
  All thy wonders I peruse.

To thy throne my hands extending
   In the spirit I complain,
And I gasp for grace descending,
   As a thirsty land for rain.

Hear me, Lord, with expedition,
   For my spirit faints with care,
Hide thee not from my contrition,
   Lest a death-like form I wear.

Early with the rising morning
   To my faith thy grace decree,
With thy word my conduct warning,
   For I lift my soul to thee.

Lord, by Christ his intercession
   From my furious foes release,
For I flee to take possession
   Thro' his merits of thy peace.

Teach me that correct behaviour
   Which is pleasing in thy sight;
For thou art my Lord and Saviour,
   Speed me to the realms of light.

Lord, from this despondence rousing,
   For the glory of thy name,
And my righteous cause espousing,
   Bring my soul from bonds and shame.

And my foes and evil neighbours,
   Lord, by charity controul;
For I dedicate my labours
   To the Saviour of my soul.

PSALM CXLIV

THE glory to the Lord I yield,
 Whose hands new strength impart,
To brave the ensanguin'd field,
 And top the warrior's art.

My hope, my Saviour, and my helm,
 My castle and my fort,
By whom my subject realm
 Themselves in peace comport.

Lord, what is man, that thou should leave
 For his concerns thy rest,
A sinful son of Eve
 So cherish'd and so blest?

Man is a thing of little worth,
 Thro' folly and misdeeds,
Resembling from his birth
 The shadow, that recedes.

Bow down the heav'ns, O Lord, in pray'r
 As I thy name invoke
Upon the mountains bear,
 And incense they shall smoke.

Cast forth thy lightnings, and disperse
 Ungodliness and gloom,
Thine arrows fiery fierce
 Shall Satan's works consume.

O send and save me with that hand
 Which all attempt controuls,
From adverse floods that land
 The foreigners in shoals.

From every loud vain-glorious fool,
  With tongue by truth unaw'd,
Whose right hand is a tool
  Of violence and fraud.

O Lord, I will an anthem chuse
  Of novelty divine,
And with thy holy muse
  The ten-string'd bass shall join.

The royal arms have peace thro' thee,
  By victory restor'd;
And David now is free
  From hostile fire and sword.

Save me from tongues of foreign stile,
  And of thy grace bereft,
Whose right hand is of guile,
  A hand of blood and theft.

So that our sons like plants may grow,
  Our polish'd daughters shine
Like cherubs in a row,
  Carv'd in the holy shrine.

So that our garners be profuse
  With much and various stores,
And that our sheep produce
  Ten thousand at our doors.

So that our oxen may be strong,
  As toil disease defeats;
That murmurs, rapes and wrong
  No more infest our streets.

Blest is the people which have got
　　Such treasure in their coasts;
Yea, blessed is their lot
　　Who serve the Lord of hosts.

PSALM CXLV

O GOD, my king, I will adore
　And magnify thy name,
To thee the praise I will restore,
And blazon ever more and more
　Thy glory, of eternal fame.

I will acknowledge day by day
　Thy grace with thankful heart;
And to thy name the praise repay,
And thine immortal worth display,
　Nor ever from the theme depart.

The Lord is infinitely great,
　And of amazing might;
His endless being knows no date,
His greatness is above all height,
　And should our utmost laud excite.

One generation shall declare
　To all succeeding times
Thy works and providential care,
Thy pow'r, which high o'er earth and air,
　And topmost heav'n itself sublimes.

As for my part, I will converse
　Upon religious themes,
Thy glory and thy praise rehearse,
And psalms upon thy word disperse,
　Which with perpetual wonder teems:

So that the language of mankind
   Upon thine acts shall dwell;
Thy works in matchless skill design'd,
And in such harmony combin'd,
   I likewise will the chorus swell.

The justly memorable tale
   Of thine abounding love,
Shall o'er malevolence prevail,
And men with songs thy truth shall hail,
   Connecting earth with heav'n above.

The Lord is of exceeding grace
   In pardon to our sin,
Long-suffering to the human race,
And great our follies to efface,
   And good our contrite hearts to win.

The Lord his tenderness extends
   To every man and beast;
His pity with his bounty blends,
To all their sustenance he sends,
   From greatest to the last and least.

Lord, all thy works thy laud include,
   The vocal and the mute;
And all thy saints elect, endu'd,
With never-failing gratitude,
   To their glad harps their numbers suit.

The glories of thine endless reign
   In hymns of praise they shew;
And sing of thy supreme domain,
Which thou transcendest to maintain
   By marvels various, great and new.

That thine uncontroverted pow'r,
   The lustre of thy throne,

And might exerted day and hour,
Which can o'er all resistance tow'r,
     Should to all human kind be known.

Thou art an everlasting king,
     In endless glory crown'd;
Truth is the signet of thy ring,
And thy dominion takes a swing
     From alpha—from omega—round.

The Lord, the grand support of all,
     From heav'n where he resides,
Recovers such as faint or fall,
And kindly listens to the call
     Of those that sink, or him that slides.

The eyes of all, O Lord, appeal,
     And heav'nwards look to thee;
And in due season thou shalt deal
For every beak and mouth its meal,
     By fixt and regular decree.

Thine hand, omnipotent to save,
     Thou open'st from on high,
And to it all things living crave,
From air, from earth, and from the wave,
     And have a plentiful supply.

The Lord has all his word fulfill'd
     In measure passing thought;
And whatsoe'er his wisdom will'd,
His matchless art has aptly skill'd,
     And to the last perfection brought.

The Lord to those is ever near
     Whose lips his aid invoke;

Yea, such as hearty faith endear
By holy meekness, and by fear,
   And yield them to his easy yoke.

He will compleat the fervent vows
   Of them that fear his laws,
He likewise will their part espouse,
And for their help his might arouse,
   And patronize their righteous cause.

The Lord is gracious to uphold
   All those that love his word;
But severs from his special fold,
And will **not** such a race behold,
   As have nor praise nor pray'r preferr'd.

My mouth shall to the Lord confess
   His meritorious praise;
Let all mankind his fear caress,
And as with holy thanks they bless
   His name for ever, ever blaze.

PSALM CXLVI

To God, my soul, exalt the strains,
   While I these active pow'rs possess;
Yea, while the life is in my veins
   I will be bound to bless.

O wait not on a prince's smile,
   Nor in a mortal put your trust,
For there's no grace of God in guile,
   Nor is there help in dust.

For as the breath and life depart
   From man returning to his mould,

Conception fails his head and heart
 When once his limbs are cold.

The man is blest who pays his court
 To Jacob's God to be supply'd;
And who for his eternal fort
 In Jesus shall confide.

The Lord, who fram'd the brilliant spheres,
 He roll'd the floods, the land he laid,
And for eternity reveres
 The promise that he made.

Which to the souls that suffer wrong
 Can their just property secure,
And helps the halt and lame along,
 And feeds the hungry poor.

The Lord is present to unbind
 The shackl'd prisoners as they pray,
The naked cloaths, and to the blind
 Restores the chearful day.

The Lord recovers from the brink
 Of hell, and from the tempter's snares,
All such as into danger sink,
 And for the righteous cares.

He takes the weary stranger in,
 And widows, orphans he defends;
And all the ways of death and sin
 He by his truth amends.

The Lord, O Zion, Christ shall lead
 Thine armies, and command thy sons,
While age from age and seed from seed
 Th' eternal series runs.

PSALM CXLVII

HOSANNA—musick is divine,
When in the praise the psalmists join,
    And each good heart is warm;
Yea, joy is sweetest so renew'd,
And all the rites of gratitude
    Are rapture to perform.

The Lord fair Salem shall replace,
And set upon his ancient base
    Hananiel's goodly tow'r;
Make captives free, the barren big,
And under his own vine and fig
    All Jacob re-embow'r.

He shall the broken heart repair,
And for all sickness and despair
    A cure in Christ provide;
And heal the wounded and the bruis'd,
His oil into their sores infus'd,
    And soothing balm applied.

Tho' their bright swarms the sand surpass,
Of every magnitude and class
    He knows th' etherial flames;
The numb'rer of their host is He,
And to his summons 'here we be',
    They answer by their names.

For God is magnitude immense,
His prowess is omnipotence
    That knows no date or end;
His wisdom infinitely great,
And all duration, depth and height,
    His mysteries transcend.

The Lord with approbation sees
The meek, and from his faithful knees
    He lifts him up on high;
But spurns the sinner and unjust,
And leaves low luxury and lust
    To worms that never die.

Sing praises all degrees and ranks,
As in the pray'r of general thanks
    The holy church commune;
As to the touch the harp revives,
Sing praises with your lips and lives
    To Christ the word and tune.

He the blue heav'n in beauty shrouds,
And ballances the plumy clouds
    Which for the rain he wrings;
He causes the mild dew to drop,
And grass upon the mountain top
    In tufted verdure springs.

For every thing that moves and lives,
Foot, fin, or feather meat he gives,
    He deals the beasts their food
Both in the wilderness and stall,
And hears the raven's urgent call,
    And stills her clam'rous brood.

And yet his maker has no need
Of the train'd ox, or prancing steed,
    Tho' thunder cloath his chest;
And man that manages the rein,
Is but a creature brief and vain
    With such proportion blest.

But God is pleas'd with duteous fear,
Men with clean hands and conscience clear,
    Which at thy mercy-gate

With ceaseless application knock,
And patient on him as their rock
    For sure redemption wait.

O Sion, praise the Lord, and thou,
Fair Salem, to his praises bow
    Thine olives and thy palms;
Are there afflicted? let them pray,
But mirth shall dedicate her day
    To hymns and festive psalms.

For by his might the Lord supports
Thy mounds, and fortifies thy forts,
    Thy brazen bars he nails;
Thy sportive children fill the streets,
Thy foe without the wall retreats,
    Nor want within prevails.

He sheathes the sword and blunts the spears,
And thy redoubtable frontiers
    Barbarian inroads scorn;
That thou may'st in thy peace possess
The blessings of a social mess,
    And flour of choicest corn.

He sends his word upon the earth
To call conception into birth,
    And kind with kind to match;
And to sustain all human race,
The blessed angels of his grace
    Make infinite dispatch.

His snow upon the ground he teems,
Like bleaching wool beside the streams,
    To warm the tender blade;
Like ashes from the furnace cast,
His frost comes with the northern blast
    To pinch and to pervade.

Like vitreous fragments o'er the field,
In ice the waters are congeal'd,
    Their liquid swiftness lost;
The breath steams on the sharpen'd air,
And who so hardy as to bear
    The quickness of his frost!

He sends the word of his command
To melt and loosen all the land,
    And let the floods at large;
He blows, and with the genial breeze,
The fount and river by degrees
    Their usual tale discharge.

His word to Jacob he disclos'd,
When he upon the stones repos'd
    And worship'd in a trance;
And laws to Israel enjoin'd
When o'er the nations of mankind
    He bade his tribes advance.

Such wond'rous love has not been shown,
But to the patriarch's seed alone
    His duty to requite;
And judgments on the rest impend,
Till Jesus make them comprehend
    His ways, his truth and light.

PSALM CXLVIII

HOSANNA to the king
    On his eternal throne,
Let heaven's high convex ring
    With pray'r and praise alone!
Praise him which treads th' etherial vault,
And with the theme your strains exalt.

Praise him, cherubic flights,
   And ye seraphic fires,
Angelical delights
   With voices, lutes and lyres;
And vie who shall extol him most,
Ye blest innumerable host!

Praise him, thou source of heat,
   Great ruler of the day,
And thou serenely sweet,
   O moon, his praise display;
Praise him ye glorious lights that are,
The planet and the sparkling star.

Praise him ye heav'ns above
   The highest heav'n sublime,
Where tun'd to truth and love
   The spheres symphonious chime;
Praise him where holy spirits lave,
Ye waters of eternal wave.

Let them to praise his name
   With choral musick flow;
For from his word they came,
   He spake and it was so;
His are the glorious, great and fair,
For he commanded, and they were.

—For he hath made them fast
   For ever and again;
For ever they shall last,
   And in their spheres remain;
In all their movements seek or shun,
The law that he commands is done.

Praise ye the Lord of earth,
   All ye that dwell therein,

And leap with active mirth,
    Ye fish of ev'ry fin;
Praise ye, that hide where ocean sleeps,
Ye dragons of unfathom'd deeps.

Ye meteors, fire and hail,
    With ev'ry cloud that snows,
As o'er the land they sail,
    And various wind that blows
The rapid terror of the storm,
At once his mandate to perform.

Ye mountains of the air,
    And hills of less degree,
And you ye groves that bear
    On ev'ry goodly tree
The summer fruits, and vernal bloom,
And lofty cedars of perfume.

Ye beasts that haunt the wild,
    From servile bondage loose,
Ye cattle tame and mild
    For man's domestic use,
Ye reptiles of the ground adore,
Ye birds sing praises, as ye soar.

Praise him, each scepter'd seer
    Advanc'd to hold the helm,
And to his praise appear,
    Ye people of the realm;
Ye princes by the world renown'd,
And judges, that the laws expound.

Ye youths the maids engage
    In melody divine,

Let infancy with age
   To praise the Lord combine,
Whose name, whose merits have no end,
But measure and immense transcend.

He shall exalt the crest
   Of his peculiar fold,
And all the wise and blest
   This festival shall hold;
Ev'n Jacob's sons and Judah's bands,
Whose faith, whose firm allegiance stands.

OR THIS

HALLELUJAH! kneel and sing
Praises to the heav'nly king;
To the God supremely great,
Hallelujah in the height!

Praise him, archangelic band,
Ye that in his presence stand;
Praise him, ye that watch and pray,
Michael's myriads in array.

Praise him, sun, at each extreme
Orient streak, and western beam,
Moon and stars of mystic dance,
Silv'ring in the blue expanse.

Praise him, O ye heights, that soar
Heav'n and heav'n for evermore;
And ye streams of living rill,
Higher yet, and purer still.

Let them praise his glorious name,
From whose fruitful word they came,

782

And they first began to be
As he gave the great decree.

Their constituent parts he founds
For duration without bounds,
And their covenant has seal'd,
Which shall never be repeal'd.

Praise the Lord on earth's domains,
And the mutes that sea contains,
Ye that on the surface leap,
And ye dragons of the deep.

Batt'ring hail, and fires that glow,
Steaming vapours, plumy snow,
Wind and storm his wrath incurr'd,
Wing'd and pointed at his word.

Mountains of enormous scale,
Ev'ry hill, and ev'ry vale,
Fruit-trees of a thousand dyes,
Cedars that perfume the skies.

Beasts that haunt the woodland maze,
Nibbling flocks, and droves that graze;
Reptiles of amphibious breed,
Feather'd millions form'd for speed;

Kings, with Jesus for their guide,
Peopl'd regions far and wide,
Heroes of their country's cause,
Princes, judges of the laws;

Age and childhood, youth and maid,
To his name your praise be paid;
For his word is worth alone,
Far above his crown and throne.

He shall dignify the crest
Of his people rais'd and blest,
While we serve with praise and pray'rs
All, in Christ, his saints and heirs.

PSALM CXLIX

Hosanna! God be prais'd,
  The song of thanks pursue;
Let ev'ry thought be rais'd,
  And ev'ry note be new;
Let saints assembl'd in his fane
The chorus of applause sustain.

Let Jacob's heart be glad
  In his Creator's name,
Ev'n him which made and clad
  His soul in such a frame;
Let Zion's grateful sons be gay,
And bless his sempiternal sway.

Praise him, ye youthful pairs,
  As ye the dance complete,
Which to the quick'ning airs
  Has wing'd your active feet,
And strike the timbrel to the strings
Of him that plays the harp and sings.

Because there is increase
  To God's eternal bliss
When men exult in peace
  To such a tune as this,
And he shall in the spirit wait
On those, whose meekness makes them great.

Let those his holy saints
   That have put off their earth,
Whom spite no more attaints,
   Rejoice in glorious mirth,
And let their gladness be imprest
On those bright mansions, where they rest.

Let hymns, of praise compos'd
   In mirth and mystic skill,
To God began and clos'd,
   Their mouths with musick fill,
And as they modulate their psalms,
Their hands present triumphant palms.

To meditate the good
   And glory of mankind,
That vice may be withstood,
   And heathens well inclin'd;
That vengeance, violence, and guile
No more the human race defile.

To make their princes bow
   To Christ's indulgent yoke,
And God's best name avow
   As they their sins uncloak;
To bid their noblemen unite
With Christians in the Lord of light.

That war, and hate, and pride,
   And ev'n the name of foe
May in that love subside
   Which Christian champions show;
For thus the holy Gospel runs,
Such honour have his saints and sons.

OR THIS

HALLELUJAH! soul of song,
 New from heav'n the notes conceive;
 Saints, assembled morn and eve,
The grateful strains prolong.

Let the people of his choice,
 Children that his heart allows,
 To their Maker pay their vows,
To Christ their king rejoice.

Let the youth his praise repeat,
 As they dance with active might;
 To his laud the tabret smite,
And harp sublimely sweet. .

For the Lord with pleasure deigns
 To behold his faithful sheep,
 As his festivals they keep,
And meekness he sustains.

Let his glorious saints from earth
 Sever'd in his faith and fear,
 Ev'ry martyr in his sphere,
Rejoice with heav'nly mirth.

For the words that Christ bequeath'd
 Let them hold the book of grace;
 Tears wip'd off from ev'ry face,
And ev'ry weapon sheath'd.

That opposers may be drawn
 To the covenant of peace,
 And that Christians may increase
From follies past and gone.

In the bond of love to bind
   Kings contending for renown,
   And their potentates to crown,
As worthies of mankind.

That as vengeance is controul'd,
   Great salvation may attend
   Truth persisting to the end,
As Christ assures his fold.

PSALM CL

HOSANNA! praise the Lord, and bless
According to his holiness,
   And let your praises tow'r;
O bless him in sublimest strains,
Where in the firmament he reigns
   Of his exalted pow'r.

The works of his Almighty hand,
Which on eternal record stand,
   With hymns of thanks review;
On his majestic glory dwell,
Whose rays all excellence excel,
   And give the praises due.

The best and boldest blast be blown
From trumpet of triumphant tone
   Abroad his praise to send;
His name upon the lute be sung,
With citerns to his praises strung,
   The work of joy attend.

Take up the trimbrel, let the sound
Extol him as the dances bound,
   And let the pipes conspire

To give his praises to the wind,
And let your organ's voice be join'd
   By minstrels on the wire.

Well order'd to a just degree
Of their most perfect melody
   With cymbals praise his name
And let the cymbals full and strong
Together and with all their song
   Aloud his praise proclaim.

Let all things that have breath to breathe
From heav'n above, from earth beneath,
   To Christ's renown repair;
O give him back your breath again,
Put all the life into the strain,
   And soar by praise and pray'r!

Hymns and Spiritual Songs for the Fasts and Festivals of the Church of England

Te decet Hymnus

שירו לו זמרו לו שיחו בכל
נפלאתיו

HYMN I

New Year

WORD of endless adoration,
   Christ, I to thy call appear;
On my knees in meek prostration
   To begin a better year.

Spirits in eternal waiting,
   Special ministers of pray'r,
788

Which our welcome antedating,
   Shall the benediction bear.

Which, the type of vows completed,
   Shall the wreathed garland send,
While new blessings are intreated,
   And communicants attend.

Emblem of the hopes beginning,
   Who the budding rods shall bind,
Way from guiltless nature's winning,
   In good-will to human kind.

Ye that dwell with cherub-turtles
   Mated in that upmost light,
Or parade amongst the myrtles,
   On your steeds of speckl'd white.

Ye that sally from the portal
   Of yon everlasting bow'rs,
Sounding symphonies immortal,
   Years, and months, and days, and hours.

But nor myrtles, nor the breathing
   Of the never-drying grove,
Nor the chaplets sweetly wreathing,
   And by hands angelic wove;

Not the musick or the mazes
   Of those spirits aptly tim'd,
Can avail like pray'r and praises
   By the Lamb himself sublim'd.

Take ye therefore what ye give him,
   Of his fulness grace for grace,
Strive to think him, speak him, live him,
   Till you find him face to face.

Sing like David, or like Hannah,
   As the spirit first began,
To the God of heights hosanna!
   Peace and charity to man.

Christ his blessing universal
   On th' arch-patriarch's seed bestow,
Which attend to my rehearsal
   Of melodious pray'r below.

HYMN II

Circumcision

WHEN Abraham was bless'd,
And on his face profess'd
   The Saviour Christ hereafter born,
'Thou pilgrim and estrang'd,
Thy name, said God, is chang'd,
   Thy lot secur'd from want and scorn.

'O Abraham, my friend,
My covenant attend,
   Which Shilo's self shall not repeal,
Chastise from carnal sin
Thy house and all thy kin,
   Thy faith by circumcision seal.'

The promis'd Shilo came,
And then receiv'd the name
   Of Jesus, Saviour of the soul;
As he the law fulfill'd
Which checks the fleshly-will'd,
   And o'er the passion gives controul.

O clean and undefil'd!
Thou shalt not be beguil'd

    By youthful heat and female art,
To thee the strains belong
Of that mysterious song
    Where none but virgins bear a part.

Come every purer thought,
By which the mind is wrought
    From man's corruption, nature's dust;
Away each vain desire,
And all the fiends that fire
    The soul to base and filthy lust.

Ye swans that sail and lave
In Jordan's hallow'd wave,
    Ah sweet! ah pensive! ah serene!
Thou rose of maiden flush,
Like Joseph's guiltless blush,
    And herb of ever-grateful green;

Ye lilies of perfume,
That triumph o'er the loom,
    And gaudy greatness far outshine;
And thou the famous tree,
Whose name is chastity,
    And all the brilliants of the mine;

Ye doves of silver down
That plume the seraph's crown,
    All, all the praise of Jesus sing,
The joy of heav'n and earth,
And Christ's eternal worth,
    The pearl of God, the Father's ring.

Let elegance, the flow'r
Of words, in tune and pow'r,
    Find some device of cleanest choice

About that gem to place—
'This is my HEIR OF GRACE,
In whose perfections I rejoice.'

HYMN III

Epiphany

GRACE, thou source of each perfection,
    Favour from the height thy ray;
Thou the star of all[1] direction,
    Child of endless truth and day.

Thou that bidst my cares be calmer,
    Lectur'd what to seek and shun,
Come, and guide a western palmer
    To the Virgin and her Son.

Lo! I travel in the spirit,
    On my knees my course I steer
To the house of might and merit
    With humility and fear.

Poor at least as John or Peter
    I my vows alone prefer;
But the strains of love are sweeter
    Than the frankincense and myrrh.

Neither purse nor scrip I carry,
    But the books of life and pray'r;
Nor a staff my foe to parry,
    'Tis the cross of Christ I bear.

From a heart serene and pleasant
    'Midst unnumber'd ills I feel,
I will meekly bring my present,
    And with sacred verses kneel.

Muse, through Christ the Word, inventive
   Of the praise so greatly due;
Heav'nly gratitude retentive
   Of the bounties ever new.

Fill my heart with genuine treasures,
   Pour them out before his feet,
High conceptions, mystic measures,
   Springing strong and flowing sweet.

Come, ye creatures of thanksgiving,
   Which are harmoniz'd to bless,
Birds that warble for your living,
   Beasts with ways of love express.

Thou the shepherd's faithful fellow,
   As he lies by Cedron's stream,
Where soft airs and waters mellow
   Take their Saviour for their theme.

Thou too gaily grave domestic,
   With whose young fond childhood plays,
Held too mean for verse majestic,
   First with me thy Maker praise.

Brousing kids, and lambkins grazing,
   Colts and younglings of the drove,
Come with all your modes of praising,
   Bounding through the leafless grove.

Ye that skill the flow'rs to fancy,
   And in just assemblage sort,
Pluck the primrose, pluck the pansy,
   And your prattling troop exhort.

'Little men, in Jesus mighty,
   And ye maids that go alone,

Bodies chaste, and spirits flighty,
   Ere the world and guilt are known.

'Breath so sweet, and cheeks so rosy—
   Put your little hands to pray,
Take ye ev'ry one a posy,
   And away to Christ, away.'—

Youth, benevolence, and beauty,
   In your Saviour's praise agree,
Which this day receives our duty,
   Sitting on the virgin's knee.

That from this day's institution
   Ev'ry penitent in deed,
At his hour of retribution,
   As a child, through him may speed.

HYMN IV

Conversion of Saint Paul

THRO' him, the chief, begot by Nun,
Controul'd the progress of the sun;
The shadow too, through him, retir'd
The ten degrees it had acquir'd.

The barren could her fruit afford,
The woman had her dead restor'd,
The statesman could himself demean
To seek the river, and be clean.

At his command, ev'n Christ I Am,
The cruse was fill'd, and iron swam;
The floods were dry'd to make a track,
And Jordan's wave was driven back.

All these in ancient days occurr'd,
The great atchievements of the Word,
By Joshua's hand, by Moses' rod,
By virtue of the men of God.

But greater is the mighty deed
To make a profligate recede,
And work a boist'rous madman mild,
To walk with Jesus like a child.

To give a heart of triple steel
The Lord's humanity to feel;
And there, where pity had no place,
To fill the measure of his grace;

To wash internal blackness white,
To call the worse than dead to light;
To make the fruitless soil to hold
Ten thousand times ten thousand fold.

To turn a servant of the times
From modish and ambitious crimes;
To pour down a resistless blaze,
'Go, persecutor, preach and praise.'

HYMN V

King Charles the Martyr

THE persecutor was redeem'd,
And preach'd the name he had blasphem'd;
But, ah! tho' worded for the best,
How subtle men his writings wrest.

Hence heresies and sects arose
According to the saint they chose,

All against Christ alike—but all
Of some distorted text of Paul.

Had not such reas'ners been at strife
With Christ's good doctrine and his life,
The land of God's selected sheep
Had 'scap'd this day to fast and weep.

Ah great unfortunate, the chief
Of monarchs in the tale of grief,
By marriage ill-advis'd, akin
To Moab and the man of sin!

When Christ was spitted on and slain,
The temple rent her veil in twain;
And in the hour that Charles was cast
The church had well nigh groan'd its last.

But now aloft her head she bears,
Accepted in his dying pray'rs;—
Great acts in human annals shine—
Great sufferings claim applause divine.

HYMN VI

The Presentation of Christ in the Temple

PRESERVER of the church, thy spouse,
  From sacrilege and wrong,
To whom the myriads pay their vows,
Give ear, and in my heart arouse
  The spirit of a nobler song.

When Hiero built, from David's plan,
  The house of godlike style,
And Solomon, the prosp'rous man,
Whose reign with wealth and fame began,
  O'erlaid with gold the glorious pile;

Great was the concourse of mankind
    The structure to review;
Such bulk with sweet proportion join'd
The labours of a vaster mind,
    In all directions grand and true.

And yet it was not true and grand
    The Godhead to contain;
By whom immensity is spann'd,
Which has eternal in his hand
    The globe of his supreme domain.

Tho' there the congregation knelt
    The daily debt to pay,
Tho' there superior glories dwelt,
Tho' there the host their blessings dealt,
    The highest GRACE was far away.

At length another fane arose,
    The fabrick of the poor;
And built by hardship midst her foes,
One hand for work and one for blows,
    Made this stupendous blessing sure.

That God should in the world appear
    Incarnate—as a child—
That he should be presented here,
At once our utmost doubts to clear,
    And make our hearts with wonder wild.

Present ye therefore, on your knees,
    Hearts, hands resign'd and clean;
Ye poor and mean of all degrees,
If he will condescend and please
    To take at least what orphans glean—

I speak for all—for them that fly,
    And for the race that swim;

For all that dwell in moist and dry,
Beasts, reptiles, flow'rs and gems to vie
    When gratitude begins her hymn.

Praise him ye doves, and ye that pipe
    Ere buds begin to stir;
Ev'n every finch of every stripe,
And thou of filial love the type,
    O stork! that sit'st upon the fir.

Praise him thou sea, to whom he gave
    The shoal of active mutes;
(Fit tenants of thy roaring wave)
Who comes to still the fiends, that rave
    In oracles and school disputes.

By Jesus number'd all and priz'd,
    Praise him in dale and hill;
Ye beasts for use and peace devis'd,
And thou which patient and despis'd,
    Yet shalt a prophecy fulfill.

Praise him ye family that weave
    The crimson to be spread
There, where communicants receive,
And ye, that form'd the eye to grieve,
    Hid in green bush or wat'ry bed.

Praise him ye flow'rs that serve the swarm
    With honey for their cells;
Ere yet the vernal day is warm,
To call out millions to perform
    Their gambols on your cups and bells.

Praise him ye gems of lively spark,
    And thou the pearl of price;

In that great depth or caverns dark,
Nor yet are wrested from the mark,
    To serve the turns of pride and vice.

Praise him ye cherubs of his breast,
    The mercies of his love,
Ere yet from guile and hate profest,
The phenix makes his fragrant nest
    In his own paradise above.

HYMN VII

Ash Wednesday
First Day of Lent

O CHARITY! that couldst receive
    The dying thief's repentant pray'r;
And didst upon the cross relieve
    Thy fellow-suff'rer there!

Tho' he revil'd among the rest—
    Before the point of utmost dread,
Grace unto pray'r was first imprest,
    And then forgiveness sped.

Alas! the more of us defraud
    The Lord of his most righteous due,
And live by guiding truth unaw'd,
    And vanities pursue.

The harlot vice with joy we clasp,
    Nor shun to meet her tainted breath;
And leave repentance to the gasp
    Of hope-retarded death;

Albeit there are appointed times
    For men to worship and to fast;

Then purge your conscience of its crimes
    At least while those shall last.

The words of vengeance threat the tree,
    And fix their axes to the helves—
Pray therefore—pray for such as flee
    Their Saviour and themselves.

Since some are but the more defil'd,
    As canons urge them to comply,
And Christ's example in the wild
    By thwarting texts deny;

Read on your knees the holy book
    That's penn'd to sooth despondent fears—
And if the Lord but deign a look,
    Remember Peter's tears.

HYMN VIII

St. Matthias

HARK! the cock proclaims the morning,
    Match the rhime, and strike the strings;
Heav'nly muse, embrace the warning,
    Raise thy voice, and stretch thy wings.

Lo! the poor, alive and likely
    Midst desertion and distress,
Teach the folk that deal obliquely,
    They had better bear and bless.

If we celebrate Matthias,
    Let us do it heart and soul;
Nor let worldly reasons bias
    Our conceptions from their goal.

As the fancy cools and rambles,
   Keep her constant, keep her chaste;
Ward from wine, and from the shambles,
   Sight and appetite, and taste.

Tho' thy craving bowels murmur
   And against thy pray'r rebell;
Yet be firmer still, and firmer
   In the work begun so well.

Sick and weakly, pris'ners, strangers,
   Cold in nakedness we lie;
Train'd in hunger, thirst and dangers,
   As in exercise to die.

All avail not to dispirit
   Toil, determin'd to succeed;
And we trust in Christ his merit,
   As we have his woes to plead.

Yea, our lot is fallen fairer
   Than the sons of wealth and pride;
While our Saviour is a sharer
   In all hardships that betide.

Hard and precious are together,
   Stripes and wounds are endless gain;
If with him the storm we weather,
   With him also we shall reign.

We shall take the traitors places,
   And their forfeit office hold,
And to Christ shall show our faces,
   Not betray'd by us or sold.

Lord, our spirits disencumber,
   From the world our hearts dismiss;

Let us reckon to the number
　　Of thy saints in fruitful bliss.

Let the few of Christ be hearty
　　In the cause they bleed to win,
And religion make her party
　　Good against the pow'r of sin.

Let us pray—by self-denial
　　Every sense to Christ resign,
Till we from the fiery trial
　　Pure as purity refine.

HYMN IX

The Annunciation of the Blessed Virgin

O PURITY, thou test
Of love amongst the blest,
How excellent thou art,
The Lord Jehovah's heart,
　　Whose sweet attributes embrace,
　　Every virtue, praise and grace.

Thou fair and good dispos'd,
'Midst glories undisclos'd,
Inspire the notes to play
Upon the virgin's day;
　　High above all females nam'd,
　　And by Gabriel's voice proclaim'd.

Glad herald, ever sent
Upon some blest event,
But never sped to men
On such a charge till then—
　　When his Saviour's feet he kiss'd,
　　To promulge his birth dismiss'd.

Hail mystery! thou source
Of nature's plainest course,
How much this work transcends
Thine usual means and ends—
    Wherefore call'd, we shall not spare
    Louder praise, and oft'ner pray'r.

But if the work be new,
So shou'd the song be too,
By every thought that's born
In freshness of the morn;
    Every flight of active wings,
    Every shift upon the strings.

To praise the mighty hand
By which the world was mann'd,
Which dealt to great and small
Their talents clear of all;
    Kind to kind by likeness linkt,
    Various all, and all distinct.

Praise him seraphic tone
Of instruments unknown,
High strains on golden wire,
Work'd by etherial fire;
    Blowing on unceasing chords,
    'King of kings, and lord of lords.'

Praise Hannah, of the three,
That sang in Mary's key;
With her that made her psalm
Beneath the bow'ring palm;
    With the dame—Bethulia's boast,
    Honour'd o'er th' Assyrian host.

Praise him faith, hope, and love
That tend Jehovah's dove;

By men from lust repriev'd,
As females best conceiv'd;
  To remount the man and muse
  Far above all earthly views.

HYMN X

The Crucifixion of Our Blessed Lord

THE world is but a sorry scene,
Untrue, unhallow'd, and unclean,
  And hardly worth a man;
The fiend upon the land prevails,
And o'er the floods in triumph sails,
  Do goodness all she can.

How many works for such a day?
How glorious? that ye scourge and slay
  Ye blind, by blinder led;
All hearts at once devising bad,
Hands, mouths against their Maker mad,
  With Satan at the head—

Are these the race of saints profest,
That for authorities contest,
  And question and debate?
Yet in so foul a deed rebell,
Beyond example, ev'n from hell,
  To match its barb'rous hate.

Behold the man! the tyrant said,
As in the robes of scoff array'd,
  And crown'd with thorns he stood;
And feigning will to let him go
He chose Barabbas, open foe
  Of human kind and good.

And was it He, whose voice divine,
Could change the water into wine,
    And first his pow'r averr'd;
Which fed in Galilea's groves
The fainting thousands with the loaves
    And fishes of his word!

And was it He, whose mandate freed
The palsied suppliant, and in deed
    The sabbath-day rever'd;
Which bade the thankful dumb proclaim
The Lord omnipotent by name,
    Till loosen'd deafness heard!

And was it He, whose hand was such,
As lighten'd blindness at a touch,
    And made the lepers whole;
Could to the dropsy health afford,
And to the lunatic restor'd
    Serenity of soul!

The daughter that so long a term
By Satan's bonds had been infirm,
    Was rescued and receiv'd;
Yea, with the foes of faith and hope
His matchless charity cou'd cope,
    When Malchus was reliev'd.

The woman in his garment's hem
Conceiv'd a prevalence to stem
    The sources of her pain;
He calls—the dead from death arise,
And as their legions he defies
    The dev'ls descend again.

His irresistable command
Convey'd the vessel to the land,
    As instant as his thought;

He caus'd the tempest to forget
Its rage, and into Peter's net,
    The wond'rous capture brought.

The roarings of the billows cease
To hear the gospel of his peace
    Upon the still profound—
He walk'd the waves—and at his will,
The fish to pay th' exactor's bill
    To Judah's coast was bound.

The wither'd hand he saw and cur'd,
And health from gen'ral ail secur'd
    Where'er disease was rife;
And was omniscient to tell
The woman at the patriarch's well
    The story of her life.

But never since the world was known,
One so stupendous as his own,
    And rich of vast event;
From love ador'd, as soon as seen,
Had not his hated message been
    To bid the world repent.

Ah, still desirous of a king,
To give voluptuous vice its swing
    With passions like a brute;
By Jesus Christ came truth and grace,
But none indulgence, pension, place,
    The slaves of SELF to suit.

The Lord on Gabbatha they doom,
Before the delegate of Rome,
    Deserted and exposed—
They might have thought on Israel's God,
Which on the sapphire pavement trod,
    To sev'nty seers disclos'd.

They might have thought upon the loss
Of Eden, and the dreadful cross
    That happen'd by a tree;
Ere yet with cursed throats they shout
To bring the dire event about,
    Tho' prophesy'd to be.

O God, the bonds of sin enlarge,
Lay not this horror to our charge,
    But as we fast and weep,
Pour out the streams of love profuse,
Let all the pow'rs of mercy loose,
    While wrath and vengeance sleep.

HYMN XI

Easter Day

Awake—arise—lift up thy voice,
    Which as a trumpet swell,
Rejoice in Christ—again rejoice,
    And on his praises dwell.

The muse at length, no more perplext
    In search of human wit,
Shall kneel her down, and take her text
    From lore of sacred writ.

My lot in holy ground was cast,
    And for the prize I threw;
And in the path by thousands past
    The Lord shall make me new.

O let the people, with the priest,
    Adorn themselves to pray,

And with their faces to the east
    Their adoration pay.

Let us not doubt, as doubted some,
    When first the Lord appear'd;
But full of faith and rev'rence come
    What time his voice is heard.

And ev'n as John, who ran so well,
    Confess upon our knees
The prince that locks up death and hell,
    And has himself the keys.

'Tis He that puts all hearts in tune
    With strings that never jar,
And they that rise to praise him soon,
    Shall win the MORNING STAR.

The morning star, and pearl of price,
    And stone of lucid white,
Are all provocatives from vice,
    To heav'n and true delight.

O GLADNESS! that suspend'st belief
    For fear that rapture dreams;
Thou also hast the tears of grief,
    And failst in wild extreams.

Tho' Peter make a clam'rous din,
    Will he thy doubts destroy?
Will little Rhoda let him in,
    Incredulous with joy?

And thus thro' gladness and surprize
    The saints their Saviour treat;
Nor will they trust their ears and eyes
    But by his hands and feet.

These hands of lib'ral love indeed
    In infinite degree,
Those feet still frank to move and bleed
    For millions and for me.

A watch, to slavish duty train'd,
    Was set by spiteful care,
Lest what the sepulchre contain'd
    Should find alliance there.

Herodians came to seal the stone
    With Pilate's gracious leave,
Lest dead and friendless, and alone,
    Should all their skill deceive.

O dead arise! O friendless stand
    By seraphim ador'd—
O solitude! again command
    Thy host from heav'n restor'd.

Watchmen sleep on, and take your rest,
    And wake when conscience stings;
For Christ shall make the grave his nest
    Till God return his wings.

He died—but death itself improv'd
    To triumph o'er the foe,
And preach'd, as God's great spirit mov'd,
    To sinners chain'd below.

The souls that perish'd in the flood
    He bid again to bliss;
And caus'd his rod with hope to bud
    From out the dread abyss.

The seventh day above the week
    Still would he keep and bless;

The pain'd to sooth, the lost to seek,
 And grievance to redress.

Yet never such a day before
 Of holy work was spent,
While hardship infinite he bore
 That malice might relent.

And whether from success exempt
 The story is not told;
But sure most glorious was th' attempt,
 Whose fame in heav'n's enroll'd.

And each man in his spirit knows
 That mercy has no bound;
And from that upmost zenith flows
 The lowest depth to sound.

And therefore David calls for praise
 From all the gulphs that yawn,
Our thoughts by greater strokes to raise
 Than e'er before were drawn.

Beyond the height that science kens,
 Where genius is at home;
And poets take their golden pens
 To fill th' immortal tome.

Ye that for psalmody contend,
 Exert your trilling throats;
And male and female voices blend
 With joys divinest notes.

By fancy rais'd to Zion's top
 Your swelling organ join;
And praise the Lord on every stop
 Till all your faces shine.

With sweetest breath your trumpets fill'd,
　　Shall forward strength and grace;
Then all your warbling measures build
　　Upon the grounding bass.

The boxen pipe, for deepness form'd,
　　Involve in strains of love,
And flutes, with inspiration warm'd,
　　Shall imitate the dove.

Amongst the rest arouse the harp,
　　And with a master's nail;
And from the quick vibrations carp
　　The graces of the scale.

The flow'rs from every bed collect,
　　And on the altar lift;
And let each silver vase be deckt
　　With nature's graceful gift.

And from the steeple's summit stream
　　The flag of golden gloss,
Exposing to the glancing beam
　　The glorious English cross;

And let the lads of gladness born
　　The ringers be renew'd;
And as they usher'd in the morn,
　　Let them the day conclude.

HYMN XII

St. Mark

PULL up the bell-flow'rs of the spring,
And let the budding greenwood ring
    With many a chearful song;
All blessing on the human race,
From CHRIST, evangelist of grace,
    To whom these strains belong.

To whom belong the tribe that vie
In what is musick to the eye,
    Whose voice is 'stoop to pray'—
While many colour'd tints attire
His fav'rites, like the golden wire,
    The beams on wind flow'rs play.

To whom belong the dress and airs
Of nature in her warbling pairs,
    And in her bloomy pride;
By whom the man of pray'r computes
His year, and estimates the fruits
    Of every time and tide.

To whom the sacred penman cries,
And as he heav'nwards lifts his eyes,
    With meekness kneels him down;
Then what inspiring truth indites,
His strengthen'd memory recites,
    The tale of God's renown.

O holy Mark! ordain'd in youth
To be historian of the truth
    From heav'ns first fountain brought;
And Christ his hand was on thy head,
To bless thee that thou shouldst be read,
    And in his churches taught.

And tho', as Peter's scribe and son,
Thou mightst a charity have done
    To cover his disgrace;
Yet strictly charg'd thou wouldst not spare
At large the treason to declare,
    And in its order place.

Thus in the church, to cleanse our sin,
By fair confession we begin,
    And in thanksgiving end;
And they that have the Lord deny'd,
Must not come there the crime to hide,
    But promise to amend.

Then let us not this day refuse,
With joy to give the Christian dues
    To Lazars at the door;
'O for the name and love of Christ
Spare one poor dole from all your grist,
    One mite from all your store!'

And those that in by-places lurk,
Invite with overpay to work,
    Thy garner'd hay to fill;
And worship on the new mown sod,
And active to the Lord thy God,
    Keep lust and conscience still.

HYMN XIII

St. Philip and St. James

Now the winds are all composure,
    But the breath upon the bloom,
Blowing sweet o'er each inclosure,
    Grateful off'rings of perfume.

Tansy, calaminth and daisies,
　　On the river's margin thrive;
And accompany the mazes
　　Of the stream that leaps alive.

Muse, accordant to the season,
　　Give the numbers life and air;
When the sounds and objects reason
　　In behalf of praise and pray'r.

All the scenes of nature quicken,
　　By the genial spirit fann'd;
And the painted beauties thicken
　　Colour'd by the master's hand.

Earth her vigour repossessing
　　As the blasts are held in ward;
Blessing heap'd and press'd on blessing,
　　Yield the measure of the Lord.

Beeches, without order seemly,
　　Shade the flow'rs of annual birth,
And the lily smiles supremely
　　Mention'd by the Lord on earth.

Couslips seize upon the fallow,
　　And the cardamine in white,
Where the corn-flow'rs join the mallow,
　　Joy and health, and thrift unite.

Study sits beneath her arbour,
　　By the bason's glossy side;
While the boat from out its harbour
　　Exercise and pleasure guide.

Pray'r and praise be mine employment,
　　Without grudging or regret,

Lasting life, and long enjoyment,
   Are not here, and are not yet.

Hark! aloud, the black-bird whistles,
   With surrounding fragrance blest,
And the goldfinch in the thistles
   Makes provision for her nest.

Ev'n the hornet hives his honey,
   Bluecap builds his stately dome,
And the rocks supply the coney
   With a fortress and an home.

But the servants of their Saviour,
   Which with gospel peace are shod,
Have no bed but what the paviour
   Makes them in the porch of God.

O thou house that hold'st the charter
   Of salvation from on high,
Fraught with prophet, saint, and martyr,
   Born to weep, to starve and die!

Great to-day thy song and rapture
   In the choir of Christ and WREN
When two prizes were the capture
   Of the hand that fish'd for men.

To the man of quick compliance
   Jesus call'd, and Philip came;
And began to make alliance
   For his master's cause and name.

James, of title most illustrious,
   Brother of the Lord, allow'd;
In the vineyard how industrious,
   Nor by years nor hardship bow'd!

Each accepted in his trial,
　　One the CHEERFUL one the JUST;
Both of love and self-denial,
　　Both of everlasting trust.

Living they dispens'd salvation,
　　Heav'n-endow'd with grace and pow'r;
And they dy'd in imitation
　　Of their Saviour's final hour.

Who, for cruel traitors pleading,
　　Triumph'd in his parting breath;
O'er all miracles preceding
　　His inestimable death.

HYMN XIV

The Ascension of Our Lord Jesus Christ

'AND other wond'rous works were done
　　No mem'ry can recall;
Which were they number'd every one,
Not all the space beneath the sun
　　Cou'd hold the fair detail of all.'

The text is full, and strong to do
　　The glorious subject right;
But on the working mind's review
The letter's like the spirit true,
　　And clear and evident as light.

For not a particle of space
　　Where'er his glory beam'd,
With all the modes of site and place,
But were the better for his grace,
　　And up to higher lot redeem'd.

For all the motley tribe that pair,
    And to their cover skim,
Became his more immediate care,
The raven urgent in his pray'r,
    And those that make the woodland hymn.

For every creature left at will
    The howling WASTE to roam,
Which live upon the blood they spill,
From his own hands receive their fill,
    What time the desert was his home.

They knew him well, and could not err,
    To him they all appeal'd;
The beast of sleek or shaggy fur,
And found their natures to recur
    To what they were in Eden's field.

For all that dwell in depth or wave,
    And ocean—every drop—
Confess'd his mighty pow'r to save,
When to the floods his peace he gave,
    And bade careering whirlwinds stop.

And all things meaner from the worm
    Probationer to fly;
To him that creeps his little term,
And countless rising from the sperm
    Shed by sea-reptiles, where they ply.

These all were bless'd beneath his feet,
    Approaching them so near;
Vast flocks that have no mouths to bleat,
With yet a spirit to intreat,
    And in their rank divinely dear.

For on some special good intent,
　　Advancement or relief,
Or some great evil to prevent,
Or some perfection to augment,
　　He held his life of tears and grief.

'Twas his the pow'rs of hell to curb,
　　And men possess'd to free;
And all the blasting fiends disturb
From seed of bread, from flow'r and herb,
　　From fragrant shrub and stately tree.

The song can never be pursu'd
　　When Infinite's the theme—
For all to crown, and to conclude,
He bore and bless'd ingratitude,
　　And insult in its worst extreme.

And having then such deeds atchiev'd
　　As never man before,
From scorn and cruelty repriev'd,
In highest heav'n he was receiv'd,
　　To reign with God for evermore.

HYMN XV

Whitsunday

KING of sempiternal sway,
Thou hast kept thy word to-day,
That the COMFORTER should come,
That gainsayers should be dumb.
While the tongues of men transfus'd
With thy spirit should be loos'd,
And untutor'd Hebrew speak,
Latin, Arabic, and Greek.

That thy praises might prevail
On each note upon the scale,
In each nation that is nam'd,
On each organ thou hast fram'd;
Every speech beneath the sun,
Which from Babel first begun;
Branch or leaf, or flow'r or fruit
Of the Hebrews ancient root.

This great miracle was wrought,
That the millions might be taught,
And themselves of hope assure
By the preaching of the poor—
O thou God of truth and pow'r
Bless all Englishmen this hour;
That their language may suffice
To make nations good and wise.

Yea, the God of truth and pow'r
Blesses Englishmen this hour;
That their language may suffice
To make nations good and wise—
Wherefore then no more success—
That so much is much to bless—
Revelation is our own,
Secret things are God's alone.

HYMN XVI

Trinity Sunday

If Jesus be reveal'd,
There is no truth conceal'd
For honour or for awe,
That tends to drive or draw
  To the hope of heav'nly bliss,
  From the dread of hell's abyss.

If oracles be mute,
And every dull dispute
Of ostentatious gloom
In Athens or in Rome;
 We should, sure, amend our ways
 By submission, pray'r and praise.

O THREE! of blest account
To which all sums amount,
For if the church has two
The work of pray'r to do,
 God himself, th' Almighty word,
 Will be there to make the third.

One Lord, one faith, one font,
Are all good christians want
To make the fiend retreat,
And build the saint compleat;
 Where the Godhead self-allied,
 Faith, hope, charity reside.

Man, soul and angel join
To strike up strains divine;
O blessed and ador'd,
Thine aid from heav'n afford;
 HOLY, HOLY, HOLY THREE,
 Which in One, as One agree.

For angel, man and soul
Make up upon the whole,
One individual here,
And in the highest sphere;
 Where with God he shall repose,
 From whose image first he rose.

Ye books, that load the shelves,
To lead us from ourselves,

Where things, in doubt involv'd,
Are rather made than solv'd;
 Render to the dust and worm
 All ye question or affirm.

Ye poets, seers and priests,
Whose lore the spirit feasts,
And keep the banquet on,
From Moses ev'n to John;
 On your truth I will regale,
 'Which is great and must prevail.'

The Trinity is plain,
So David's psalms maintain,
—Who made not God his boast
But by the HOLY GHOST;
 Thence prophetick to record
 All the suff'rings of the Lord.

Yet all the Scriptures run
That God is great and one,
Or else there is no cause
Of nature or her laws;
 To controul and comprehend
 All beginning, course and end.

HYMN XVII

The King's Restoration

ALMIGHTY Jesu! first and last,
 The sole original and cause
Of all heroic actions past,
 The God of patriot deeds and gracious laws;
Which didst at sea this western empire found
The chief, the lords and people in thy love renown'd.

We thank thee that we were despis'd,
   And as unblest barbarians held;
For then and therefore thou devis'd
   All things in which we have the rest excell'd;
The progeny, that God's free woman bare,
In all their leagues and dealings faithful, just and fair.

We thank thee for the spacious stream,
   Thrice rolling thro' the sounding arch;
O'er which the dome of CHRIST supreme
   Sees George's gallant horse exalt their march,
And thence their prosp'rous embarkation speed,
Against the fraud and pride of Moab's spurious seed.

We thank thee for the naval sway
   Which o'er the subject seas we claim;
And for the homage nations pay,
   Submissive to the great Britannic fame;
Who soon as they thy precious cross discern,
Bow lowering to the staff on our imperial stern.

We thank thee for Eliza's reign,
   When to the realm thy spirit spake;
And for thy triumphs on the main
   By Howard, Frobisher, and glorious Drake;
Whose heart was offer'd, resolute and free,
To bleed for Englishmen, but that was done by thee.

We thank thee for thy pow'r divine,
   By which our ships were mann'd from heav'n;
What wonder then if three should join
   To play their destin'd balls and conquer scorn,
That Forest, Suckling, Langdon should prevail,
When thou hadst weigh'd the combat in thy righteous
    scale.

The glory to thy name we yield,
   By which the vast exploit was done;

At Poictier's and in Cressey's field
   Against vain Moab must'ring ten to one,
'Enough to kill, to take and put to flight,'
By faith of Englishmen in God's redoubted might.

The glory to thy name for Cam,
   Immortal from the hour he bled,
Who stoutly fixt himself to dam
   The torrent, rushing on his LEADER's head;
The glory to thy name, for each and all,
Of Henry's gifted sword, or Edward's noble stall.

The glory to thy name for Ann,
   And for the houses that she built;
And for that great victorious man,
   Who ran profane oppression to the hilt;
Born HIS sublime atchievement to fulfill,
Which bids IMPOSSIBLE make speed to do his will.

The glory to thy name for Ann,
   Sweet princess, with thy grace endu'd;
And for that charitable plan,
   By which the poor may preach, and have his food;
And for the special pray'r that she preferr'd,
Which for the famous march of deathless Webb was
    heard.

The glory to thy name for Ann,
   Again a princess, and most sweet,
To meet her Saviour Christ she ran,
   And gently stoopt to wash the poor man's feet;
Queen of the wave, to cherish with her wing
A Russel, Shovel, Rook, a Benbow, and a Byng.

We give the glory for the means
   By which the reformation rose;
Thy grace to stop the bloody scenes
   Of pride and cruelty, thy deadly foes;

Whence now the church in dignity sublimes,
The simple truth of Christ, and praise of pristine times.

We give the glory for thy word,
   That it so well becomes our tongue;
And that thy spirit is transferr'd
   Upon the strains of old in Hebrew sung.
And for the services dispers'd abroad,
—The church her seemly course of practic pray'r and
     laud.

We give the glory for the eyes
   Of science, and the realm around;
The two great rivals for the prize,
   Ingenuous to a blessing on the sound.
Well may their schools and num'rous chapels teach,
'The word is very Christ, that we adore and preach.'

O fair possessions! ghostly wealth!
   Nigh laid and lost on Charles's block,
What time the constitution's health
   Was broke, and ruin'd by the general shock;
Till God was with the loyal pray'r implor'd,
And THIS DAY saw the heir acknowledg'd and restor'd.

On this day, therefore, we support
   The joy with such applause begun,
Which sounding from th' imperial fort,
   Redoubles clam'rous roar from gun to gun.
Controuling unto good the sulph'rous blaze,
And making Satan's wrath benevolent of praise.

Lift!—as ye bless at each discharge,
   Remember where the glory's due
(In every house, and bow'r and barge)
   To Christ his love for everlasting true.

Accordant to the prophecies express,
His people to redeem, revisit and redress.

Remember all the pious vows
   Made by our ancestors, for us,
That we should thus dispose the boughs,
   And wear the royal oak in triumph thus;
And to the skies, the caps of freedom hurl'd,
Should thus proclaim the queen of islands and the
    world.

Ye soldiers reverend with scars,
   Remember Chelsea's pleasant groves;
And you, ye students of the stars,
   Remov'd from seaman's toils to fair alcoves;
Remember Edward's children train'd in art,
Which now can con the card, and now can plan the
    chart.

Remember all ye may of good,
   Select the nosegay from the sod;
But leave the brambles in the wood—
   Remember charity is God—
Which, scorning custom, her illib'ral crowds
Brings virtue to the sun, while slips and crimes she
    clouds.

HYMN XVIII

St. Barnabas

DARING as the noon-tide ray
On the summer's longest day,
   Is the truth of Christ supreme;
Proving at its sacred touch,
Whether Ophir's gold be such,
   Or a shift to seem.

Joses, who can doubt thee now,
Who will not thy faith allow,
　　With thy lands, for Christ, at sale?
By foul lucre undefil'd,
In the spirit Jesus' child,
　　Son of comfort, hail!

For a substance to endure
Hast thou listed with the poor,
　　Triumph o'er thyself atchiev'd—
Thee thy Saviour God inrolls
In the calendar of souls,
　　Sainted and receiv'd.

Heroes of the Christian cause,
Candidates for God's applause,
　　—Leaving all for Christ his sake;
Scorning temporal reward,
Ready to confess the Lord
　　At the cross or stake.

Shew your everlasting store
To one great believer more,
　　And your [ghostly] gifts impart—
Grutching treasures for the moth,
To the Lord he pledg'd his troth,
　　And ally'd his heart.

Hence instructed, let us learn
Heav'n and heav'nly things to earn,
　　And with want by pray'r to cope;
To the Lord your wealth resign,
Distribution is divine,
　　Misers have no hope.

HYMN XIX

The Nativity of St. John the Baptist

GREAT and bounteous BENEFACTOR,
  We thy gen'rous aid adjure,
Shield us from the foul exactor,
  And his sons, that grind the poor.

Lo the swelling fruits of summer,
  With inviting colours dy'd,
Hang, for ev'ry casual comer,
  O'er the fence projecting wide.

See the corn for plenty waving,
  Where the lark secur'd her eggs—
In the spirit then be saving,
  Give the poor that sings and begs.

Gentle nature seems to love us
  In each fair and finish'd scene,
All is beauteous blue above us,
  All beneath is cheerful green.

Now when warmer rays enlighten
  And adorn the lengthen'd time,
When the views around us brighten,
  Days a rip'ning from their prime,

She that was as barren reckon'd,
  Had her course completely run,
And her dumb-struck husband beckon'd
  For a pen to write a son.

JOHN, the child of Zacharias,
  Just returning to his earth,
Prophet of the Lord Messias,
  And fore-runner of his birth.

He too martyr'd, shall precede him,
    Ere he speed to heav'n again,
Ere the traitors shall implead him,
    And the priest his God arraign.

John beheld the great and holy,
    Hail'd the love of God supreme;
O how gracious, meek, and lowly,
    When baptiz'd in Jordan's stream!

If from honour so stupendous
    He the grace of pow'r deriv'd,
And to tyrants was tremendous,
    That at fraud and filth conniv'd;

If he led a life of rigour,
    And th' abstemious vow obey'd;
If he preach'd with manly vigour,
    Practis'd sinners to dissuade;

If his voice by fair confession
    Christ's supremacy avow'd;
If he check'd with due suppression
    Self-incitements to be proud.

Vice conspiring to afflict him
    To the death that ends the great,
Offer'd him a worthy victim
    For acceptance in the height.

HYMN XX

St. Peter

HIGH above the world's pursuit,
    Far beyond the fool's conceit,
Where the cherub plays her lute,
    Dwells the man of God complete.

Greatness here severely shunn'd,
   Falls in heav'n to virtue's share,
And the poor man finds a fund
   Of eternal treasures there.

To the Lord is not access
   But by magnitude above,
And exalted strength must bless
   In yon upper flights of love.

Peter from repentance rose
   To the magnitude requir'd,
First of all his master chose
   In celestial pomp attir'd.

But he is a stranger still
   To the Roman frauds and fees;
He nor sold to vice her will,
   Nor to Mammon left his keys.

Hence the practice, prais'd at Rome,
   Christian principle confounds—
What! at eminence presume,
   And not skill to know the grounds?

What! can pride and kingly pow'r,
   With the soldier kept in pay,
And a crown like Babel's tow'r,
   Suit the sons of YEA and NAY?

YEA is Christ avouch'd by truth,
   Sharing hardship with her prince,
Feed my lambs—instrust the youth—
   Feed my sheep—the old convince.

NAY is quit thy house and land,
   And all carnal things abjure;

NAY is neither rich nor grand,
   But refuses for the poor.

Peter, when with Christ he went,
   Made this excellence his plea—
'Here we are, and rest content,
   Quitting all, and tending thee.'

Wherefore he was worthy deem'd
   On the mountain-top to tread,
While surpassing glories beam'd
   On his master's hallow'd head.

Wherefore too this day we hold
   As of honourable note,
We of Christ's peculiar fold,
   That protest against the goat.

Wheresoe'er we are dispers'd,
   In the ocean, or ashore,
Still the service is rehears'd,
   Still we worship and adore.

Thanks to God we have a form
   Of sound words abroad the ship,
In the calm, or in the storm,
   To exalt him heart and lip.

There Jehovah's dove may perch
   On the topmast as she swims—
Ev'ry vessel is a church
   Meet for praise, for pray'r, and hymns.

HYMN XXI

St. James

Sure a seaman's lot is bless'd,
   Gen'rous, faithful, frank, and brave,
Since the Lord himself possess'd
   Of disciples from the wave.
Sure a realm, whose fame depends
On their deeds the rest transcends.

Yea, from fishers on the coast,
   Poor, and by the nations scorn'd,
With our navy's gallant host
   Seas are crouded and adorn'd,
Wheresoe'er the billows toss,
Bearing Christ's triumphant cross.

Lo! the Lord is on the cliff,
   Peter's partner, come away;
Leave thy tackle and thy skiff
   For a life to preach and pray—
James shall answer the command,
Soon as he can make the land.

Let the net no more be hawl'd,
   Zebedee, thy sire neglect
Now, the son of thunder call'd,
   E'en the word of God direct—
Thou disputing sects shall foil,
And conviction bless thy toil.

Having now obtain'd release
   From thy low concerns and cares,
Go, and preach the Spaniard peace,
   Teach ambitious pomp her pray'rs,
Fav'ring still, in Jesus' stead,
God in England at the head.

O that all the human race
  In what region, clime, or zone,
Would the genuine faith embrace,
  As in these thy kingdom's known;
Prosper thou the pilgrims sent
To prepare the great event.

Prosper thou, O God of light,
  Them which propagate thy word
In the realms that fiends benight—
  By no seas or toils deterr'd;
More and more in this employ
Thy cherubic guard convoy.

God of heartiness and strength,
  God of English pray'r and laud,
May good-nature speed at length,
  Join'd with grace, to foes abroad,
Thou that lend'st a special ear
To the simple and sincere.

HYMN XXII

St. Bartholomew

'BEHOLD an Israelite indeed,
    In whom there is no guile,'—
Whom neither wordly ways mislead,
    Nor treach'rous thoughts defile.

SINCERITY, belov'd of Christ,
    For him herself has kept,
And neither purchas'd, nor intic't,
    With him has smil'd and wept.

832

Her Jesus in his arms infolds,
    And to his church ascribes—
She wears the precious ring that holds
    Each jewel of the tribes.

Gold is not very gold, nor myrrh
    True myrrh, nor rubies glow,
If first not try'd and prov'd by her
    That they indeed are so.

She is a fountain from the truth,
    And floods embracing all;
Hypocrisy shall gnash its tooth
    Whene'er it hears her call.

Who then amongst mankind can thrive
    That has such ghostly worth?
The saint must needs be slay'd alive,
    Possessing her on earth.

Come then, or sword, or fire, or ax,
    Devour me branch and stem.
I will not fail to pay the tax
    Of life for such a gem.

HYMN XXIII

St. Matthew

Ev'n exactors of the toll,
    And the harlot of the stew,
    Sooner give the Lord his due
Than men disguis'd of soul.

Matthew made the Lord a feast,
    Wealth and business left behind,

Of his tribe, and of his kind,
Among the worst and least.

Yet he had an eye to God
  Soon as Jesus Christ drew near,
  And with meekness, faith, and fear,
He worship'd to his nod.

Humbl'd therefore by the shame
  Of his wordly filth and guilt,
  By his hand the Lord has built
A pillar to his name.

One for ev'ry point are four,
  Matthew for an obvious praise,
  His in Hebrew chose to raise,
That easterns might adore.

Of a meaner order, Mark,
  As he would the north address,
  Yet his word of God express
Illuminates the dark.

Luke diffusive takes a sweep,
  Rising to command the west,
  And by Jesus Christ is blest,
Historic high and deep.

John, above the rest divine,
  In the church her southern isle,
  Stands of plain majestic stile,
Where warmth and brightness join.

These combin'd the church sustain,
  But this day assigns to thee,
  Matthew, rather than the three,
The heav'n directed strain.

Sure the mother-tongue is great,
　　Since it is what seraphs use;
　　Since with that the cherub woos
To mutual praise his mate.

HYMN XXIV

St. Michael and All Angels

ANGELIC natures, great in arms
　　Against the dragon and his pow'rs,
Whom Michael's excellence alarms
　　From highest heav'n's imperial tow'rs;

Ye that in Christ his church attend
　　What time the services are sung,
And your propitious spirits blend
　　With our united heart and tongue.

O come, celestial watch and ward,
　　As in the closet I adore
My fellow-servants of the Lord,
　　To whom these measures I restore.

If Satan's malice was withstood
　　Where Moses cold and breathless lay,
Give Michael, patient, meek, and good,
　　Through Christ, the glory of the day.

If Tobit's charitable soul,
　　A type of Jesus Christ to come,
Was blessed from the poor man's dole
　　Ev'n to the social sparrow's crumb;

If to the living and the dead
　　His hand was rich in deeds of love,

First Raphael from his Master fled
 By mandate in the heights above.

If Zacharias was inform'd
 That God his pious pray'rs should crown,
The barren womb to ripeness warm'd,
 'Twas Gabriel brought the tidings down.

Hail mighty princes in the height,
 Which o'er stupendous works preside
Of vast authority and weight—
 But there are other pow'rs beside.

These, one for every man, are sent
 God in the spirit to reveal,
To forward ev'ry good event,
 And each internal grief to heal.

HYMN XXV

St. Luke

LUKE, physician of the wound,
 Where the troubl'd conscience stings,
Far beyond the skill profound
Of the graduates here renown'd,
 Or the costly springs.

Thy conversion soon is wrought,
 When thou seest thy Saviour's cures,
So surpassing human thought,
What thy books from Greece have taught,
 Or thy hope assures.

Henceforth, without scrip or purse,
 Go on embassage divine,

Med'cines of the soul disperse
To the wicked and perverse
    Thou wert wont to join.

Thee thy Saviour shall allot
    His great actions to relate,
And thy brethren's sins to blot;
Greater blessing there is not
    In a mortal state.

Thou shalt also tell the deeds
    Of that apostolic band,
While the happy convert reads
How in Christ the pris'ner pleads
    By a master's hand.

Sure thy skill in picture came
    To th' assistance of thy pen,
If she was of heav'nly flame,
That is now a sin and shame,
    By the frauds of men.

Her the hypocrites adore
    In the fane of modern Rome,
And from shadow's aid implore,
That they may blaspheme the more,
    And the more presume.

Christ from such detested arts
    Guard thy church with watchful eyes,
Keep from Satan's snares and darts,
Innocent as doves our hearts,
    But as serpents wise.

HYMN XXVI

The Accession of King George III

By me, says Wisdom, monarchs reign,
    And princes right decree;
The conduct of the land and main
    Is minister'd by me.

Where neither Philip's son was sped,
    Nor Roman eagles flew,
The English standard rears its head,
    To storm and to subdue.

Our gallant fleets have won success,
    Christ Jesus at the helm,
And let us therefore kneel and bless
    The sovereign of the realm.

This day the youth began his race,
    With angels for allies,
And God shall give him strength and grace
    To claim the naval prize.

His righteous spirit he fatigu'd
    To speak the nation's peace;
Yet more and more the Papists leagu'd
    To mar the world's increase.

The Lord accept his good intent,
    And be his great defence,
And may his enemies repent
    At no prescrib'd expence.

As yet this isle the proof has stood,
    Which God from all disjoins;
O make him singularly good,
    And bless with fruit his loins.

His eastern, western bounds enlarge,
　　Which swarms in vain contest,
And keep the people of his charge
　　In wealth and godly rest.

HYMN XXVII

St. Simon and St. Jude

PEACE be to the souls of those
　　Which for Jesus Christ have bled,
Or that triumph'd o'er their foes
　　With the coals upon their head.

Which for him have undergone
　　Any other dread or death,
Crucify'd, or stabb'd, or sawn,
　　Blessing to their latest breath.

Simon well may claim a place
　　In our book of Common Pray'r;
Here he likewise planted grace
　　By his apostolic care.

He his pilgrimage perform'd
　　Far as the Britannic coast,
And the ready converts swarm'd
　　To receive the Holy Ghost.

Fair sincerity's the ground
　　For the Lord to sow his seed,
That will flourish and abound
　　With a goodly crop indeed.

Christ is pow'rful to renew
　　Men so quick his will to know,

Whence ten thousand churches grew,
   And ten thousand more shall grow.

Farther yet, and farther east,
   English sails shall be unfurl'd,
Wafting many a pious priest
   To protest against the world.

Farther yet, and farther west,
   We shall send the faith abroad,
Against nations to protest,
   That are still by Christ unaw'd.

We shall cite from holy Jude
   Wholesome texts to mend their way,
Whom our praise and pray'rs include
   In the duty of to-day.

He is full of just complaint,
   As foul deeds his wrath provoke;
And they massacred the saint
   For the cutting words he spoke.

Let us therefore well provide
   This good festival to hold,
Lest to us they be apply'd
   As to wand'rers from the fold.

Lo! the church herself attires
   For the work of pray'r and song;
To the strains that Christ inspires
   Crowds of either sex shall throng.

HYMN XXVIII
All Saints

MANY male and female names,
From the cross, the sword, and flames,
To their blessed Saviour dear,
Have escap'd memorial here.

These are all the Lord's elect,
Which the church must not neglect,
But appoints a day to raise
Anthems for a gen'ral praise.

Stars of the superior class,
Which in magnitude surpass,
From the time they rose and shone,
Have their names and places known.

Mazaroth his circuit runs,
With Arcturus and his sons;
Pleiad twinkles o'er the streams
Of Orion's bolder beams.

But what glories in array
Brighten all the milky way,
Where innumerables vie,
Told alone by God Most High!

Enoch of exceeding grace,
Abr'ham of unnumber'd race,
Jael bursting into fame,
Joab of stupendous name.

These the seers of God commit
To the rolls of holy writ,
With a multitude of note,
Which our children have by rote.

There are thousand thousands more,
   Like the sand upon the shore,
Through the love of Christ reveal'd,
   All in heav'n receiv'd and seal'd.

HYMN XXIX

The Fifth of November

WHAT impression God and reason
   Had on some abandon'd times,
Was made evident by treason,
   And the most flagitious crimes.

England lay dissolv'd in slumber,
   Toil and emulation ceas'd,
Till the malice, strength, and number
   Of her foes were all increas'd.

Eat and drink, and die to-morrow,
   From the cottage to the helm,
Till the blessed man of sorrow
   Was not heard in all the realm.

This was deem'd a fit occasion
   For the Papists to be bold,
For the children of evasion
   To come sneaking from their hold.

What a plan of devastation,
   That the dev'l alone could start,
How at once to crush the nation
   In the bowels, head, and heart!

There is no such great perdition
   In the story of mankind,

Not by craft and superstition,
  Yea, and cruelty combin'd.

God, in a stupendous manner,
  Bade a spendthrift nation home—
Let us therefore fix the banner
  On the high cathedral's dome.

Play the musick—call the singers—
  Open wide the prison door—
Make a banquet for the ringers—
  Give to poverty the store.

Fire away the joyful volley,
  Deck your houses, bless your wine;
Triumph o'er the Papists folly,
  Who their God would undermine.

HYMN XXX

St. Andrew

O LORD, thou God of bliss,
  Which highest natures leave
To rectify the things amiss
  Amongst the sons of Eve.

From time to time they came
  To warn and to correct;
But ah! the dreadful sin and shame,
  With small or none effect.

At length no more with-held
  By seraph's tears and pray'r,
The God of heav'n himself compell'd
  This fleshly veil to wear.

But how to find a friend
   In poverty and woe,
Omnipotence must needs attend
   His steps where'er they go.

When John his Saviour spy'd,
   Behold the LAMB (said he).
If it be so, St. Andrew cry'd,
   No more I follow thee.

His teacher he forsook,
   And on his face he fell,
And instantly himself betook
   To life's eternal well.

Then from a life reform'd,
   He spread example wide,
And multitudes with zeal he warm'd
   To take their Saviour's side.

At length the words prevail
   Which Christ prophetic spake,
And to the cross the saint they hale
   That ruffian traitors make.

Tormented, tried, and bound
   Two well-supported days,
His life his dying accents crown'd,
   E'en to their last essays.

His body was remov'd
   From Patræ to the Turk,
Where it, through Christ, shall be improv'd
   To do a glorious work.

The Spirit shall descend,
   And churches shall aspire,

—And they that now the mosques attend,
  Of Jesus shall inquire.

Yea Edom one and all
  Shall choose the Lord their chief;
And he shall finally recall
  The sons of unbelief.

HYMN XXXI

St. Thomas

AH! Thomas, wherefore would'st thou doubt,
  And put the Lord in pain,
And mad'st his wounds to spout
  Anew from ev'ry vein?

Lo! those of God are blessed most,
  Which, simple and serene,
Believe the Holy Ghost,
  That operates unseen.

This is that great and prior proof
  Of God and of his Son,
Beneath whose sacred roof
  To-day the duty's done.

Tho' seventeen hundred years remote,
  We can perform our part,
And to the Lord devote
  The tribute of our heart.

O Lord, the slaves of sin release,
  Their ways in Christ amend,
Our faith and hope increase,
  Our charities extend.

Make thou our alter'd lives of use
　　To all the skirts around,
And purge from each abuse
　　Thy church, so much renown'd.

Enlarge from Mammon's spells her priests,
　　And from all carnal cares,
And bid to ghostly feasts,
　　To pure cherubic airs.

Thy people in that choir employ
　　Whose business is above,
In gratitude and joy,
　　In wonder, praise, and love.

HYMN XXXII

The Nativity of Our Lord and Saviour Jesus Christ

WHERE is this stupendous stranger,
　　Swains of Solyma, advise,
Lead me to my Master's manger,
　　Shew me where my Saviour lies?

O Most Mighty! O MOST HOLY!
　　Far beyond the seraph's thought,
Art thou then so mean and lowly
　　As unheeded prophets taught?

O the magnitude of meekness!
　　Worth from worth immortal sprung;
O the strength of infant weakness,
　　If eternal is so young!

If so young and thus eternal,
　　Michael tune the shepherd's reed,

Where the scenes are ever vernal,
   And the loves be love indeed!

See the God blasphem'd and doubted
   In the schools of Greece and Rome;
See the pow'rs of darkness routed,
   Taken at their utmost gloom.

Nature's decorations glisten
   Far above their usual trim;
Birds on box and laurels listen,
   As so near the cherubs hymn.

Boreas now no longer winters
   On the desolated coast;
Oaks no more are riv'n in splinters
   By the whirlwind and his host.

Spinks and ouzles sing sublimely,
   'We too have a Saviour born,'
Whiter blossoms burst untimely
   On the blest Mosaic thorn.

God all-bounteous, all-creative,
   Whom no ills from good dissuade,
Is incarnate, and a native
   Of the very world he made.

HYMN XXXIII

St. Stephen

O MAKER! of almighty skill,
Whose word all wonders can fulfil,
Where'er the sun, where'er the planets shine,
Exertion and effect at once are thine.

God! great and manifest around,
In earth, and air, and depth profound,
In every movement, animals that breathe,
And all the beauties visible beneath.

But nobler works about his throne,
And brighter glories are his own,
Where high o'er heav'n the loves his Spirit mates,
And virtues, graces, mercies he creates.

A saint is a stupendous thing,
Sublimest work of Christ the king;
For ere his blessed Saviour can succeed,
How many foes to foil, and veins to bleed!

Soon as the Lord resum'd the skies,
He put up his immortal prize,
And in a full maturity of soul,
Great Stephen ran the first, and past the goal.

His therefore is the champion's crown—
And his the firstlings of renown—
O GRACE, thou never rais'd a sweeter flow'r.
Which sprang, and gemm'd, and blossom'd in an hour.

Then welcome to a quick reward,
Ev'n in the bosom of the Lord,
To hear, 'Well done, thou good and faithful friend,
Receive thy Saviour's joy, that knows no end.

'Beyond the bliss of ear or eye,
Beyond the heart's conception high,
Beyond the topmost flight of mortal ken,
Hosanna! halelujah! and amen.'—

HYMN XXXIV

St. John the Evangelist

HOSANNA! yet again,
  Another glorious day,
  Ye cherubs sing and play,
Ye seraphs swell the strain.

Hail! highly favour'd man,
  Thy name and lot transcend
  All praise that e'er was penn'd
Since first the verse began.

O dear to Christ supreme,
  His bosom friend declar'd,
  And yet for all he car'd
With tenderness extreme.

As Benjamin was blest,
  When he to Egypt came,
  By Joseph full of fame,
And honour'd o'er the rest.

But Christ was meek and poor,
  No chariot his to ride,
  No Goshen to divide,
No favours to procure.

Yet in his realms above,
  Which are the highest heav'n,
  First of th' elect elev'n,
Thou claim'st thy master's love.

HYMN XXXV

The Holy Innocents

LOVE and pity are ally'd,
So are cruelty and pride;
But they never met till now,
As in Herod's hellish vow.

Ev'ry tyrant of his time
Stands abash'd at such a crime;
Not a monster since the flood
Was in equal guilt of blood.

Rachael, with a mother's grief,
Sees the ruffians and their chief,
Piercing heav'n and earth with cries,
For her children's rescue tries.

'Cherubs lend your aid in air;
Seraphim, ye shall not dare
Such a scene as this to see,
And not succour God and me.'

Woman, speed thee back to bliss—
At a greater price than this,
Ere the plan of Christ we build,
Prophecies must be fulfill'd.

Blessed be the Lord's escape,
When the gulph began to gape,
And the fiends from hell were sent,
Man's salvation to prevent.

By the hope which prophets give,
By the psalmist 'he shall live',
Sav'd for a sufficient space
To perform his work of grace.

Though the heav'n and earth shall fail,
Yet his spirit shall prevail,
Till all nations have concurr'd
In the worship of the WORD.

The Parables of Our Lord

PARABLE I

The Sower and the Seed

'TWAS thus the Light of Light, the Son
Of GOD, his moral tales begun.
Behold, the parable I show:
A sower went his way to sow,
And, as the kindly grain he threw,
Some by the beaten path-way flew,
And there, neglected as it lay,
Fell to the birds an easy prey.
Some upon stony places fell,
Where, as it was not rooted well,
For lack of depth it soon appear'd:
But, when the sun the vapours clear'd,
It perish'd by the scorching air,
Because it wanted ground to bear:
And some amongst the thorns was cast,
Which choak'd them, growing up too fast.
But some upon a kindly soil
Fell, and repaid the workman's toil.
And these an hundred fold increas'd,
Those sixty, thirty ev'n the least.
He, to whom God has giv'n an ear,
Let him attend the word in fear.
He spake—and as he made a pause
His scholars came, and ask'd the cause—
'Why dost thou parables recite,

Nor speak'st thy gracious will out-right?'
Because it is reserv'd for you,
He cries, God's glorious light to view;
But from the race, that have rebell'd,
Are heav'nly mysteries with-held;
For those that deathless treasures store
Are sure to reap the more and more,
While him, that makes his little less,
I finally shall dispossess.
I therefore parables devise—
Because, altho' I made them eyes,
Yet is not their discernment clear,
Nor have they for the truth an ear;
That in the hardned and self-will'd
Isaiah's words might be fulfill'd:
'In hearing shall your ears be blest,
And not one word shall ye digest;
And seeing ye your God shall view,
Nor shall ye know him, when ye do.
For callous hearts this race have got,
Their ears are clogg'd, their eyes are not:
Lest, when the season is at hand,
They see, and hear, and understand,
And all at once be converts found,
And I should heal their inward wound.'—
But blessed are your eyes, that see,
And ears, that hear in verity.
For many kings and patriarchs too
(So great the grace indulg'd to you)
And prophets by the word inspir'd,
Have with all fervent pray'r desir'd
To see the things, which ye behold,
And hear the myst'ries, I unfold,
And all their vows, and earnest suit,
Were premature, and bore no fruit.
Hear, then, and note the mystic lore
Couch'd in the story of the sow'r.

When a man hears, not to retain,
The word of Christ's eternal reign,
Then comes the fiend, and takes away
The grace his heart could not obey.
This is the seed that was imply'd
As wasted by the path-way side.
But that receiver of the grain
Sow'n on the stony-ground in vain,
Resembles one of chearful heart,
Who hears and acts a christian's part,
By bearing instantaneous fruit,
But having neither depth nor root,
By scourge of pow'r, or worldly loss,
Straight is offended at the cross.
He likewise that receiv'd the seed
'Mongst many a thorn, and many a weed,
Is he, that hears the word, and trusts,
But treach'rous wealth and worldly lusts
Choke up his heart with carnal care,
Till all is naught and barren there.

But men of upright hearts and sound
Receive the seed on kindly ground;
The word, which they are apt to hear,
Is to their understanding clear.
These at the harvest we behold
Some bearing fruit an hundred fold,
Some sixty, for the bridegroom's feast,
And thirty ev'n the last and least.

PARABLE II

*The Kingdom of Heaven compared unto a Man
who sowed good Seed in his Field*

CHRIST'S reign (again the Lord began)
Is liken'd to a certain man,

Who plow'd in hope, and sow'd his field
With seed most promising to yield.
But in the night his foe arose,
What time mankind indulg'd repose,
And having sown amongst the corn
Some tares, made off before the morn.
But when the blade grew up and stood
Bidding for harvest rank and good,
Then too the tares, with heads uprear'd,
Amongst the goodly crop appear'd.
His servants therefore came to know—
'Good seed, my Lord, didst thou not sow?
Thy land what ails it, that it bears
A mingled crop of wheat and tares?'
It is an enemy, he said,
Has this adult'rous mixture made.
Then did his men for licence plead
The bad from out the good to weed.
But he rejoin'd, 'My children, nay,
Lest while the tares ye take away,
Ye gather too the wheat with them,
And mar my harvest ear and stem.
Stay till the season is at hand,
When I my reapers shall command,
First those vile tares in bundles bind,
And be they to the flames consign'd:
But that good wheat collect with care,
And to my granary repair.'—
He spake—the multitude retired;
Then by the Twelve he was desir'd
The secret meaning to unfold
In all, that of the tares, he told.
He answers—it is Christ alone
By whom the genuine seed is sown:
The field's the world, the genuine seed
Are God's true heirs in word and deed.
By tares amongst the corn, you trace

The prince of darkness and his race.
The harvest is the last event;
By reapers are the Angels meant.
The tares into the flames are cast—
So must it needs be at the last.
The Son of man his host shall send
To take out all things that offend,
The race of base injurious men,
And hurl them to the infernal den:
There in the realms of death and pain
They wail and gnash their teeth in vain.
Then shall the righteous seed display
Their glory like the blaze of day,
And in their Father's realm appear—
Ye, that have ears for doctrine, hear.

PARABLE III

The Kingdom of Heaven compared to a Grain of Mustard-seed

THEN did he to the throng around
Another parable propound.
So fares it with the heavenly reign
As mustard-seed, of which a grain
Was taken in a farmer's hand
And cast into a piece of land.
This grain, the least of all that's sown,
When once to full perfection grown,
Outstrips all herbs to that degree
Till it at length becomes a tree,
And all the songsters of the air
Take up an habitation there.

Christ laid (at first an infant boy)
The basis of eternal joy;

And from humility, his plan,
Arose the best and greatest man,
The greatest man that ever trod
On earth was Christ th' eternal God,
Which as the branch of Jesse's root
Ascends to bear immortal fruit.
From contradiction, sin and strife,
He spreads abroad the tree of life;
And there his servants shall partake
The mansions, that the branches make;
There saints innumerable throng,
Assert their seat, and sing their song.

PARABLE IV

The Kingdom of Heaven compared unto Leaven

ONCE more—The kingdom nam'd of heav'n
Bears a similitude to leav'n,
Which in three measures of her meal
An housewife happen'd to conceal;
Till light and good was all her flow'r
By that communicative pow'r.

The bread of life is God's free grace,
Which, first in an especial place,
Reveal'd to Peter, *and a few,*
Soon marvelously spread and grew,
And shone till it illum'd the blind,
And shall enlighten all mankind.

856

PARABLE V

The Kingdom of Heaven compared unto a Treasure hid in a Field

HE yet a parable declar'd—
The reign of Christ may be compar'd
To treasure hid within the ground,
Which when a certain man had found,
In hasty joy he went by stealth,
And selling all his worldly wealth,
With ev'ry farthing he had got
He made a purchase of the spot.

This treasure's Christ's eternal worth,
That time obscur'd upon the earth,
Which whoso had the grace to find,
And on such riches set his mind,
Held carnal wealth and fame as dross,
And sold the world, and bore the cross.

PARABLE VI

The Kingdom of Heaven compared unto a Merchantman seeking goodly Pearls

AGAIN—'tis like a man that made
The search of precious stones his trade,
Who when he found a *pearl indeed*,
Of price all others to exceed,
He chose from all his wealth to part,
And bought the jewel of his heart.

All parts must center in the whole.
This pearl's salvation of the soul,
And he that stedfastly denies

To deal in pomp and vanities,
Shall gain by tenure not to cease,
His Saviour and eternal peace.

PARABLE VII

The Kingdom of Heaven compared unto a Net cast into the Sea

AGAIN—the kingdom's like a draught
Of fishes in the ocean caught;
With which of every kind well stor'd,
The net they on the strand explor'd,
When some in vessels they collect,
And some they sever and reject.
　So shall it happen in the end,
The Lord th' angelic host shall send
To sever from amongst the just
Those, that attentive to their lust,
Were dead to Jesus preaching truth,
Now doom'd to wail and gnash the tooth.

PARABLE VIII

The Scribes and Pharisees reprov'd

THE scribes and pharisaic race,
Abiding in the holy place,
Did to our blessèd Lord repair,
And question'd him on this affair—
Why have thy followers rebell'd
'Gainst laws traditionally held,
And wash not e'er they take their bread?
To which the Lord in answer said—
'Why by tradition have ye broke

God's great commandment, for he spoke
Give either parent honour due,
And he that does not let him rue.
Tradition works another way:
As whoso to his sire shall say,
Whatever profit shall accrue,
Or to my mother, or to you,
Is my free gift, and not the fruit,
Of God's commandment absolute;
Him you acquit by your decree,
And make a mock of God and me.
Ye hypocrites, how well of old
Esaias of your ways foretold?
With words and mouths this froward race
Adore me, and approach my face,
And their lip-service they devote,
While all their hearts are far remote.
But all that worship is in vain,
Which for your Maker you would feign;
While you would have bye-laws injoin'd
Of frail and fallible mankind.'

   He therefore bade the throng draw near,
And said unto them, learn and hear:
Not outward things, however vile,
Receiv'd into the man, defile;
But that which cometh from within
Pollute the human soul with sin.

   Then came the Twelve around and said,
Lord, what you urg'd upon this head,
Gave great offence, as we descry'd,
To pharisees—The Lord reply'd;
Whatever plant does not exist,
As set by God the Arborist;
Such must be rooted up and fall—
Let them alone, for one and all,
They're guides to whom no light's bestów'd,
Yet take the lead and show the road.

When to the blind the blind commit
Themselves, they all must to the pit.

Then did St. Peter interpose,
Lord, thy last parable disclose.
Then Jesus—dull, and taught in vain,
Can ye not fathom truths so plain?
Whatever in the mouth one takes,
Its passage to the stomach makes,
And thence into the draught descends:
But that in which a man offends
Must from a tainted heart arise;
Thence evil thoughts, that they devise,
Thence murder, fornication, fraud,
Thence blasphemies are spread abroad.
Such things all purity defeat,
Not with unwashen hands to eat.

The blessed men our Saviour chose
To hear his doctrine, share his woes,
Still as they waited by his side
Were by his glory purified.
No limpid rill, no polish'd vase,
But were unclean before his face.
Where'er he travell'd, or remain'd,
Inevitable sweetness reign'd;
And by his very word applied,
He cleans'd, he bless'd, and sanctified.

PARABLE IX

The unmerciful Creditor

How oft (says Peter) Lord, I pray,
Shall ev'n my brother err and stray,
And I forgive repeated crimes,

Must it be done till seven times?
   Not until seven times a-day,
(The Man of Mercy cries) I say,
But until seventy times by sev'n.
Wherefore the reign of Christ from heav'n
Is liken'd to a certain king,
What time he set about to bring
His servants each to his account,
When one was found upon th' amount
Ten thousand talents in his debt,
Which sum as he could no where get,
His lord gave instant charge, that he,
His goods, his wife, and family,
Should in the public mart be sold,
And thence the talents to be told.
His servant then before his feet
Fell down his mercy to intreat—
'Have patience, Lord, thy wrath controul,
And I will fairly pay the whole.'
His master soon inclin'd to yield
Compassion, not alone repeal'd
The condemnation of a slave,
But frankly all the debt forgave.
   Yet this same fellow, nothing taught,
Went, and another servant caught
Fierce by the throat in rank offence,
That ow'd him but an hundred pence;
'Let my debt instantly be paid.'
His brother therefore meekly pray'd—
'Have patience, and thy wrath controul,
And I will fairly pay the whole.'
Yet he would not attend his plea,
But cast him into jeopardy,
His bondage not to be enlarg'd,
Until the total was discharg'd.
So all the household in disgust,
Of guilt thus cruel and unjust,

The matter to their lord relate,
Who calling in the base ingrate,
Cried, 'Traitor, did not I forbear
Relenting at thine earnest pray'r,
And should'st not thou have had the grace
To weigh a less offender's case,
And to his debt have pity shown,
So late forgiven all thine own?'
   Then justly wroth his lord ordains
For him the torture and the chains,
Till he should answer his demand—
Thus likewise shall the reck'ning stand
Betwixt my heav'nly Sire and you,
Unless your hearts all hate subdue,
And spare your brother ev'ry one,
Whatever trespass he has done.

PARABLE X

The Lord of the Vineyard and the Labourers

My kingdom in another view
(Says Christ) has this resemblance too,
A certain man at early day
Agreed with labourers for pay,
Who for a penny each content
Were straightway to his vineyard sent.
At the third hour again he hied,
And idlers in the market spy'd,
To whom he his command injoins,
'Go ye likewise and dress my vines,
And what in reason is your due,
That will I pay'; so they withdrew.
At the sixth hour he likewise came,
And at the ninth, and did the same.
About th' eleventh he chanc'd to meet

With other loit'rers in the street,
To whom, 'Why stand ye thus?' he cry'd;
No man has hir'd us, they reply'd.
'Ye likewise to the vineyard go,
And what is right I will bestow.'—

His servant therefore at the eve
Made, by command, the men receive
What to each labourer should fall,
Beginning with the last of all.
So they, that at th' eleventh were hir'd,
Each man with pence a-piece retir'd:
But when the first were also come,
They thought to have a greater sum,
And they but pence a-piece receiv'd,
At which they murmur'd and were griev'd,
And the good man of fraud arraign'd—
'Lo! we that all the day sustain'd,
And brav'd the sun's meridian pow'r,
Fare ev'n as those that wrought an hour.'—
But he the loudest thus address'd,
Friend, thou by no means art oppress'd.
Did ye not all agree for pence,
Take that is thine, and get thee hence.
This last shall have as much as thou—
What not my property allow,
And shall thine evil heart repine
At God's benevolence in mine?

The last shall thus the first precede,
For tho' a multitude indeed
Are call'd to hear the common word,
Yet few are chosen, and preferr'd.

According to the Lord's intent
By this same penny here is meant,
The crown of him that wins the race;
The time of day's the time of grace.
Some from their infancy begin

To cleave to Christ, and flee from sin,
As Samuel *walk'd to God well known*
As soon as he could walk alone:
Some must be strengthened e'er they thrive
In Christ, and ev'n their prime survive.
Some are religious not before
Their knees are weak, and heads are hoar.
And others on a sick-bed lie,
And there first call on Christ, and die.
God's property is mercy still,
And he can grant it when he will.
He knows man's talent, and his pow'r:
Some lab'rers earn more in an hour
Than others in a tedious space,
And frustrate love and thwarted grace
Thro' Christ the final doom may stave,
And rise fructif'rous from the grave.

PARABLE XI

The Father and his Two Sons

A CERTAIN man, whose sons were twain,
Who had a vineyard to maintain,
Address'd the first 'My son, away,
To work, and prune my vines to-day.'
He said, I will not go, but went
When wrought by conscience to repent.
The second had the like command,
And said, 'I go, sir, out of hand,'
But did not stir—which of these two
Had grace the father's will to do?
They answer, Lord, the first—if so,
The Lord reply'd, for certain know,
As touching Christ's eternal mead,
Harlots and publicans precede

You, elders—for when John express
Came in the way of righteousness,
Him whom nor priest nor scribe believ'd,
Harlots and publicans receiv'd.
And when his ways and works were known,
Yet would ye not amend your own;
Nor did your froward hearts dispose,
Nor unto faith repentance chose.

Christ in the parable decries
A mere professor's life of lies,
Who's bold to preach and reprimand
In words magnificent and grand,
The pompous self-applauding saint,
All inward filth and outward paint;
But conscious meekness, which appears
To give the glory voice and tears,
At once uncloaking all offence
By duty and by diffidence,
Not only brings the pardon down,
But gains th' incorruptible crown.

PARABLE XII

The Householder and Husbandmen

ATTEND to what I yet relate—
A certain man of an estate,
When he had plann'd and planted out
A vineyard, fenc'd it round about,
And made a wine-press on the spot,
And tow'r—and let it out by lot,
And in a foreign realm sojourn'd,
But when th' in-gathering time return'd,
He to the husbandmen deputes
His servants to receive the fruits.

But they those servants roughly treat,
And one they stone, and one they beat.
Then thinking he had sent too few,
He more dispatch'd, and them they slew.
But last he bade his Son appear—
'Him they will certainly revere.'
Whom when the husbandmen beheld,
They all united and rebell'd.
'This is the heir, come, him destroy,
And we shall all th' estate enjoy.'
Then seizing him, they basely wound,
And slay, and cast from out the ground.
But when the Lord himself arrives,
What shall he do for all these lives?
They say, he surely will consume
Those wretches in a dreadful doom,
And let his vineyard out at last
To lab'rers of another cast,
Who shall restore the Lord his due
In season, and with rev'rence too.—

By that fenc'd vineyard mention'd here
Let out to lab'rers by the year,
The Lord the Holy Land describes,
The husbandmen are all the tribes.
By the Lord's servants are inferr'd
The priests and prophets of the word,
Which still were sent from time to time
Upbraiding Israel with his crime,
That all his sons were gross ingrates,
Nor gave the praise, nor paid the rates,
Nor heeded fast or feast to keep,
Nor let the land in sabbath sleep.
These some were beat, and some were slain,
All made their embassy in vain.—
The son commission'd in the end—
By him does Christ himself intend,
And prophecies of his decease—

866

O God, do thou our faith increase,
That we be worthy workmen found
To dress the vine and till the ground,
And yield thy fruits in season due,
Nor imitate th' apostate Jew;
And Zion's forfeit place retake,
Thro' Christ his aid, and for his sake.

PARABLE XIII

The Marriage Feast

AND Jesus yet again pursu'd
His theme by parables renew'd.
The charter, which from heav'n I bring,
Is like a certain earthly king,
Who did his son a feast provide
The day on which he took a bride,
And sent his servants to invite
Such guests as had the greatest right;
But not a man of them would come.
Again he sent out other some,
'Tell them (I charge you) that are bid,
My beeves, my fatlings, lamb, and kid,
I for your company prepare,
Attend the feast, and take your share.'
But they contemn'd the joyful day,
And went in scoff another way,
One going to his rural grange,
And one into the throng'd exchange.
But for the remnant—they revile
His men and kill them—in a while
When the king heard thereof, enrag'd
He sent forth armies, that engag'd
Those murderers, and overcame,
And set their city in a flame.

Then to his servants he declar'd,
'The wedding is indeed prepar'd;
But they, who first were bidden here,
Were most unworthy my good cheer.
Go, therefore, to the common road,
Where whomsoe'er you find bestow'd,
Bid welcome.'—So the servants went
To the highways on such intent,
And good and bad, and one and all,
They brought, and plac'd them in the hall:
So that the wedding-feast was stor'd
With guests that fill'd the social board.
And when the king came in to see
The guests, a man there chanc'd to be
Without a garment made to grace
The rapture of the day and place.
'Friend, said the king, how durst thou come
Without a robe?' and he was dumb.
Then said the sov'reign to his men,
Bind him, and take him to the den
Of outer darkness, there to rail
At goodness, gnash his teeth and wail,
And fitter so his thoughts employ
In sorrow, unarray'd for joy.

God is the king, his son is Christ,
The marriage-feast the eucharist.
By servants here are understood
God's priests, ambassadors for good.
Th' invited guests, that did refuse,
Are worldlings that the church disuse.
The wretches, that in discontent
Murder'd the servants that were sent,
Are such as not alone reject,
But persecute the Lord's elect.
The people brought from public ways
Are such as yield the pray'r and praise,

Where God's communicants agree;
The wedding-garment's charity,
Which whoso does not love and wear
Can give no praise, can make no pray'r,
And last of all should dare come up
To eat that bread, and drink that cup.

PARABLE XIV

The Fig-tree

HARD on the great tremendous day
Of tribulation, and dismay,
Thick darkness shall the sun-beams veil,
And all the lunar brightness fail;
Each star shall fall from out his sphere,
The pow'rs above shall quake with fear:
Then they in heav'n the SIGN shall view
Of him, they crucify'd and slew.
Then shall the nations weep and sigh
To see the Son of Man on high,
With all the host of heav'n around,
And in stupendous glory crown'd;
And then he shall th' angelic band
With the shrill trumpet's voice command,
To call and congregate the blest
From north to south, from east to west.
Now learn a parable in brief
About the fig-tree and its leaf,
Which tree while it is tender now,
And puts forth verdure from each bough,
Ye hail the token, and descry
At once, that summer-time is nigh.
So when ye see these things, my friends,
Know ye, the dreadful day impends;
Attend ye, for in very deed
The present race shall not recede

Before these things you hear from me,
Shall be fulfill'd in a degree.
The heav'n and earth shall pass away,
But not one word of what I say.

PARABLE XV
The Ten Virgins

THE heav'nly kingdom at the last,
When man's account is to be cast,
Shall to ten virgins likeness bear;
Which virgins did their lamps prepare,
And went upon the wedding-day
To meet the bridegroom in the way.
Now five were wise, and five were weak,
With lamps, but had their oil to seek;
While the five prudent ones produce
Their lamps replenish'd from the cruse.
And as the ling'ring bridegroom kept
Away, they laid them down and slept:
And in a while, about the dead
Of night, a great alarm was spread—
'The bridegroom comes—ye damsels fly,
With joy to meet him!' was the cry.
Then all arose with one consent,
And trimm'd their lamps in haste, and went.
Then the fond maids besought the wise,
'Give us such oil as may suffice
From out your lamps, for ours we've burn'd.'
Not so, the wary ones return'd,
Lest there be scarce for either train—
But go ye rather back again,
And buy of those that sell the same:
But while they went, the bridegroom came.
And as all those that had address
To hold themselves in readiness,

870

Went in, each maid a welcome guest,
The door was barr'd against the rest.
Anon the foolish ones appear'd,
Whose cries were at the threshold hear'd,
'Lord, Lord, receive thy handmaids in!'
But he reply'd, 'I know not sin.'—
Watch therefore, for the hour's not known,
When Christ shall come to claim his own.

In these ten virgins Christ recites
Five senses in two diff'rent lights.
The wise are passions kept on guard;
The foolish ones are mercies marr'd.
The touch, the taste, the sight, the smell,
The sense of hearing will rebell,
Not kept from wand'ring and mischance
By all attentive vigilance:
So they that every sense degrade,
What time the thoughts of death invade,
On any crutch, however mean,
In spite of Christ the word would lean:
Hence idleness itself subsists
On spiritual œconomists.
Invidious folk with evil eyes,
Bad tongues, and list'ners unto lies,
Who keep not the Lord's body chaste,
Gluttons, that mar th' intent of taste,
Those that defile the human breath
With oaths and curses unto death,
And spoil that incense God desires,
Which through the lips to heav'n aspires;
Wretches like these would all to Rome,
And go to them that sell perfume,
And to the man of sin *apply,*
There pardons and indulgence buy:
But Christ against the fools, that put
Their trust in man, his door has shut.

PARABLE XVI

The Traveller and the Talents

THE heav'nly kingdom's like the case
Of one that sought a foreign place,
And call'd his servants to receive
Such goods as was his mind to leave.
Five talents he on *this* conferr'd,
And *that* had two, and one a third:
Each man, according to his skill;
Then went his purpose to fulfill.

Now he, to whom were five convey'd,
Employ'd the same in useful trade,
Until to other five they grew.
Likewise the next increas'd the two,
With which at first he had begun:
But he, whose talent was but one,
Went forth and dug into the dust,
And there deposited his trust.

Their lord, a tedious season past,
Came home, and reckon'd at the last:
Then he to whom the most was giv'n,
Said, Lord, behold thy five have thriv'n
Till there are other five beside—
'Thou good and faithful man, he cry'd,
Thou that a little hast inhanc'd,
To a great charge shall be advanc'd,
And thy superior gifts employ:
Receive thy lord's exceeding joy.'
He likewise that receiv'd the twain,
Cry'd, Lord, behold thy gold again,
Also with other two I come,
As int'rest for th' intrusted sum.
'Thou good and faithful man, he cry'd,
Who hast thyself so well apply'd,
More talents shall such gifts employ:
Receive thy lord's exceeding joy.'—

Then said the man to whom there fell
One talent, Lord, I knew thee well
A rig'rous man, that claims his own
Where he has neither straw'd nor sown;
And I was fearful to be chid,
So in the earth thy talent hid;
Behold, that talent I restore,
Here take it, neither less nor more.
His lord reply'd, 'Thou slothful slave,
If I deserve the word you gave,
A rig'rous man, that claim my own
Where I had neither straw'd nor sown,
Thou, therefore, should'st have set about
To put thy master's money out,
That he might have been repossess'd
With capital and interest.
Take then the talent from the worst,
And give to him that was the first.
For he that by improvement gains,
Shall have abundance for his pains:
But he, that wretch, that could not use
His little, shall that little lose.
So take the worthless slave away,
And into outer gloom convey,
Where midst the refuse of mankind
Fiends bellow, and their teeth they grind.'
For when the Son the second time
Shall come in majesty sublime,
By Cherubs and by Seraphs own'd,
And in his glory sit enthron'd,
Before his face and awful state
Shall all the nations congregate,
And he shall sever them in two,
Ev'n as the sheep the shepherds do,
And from the filthy goats divide,
The sheep shall on his right abide,
The goats shall to the left depart.—

Then shall the King declare his heart,
And thus them on the right address,
'Ye, whom my Father loves to bless,
Come, take the substance that endures,
And crown, from the beginning yours.
For hungry, and without a crumb,
To me ye did with nurture come;
Athirst, and ye my drought reliev'd;
A stranger, and ye me receiv'd;
Upon my shiv'ring limbs and bare
Ye threw the garment that I wear;
When I was sick, you visits paid;
And when a pris'ner, came to aid.'
Then shall the righteous race rejoin,
Lord, when with hunger didst thou pine,
And we the least assistance show'd?
Or to thy thirst a drop bestow'd?
Or took thee trav'ling in distress?
Or cloth'd at all thy nakedness?
When wert thou sick, or in a jail,
And we too there thy hap to wail?
Then shall the Lord this answer make,
'Since to my brethren, for my sake,
Ev'n to the least, you've done these things,
You've done them to the King of kings.'

Then shall he turn him to the left,
'Away from me, of grace bereft,
Depart ye to eternal hell,
Where satan and his legions dwell.
For hungry, and without a crumb,
To me with food ye did not come;
Athirst, ye did not me relieve,
Nor when a stranger, would receive;
Upon my shiv'ring limbs, and bare,
Ye brought no cloaths for me to wear;
When I was sick, no visits paid,
Nor when a pris'ner, came to aid.'

They too shall answer like the first—
When wert thou hungry, or athirst,
A stranger, naked, sick, confin'd,
And we were not to help inclin'd?
Then shall he tell them, 'Be ye sure,
If ev'n the least of all my poor
Was not with needful things supply'd,
Your Saviour also was deny'd.'—

Then to their bliss the good shall go,
The bad to everlasting woe.

PARABLE XVII

The Seed cast into the Ground secretly

CHRIST form'd his kingdom on a plan
Of liberty. As if a man
Should cast some seed into the ground,
Then go his way, and sleep profound,
And rising duly night and day,
Direct his course another way,
Until the seed should spring and grow,
But in what wise he does not know.
For earth, productive by degrees,
Brings forth spontaneous fruit with ease:
And first the blade, and then the ears,
And last the perfect corn appears.
But, when the fruit mature is found,
He brings his sickle to the ground,
Nor longer at a distance keeps,
But when 'tis harvest, then he reaps.

The Lord descends and gives his charge,
Then leaves the human will at large;
Withdraws himself, and winks a while:
Mean time in hearts, devoid of guile,

Spring forth his grace, and saving health,
Whose first exertions act by stealth;
But soon from such an hopeful root
Arise the blades, and bid for fruit,
And flourish, till the Lord dismiss
The ripen'd soul to endless bliss,
And at his harvest-home comes down,
And brings his sickle, and his crown.

PARABLE XVIII

The wealthy Self-deceiver—of taking no Thought of the Body—and of Watching

A CERTAIN wealthy man had ground
Which did with golden crops abound,
And he debated in his breast
'How shall I manage for the best,
Since I've no room to stow my fruits?'
At length he says, 'This method suits,
I will pull down my barns, and build
Much greater, and they shall be fill'd
With all this wealth, in which I roll,
And I will say unto my soul,
Soul, thou hast plenteous goods in store
For this and many a season more;
Repose thyself, indulge good cheer,
Eat, drink, and mirthful spend the year.'
But God within his conscience said,
'This night, thou fool, thou shalt be dead,
And I thy sinful soul demand;
Then whose are all these goods and land?'
This is the case of one who thrives,
And for his carnal lust contrives;
Rich to himself, and mammon's leav'n,
But poor to Jesus Christ and heav'n.

Therefore the Lord his scholars taught,
'Take for your mortal lives no thought,
What sustenance ye have to-day,
Or how ye shall your limbs array.
The life, far more than meat, above
Is God's communicated love;
The body there is more than dress'd,
With light encompassed and bless'd.
Consider how the ravens feed,
Nor sow nor reap they for their need,
Nor have they barns their store to hive,
But God preserves their race alive:
How much more worthy of his care
Are ye than birds that haunt the air?
Can ye by anxious thought devise
To add one cubit to your size?
If then in that is least ye fail,
What can solicitude avail?
Observe the lillies how they grow,
They toil not, nor the distaff know;
And yet believe what I relate,
That Solomon in all his state,
Deck'd with much gold, and many a gem,
Was not array'd like one of them.
If then your God so clothes the flow'r,
Whose being's of the present hour,
But on the morrow burnt with fire;
How much more shall he you attire?
O scant of faith! Then do not seek
For drink to draw, nor bread to break,
Nor do ye entertain a doubt,
For all the race, that be without,
Are anxious after things like these,
And your Almighty Father sees,
And helps your cravings from his throne—
Then seek ye Jesus Christ alone,
And wait for his eternal mead,

And all things meaner shall accede.
Fear not, my faithful flock, at all,
Although your number be but small;
For God's benevolence be prais'd,
To heav'nly thrones ye shall be rais'd.
Sell what ye have, and give away;
Provide ye bags which ne'er decay,
A heav'nly treasure, not to fail,
Where neither moth nor rust assail;
For where your treasure is, your heart
Will never from that place depart.
Your tapers light, your loins adjust,
And be ye like to men of trust,
And tarry for the Lord at home,
'Till from the wedding he shall come,
That when he knocks he may not wait,
But find the door wide open straight.
Those servants of the Lord are blest,
Whom he shall find disdaining rest;
In truth he shall his loins begird
And feed them to himself preferr'd.
If at the second watch he speed,
Or at the third, then blest indeed
Are all those servants, that retard
Their peace, and stand upon their guard—
And this for certain ye may hold,
If the good man had been foretold
What time the thief broke thro' the wall,
He would have watch'd, and sav'd his all.
Be ready, therefore, and take care,
The hour, of which you're not aware,
May be the Lord's appointed time
To crown thy toil, or charge thy crime.'

    Then Peter interrupts him thus—
Speak'st thou this parable to us?
Or is it, Lord, a gen'ral call
And warning, giv'n alike to all?

But, waving him, the Lord replies,
Who is that steward just and wise,
To whom his lord shall give the lead,
And charge him all his house to feed?
He's at his lord's arrival blest,
Detected doing of his best.—
His master, ('tis the truth I say)
Shall justly bid him bear the sway.
But, if within himself he says,
My master his return delays,
And then each man and maiden beats,
And drinks to gross excess, and eats.
The day, the hour, he never thought,
He by his master shall be caught,
Who will the wretch in pieces hew,
And rank him with the godless crew.—
And he, that knew his master's will,
Yet was not ready to fulfil,
Shall, heedless of a plain command,
To many stripes a victim stand.
But he, without precaution rash,
Altho' he's worthy of the lash,
Shall be corrected with a few:
Where much is giv'n, much is due;
And men, to whom they much commit,
Will not but still for more acquit.

PARABLE XIX

The Barren Fig-Tree

This parable he then did add—
A man within his vineyard had
A fig-tree set, when he was bound
In search of fruit, but none he found;
Then to his dresser thus he spake—

Lo! three years I my journey take
In quest of fruit from off this tree,
And not a single fig I see—
Then cut it down, for nothing worth,
Why should it load the useful earth?
But he reply'd—Lord, I implore,
Forbear it also one year more,
'Till I shall dig about the root,
And dung it still in hopes of fruit,
Which, if it should my labour crown,
'Tis well; if not, then cut it down.

God's sov'reign justice must decree
To cut off, as an useless tree,
Each sinful man—but mercy pleads,
And hope, thro' Jesus Christ, she feeds.
Another and another year—
Perhaps the wretch, thro' love or fear,
Himself to grace may recommend,
And be accepted in the end.

PARABLE XX

The Lost Sheep

THEN all the Publicans drew near,
And profligates, his word to hear;
Which congregation did displease
And grieve the Scribes and Pharisees;
Who said, the sinner this man joins,
And with th' exactor sits and dines.

Then he this parable began—
Is there of you a single man,
If worth a hundred sheep in stock
And lose but one of all the flock,

Who does not quit the ninety odd,
Left to the providence of God,
And hies him to regain his loss?
Which, when he finds it, thrown across
His shoulders, joyful home he bends,
And calls his neighbours and his friends,
'Rejoyce with me, for I have made
Discov'ry of the sheep that stray'd.'
So likewise joy in heav'n shall be
More for one sinner's contrite knee,
Than ninety-nine without offence,
Who have no need of penitence.

PARABLE XXI

The Piece of Silver

OR thus,—What woman, that retains
Ten silver pieces, all her gains,
And loses one, does not explore,
With candle light, and sweep the floor,
And use all diligence, to find
The coin on which she sets her mind;
And, when she finds it, does not call
Her friends and neighbours, one and all,
'Your gratulations here be paid,
I've found the piece that I mislaid!'
Likewise there's joy, you may rely,
Before th' angelic host on high,
If one poor sinner meekly prays,
Repenting all his evil ways.

PARABLE XXII

The Spiritual Œconomist

CHRIST call'd the throng—These things ye
    hear,
But do ye comprehend them clear?
They say unto him, 'Lord, we do.'
Then did he his discourse renew—
'On this account each learned scribe,
That can Christ's heav'nly truths imbibe,
Hence shall his ghostly charge subsist,
And act the good œconomist,
While new and old, from all his store,
He gives each guest, that haunts his door.'

The Lord would here his converts teach
How his good saints should read and preach,
By copying all his faith and force,
As he sets off his plain discourse;
Brings forth new truths, the old he cites,
Puts diff'rent things in various lights;
Disposes all things for the best,
And treats his hearers as his guest.

PARABLE XXIII

The Prophet without Honour in his own Country

THE Lord, as he had made a pause
From all these parables, withdraws,
And as his destination tends,
Seeks his own country, and his friends;
And in their synagogue he taught,
'Till all the throng amazement caught.
And whence (exclaim'd the traitors) springs
This wisdom, and these mighty things?

Is Mary not his mother's name,
Who from the vile mechanic came?
And are not Simon, Joses, James,
And Jude, his brethren by their names?
His sisters too before our eyes?
Whence, therefore, can these things arise?
And they in rank offence decry'd
His works.—But Jesus Christ reply'd,
And said unto them all—'A seer
Is not without respect e'en here,
(Unless before his native land,
And his own family he stand.)'
And there, as they would not believe,
He did few miracles atchieve.

By envy was Christ Jesus try'd,
By envy cast and crucify'd;
This had not been the case at Rome
Or Athens, *if one may presume.*
Joseph *with many-colour'd vest,*
That child o'er all his brethren blest,
A type of Christ our Saviour sent,
God's Son, in whom he was content;
At home condemn'd to death and shame,
In foreign Egypt *found his fame,*
'Till he at Pharaoh's *right-hand stood,*
As Christ at God's supremely good.

PARABLE XXIV

The Prodigal Son

Two youths a certain father rear'd,
Of which the youngest son appear'd,
And ask'd him, 'Sir, to me consign
What portion of the goods is mine.'

Then shared he, without more ado,
His livelihood betwixt the two.
But e'er a many days were pass'd,
The younger all his wealth amass'd,
And took his journey far away,
Where soon, inordinately gay,
He wasted all he did possess
In rioting and rank excess;
And when with all he'd made an hand,
There rose a famine in the land,
And he began to be in need:
He therefore with himself agreed
A certain foreigner to join,
Who sent him forth to feed the swine,
And he thro' want began to crave
The husks that to the herd he gave;
And to his want none had respect—
But when he did at length reflect,
'How many a servant man, he said,
My father hires, abounds with bread,
Nay, can the neighb'ring poor supply,
And I am at the point to dye:
I will arise, and thus accost
My father; father, I am lost
By grievous sin to heav'n and thee,
Not worthy in the least degree
That thou should'st as a son embrace
Me, therefore 'mongst thy servants place.'
Then he arose, and left the trough,
And when he was a great way off,
His weeping father knew him well,
And ran, and on his neck he fell,
And kiss'd him.—Then he did accost
His father, 'Father, I am lost,
By grievous sin to heav'n and thee.'—
But raising him from off his knee,
His father bade the servants bring

The goodliest vestment, and a ring
To put upon his hand, and shoes
Upon his naked feet, and loose
The fatted calf, which they should kill,
Of mirth and cheer to have their fill:
For this, my son, tho' dead to me,
Once more alive again I see,
And my lost hope I have regain'd.—
Then all were glad and entertain'd.
Now all the while that this was done,
It happen'd, that the elder son,
Who then was in the field, advanc'd
And heard them, as they sung and danc'd,
And calling of a servant out,
Inquir'd what they was about.—
He said, thy brother's come again,
Thy father has the fattling slain,
As he is safe and sound receiv'd.—
Then he was very wroth and griev'd,
Disdaining to go in a doors.
Then comes his father, and implores
His presence.—But he answ'ring said
Behold! now many years are fled,
Since thee with all my heart I serv'd,
Nor ever from thy mandates swerv'd,
And yet I never had th' amends
Of one poor kid to treat my friends;
But soon as this thy son was come,
Who has embezzled such a sum
In lust, and thy affairs distress'd
For him the fatted calf is dress'd.
But he returning, Son, reply'd,
With me you ever do reside,
And all I have is thine—'twas meet
This day with joy and mirth to greet,
For this thy brother, tho' esteem'd
As dead, 's alive, tho' lost, redeem'd.

PARABLE XXV
The Unjust Steward

THIS parable, as he convers'd
With his disciples, Christ rehears'd.—
    A certain man of wealth maintain'd
A steward, and he was arraign'd,
That he had of his goods made waste;
He therefore call'd him up in haste,
And said, 'What is this thing I hear?
Let your accounts be stated clear:
Thou from thine office must depart.'—
Then said the steward in his heart,
'Thus stripp'd, how grievous is my task?
I cannot dig, and scorn to ask.
I am resolv'd what step to take,
That when my post I must forsake,
I somewhere may reception win.'
On which he call'd one debtor in,
And ask'd, how much he was in debt
In that he had not settled yet?
'An hundred measures, I confess,
I owe, sir, from the olive-press.'
Then haste (he said) and sit thee still,
And write down fifty in thy bill.—
He of a second next would know,
How much? 'An hundred bowls I owe
Of wheat from out the threshing-floor.'
Then take thy bill and write fourscore.—
The Lord moreover in the end
Did this same man of guile commend
For acting of a prudent part:
Since all the race, that set their heart
On worldly things, are wiser far,
In what concerns them, where they are,
Than children of the light can be,
Train'd in the Lord's simplicity.

Then, (in griev'd irony he spake)
Friends, of unrighteous mammon make
That when you fail, from wealth and pride,
You heav'nly mansions may provide.

This lecture seems to have been read
After the twelve the Lord had fled,
And went about with carnal eyes
In quest of temporalities;
Perhaps indulging vice her way;
Perhaps remitting sins for pay;
With Judas selling Christ his worth;
With Peter sav'ring things on earth:
But Christ explicitly declares
Against the world and its affairs.

Two lords no minister can serve:
For or of one he'll well deserve,
The other hate in servile fear;
Or else he will to *this* adhere,
And *that* will disobey and scorn:
You're not for God and mammon born.

PARABLE XXVI

The Rich Man and Lazarus

A CERTAIN man of wealth possess'd,
In purple and fine linnen dress'd,
Did proudly pass each live long day
In sumptuous banquetings away;
At whose uncharitable doors
A certain beggar, full of sores,
Was station'd, Lazarus by name,
And all the wretched suppliant's aim
Was, of the crumbs but to be fed

Of the great lord's superfluous bread:
But he the beggar's pray'r deny'd;
'Till, nearer with their God ally'd
In charity, the very hounds
Came up and lick'd the poor man's wounds.
He, therefore, died for lack of aid,
And by the angels was convey'd
To Abraham's bosom for his peace.
The greedy Epicure's decease
In a short season too occurr'd,
And he was pompously interr'd:
Then lifting up his baleful eyes,
Tormented with hell's agonies,
He did poor Lazarus survey
In Abraham's bosom, where he lay,
And, 'Father Abraham, he said,
Have mercy on me, thus dismay'd,
And send back Lazarus to dip
In the cool stream his finger's tip,
That he may so relieve my tongue,
Which in tormenting flames is stung.'
Then Abraham said, Remember, son,
What in your mortal state was done:
How thou the goods of life hadst got,
And Lazarus an evil lot:
Whence heav'nly comforts bless the poor,
Whilst thou must agonies endure.
Add to the certainty of this,
Betwixt the seats of pain and bliss
There is a gulph they may not shoot,
Nor I from hence my sons depute,
Nor can they come with us to class,
Who would from your allotment pass.
'I therefore (he renew'd his pray'r)
Beseech thee, that he may repair
Unto my father's house, where five
Of my own brethren still survive,

And testify unto them all,
Lest they to this perdition fall.'
There's Moses (Abraham in return)
And Prophets, let them read and learn.
'Nay, father Abraham, (he said)
If one went to them from the dead,
They will repent themselves and fear.'
He answer'd, If they will not hear
What Moses and the Seers maintain,
The dead themselves would rise in vain.

All Prophets, since the world began,
Foretold our Saviour God and Man.
And when the Jews would not collate
The scriptures with our Lord's estate,
But all the miracles atchiev'd
By doubt stupendous disbeliev'd;
They were not likely to repent
By things however evident.
Our Saviour, therefore, did not shew
Himself, when ris'n, but to a few,
Which for that purpose he had chose,
All evidence to crown and close.

PARABLE XXVII

Faith as a Grain of Mustard-seed

The Twelve to Christ, their Master, cry'd,
'Increase our faith!' The Lord reply'd,
If you had lively faith, indeed,
But as a grain of mustard-seed,
You might this sycomine command
To grow by sea and quit the land.
But whatsoe'er by faith is known,
Or done by works, is God's alone.

For which of you shall have a HAND,
That plows and fodders at command;
And to him thus anon shall say,
Loos'd from the labour of the day,
'Go, get thee in, and take thy mess';
And shall not rather thus address,
'Make ready that on which I sup,
And gird thyself, and bring it up;
And when thou'st serv'd my bowl and meat,
Then likewise thou shalt drink and eat.'—
What are the Master's thanks conferr'd
On him, who thus obey'd his word?
Not they, I trow—So likewise you,
That done you were enjoin'd to do,
Shall better with submission own
Before your Master's awful throne,
'Our duty is but barely paid,
And 'twas by force that we obey'd;
And all our services are vain
In which are neither grace nor gain.'

PARABLE XXVIII

The Importunate Widow

THIS parable he likewise spoke,
Religious ardour to provoke,
That men their constant pray'r should plead,
Nor e'er grow languid, or recede.

There in a certain city dwelt
A judge, whose heart no pity felt,
Nor did he God Almighty fear,
Or any man on earth revere.
On him a widow of that place
Attended, and referr'd her case:

'Avenge me of my foe,' she cry'd,
Which for long while the judge deny'd:
But when a certain time was past,
He argued with himself at last,
'Although the Lord I do not fear,
Nor any man on earth revere;
Yet since this widow day and night
Is urgent, I will do her right,
Lest by her coming without end,
She weary me to death.'—Attend
To what th' unrighteous judge admits,
And shall not God Supreme, that sits
Enthron'd in righteousness, respect
And vindicate his own elect,
Which day and night prefer their pray'r,
Though for a long time he forbear?
I tell you of a truth, indeed,
It shall be done, and done with speed.

PARABLE XXIX

The Pharisee and Publican

HE too this parable address'd
To men, that pompously profess'd
Themselves in their own works to pride,
And scorn all other folk beside.
Two persons, to prefer their pray'r,
Did to the house of God repair;
One of the Pharisaic clan,
And one a sinful publican.
The Pharisee stood up and pray'd,
And thus within himself he said,
'I thank thee, God, that I am free
From sins, in which the rest agree,
That are extortioners, unjust,
Or giv'n to foul adult'rous lust,

Or like this publican to gold;
Twice ev'ry week the fast I hold,
And give of all that I possess
The tithe in perfect righteousness.'
Mean time the publican withdrew
To a more distant point of view,
Nor durst to heav'n exalt his eyes,
But smiting on his breast he cries,
'The Lord be merciful to me
A sinner in the worst degree.'
I tell you fairly of the twain,
The publican went home again
More sure of pardon for his fault.
For those that would themselves exalt,
Shall fall, while heav'n-accepted sighs,
And humble penitents, shall rise.

PARABLE XXX

The Camel and the Needle's Eye

A CERTAIN ruler came to ask,
'Good Master, what must be my task
To gain heav'n's infinite reward?'
Why callest thou me good? the Lord
Reply'd: no person has a claim,
Save God alone, to such a name.
Thou know'st the statutes what they be,
Do not commit adultery;
And, Do no murder; Do not steal;
Nor in false testimony deal;
Thy parents reverence.—He cry'd,
'With these from youth have I comply'd.'
Now Jesus hearing this, return'd,
Yet one thing is there to be learn'd;
Give all thou hast unto the poor,
And thou shalt heav'nly wealth insure,

And one to my disciples add.
This said, he was exceeding sad,
For he much opulence possess'd.
When Jesus saw him thus distress'd,
He said, How hardly shall they go
To heav'n who have their wealth below:
For ev'n the camel may go thro'
The needle's eye with less to do,
Than men, that doat on mammon's rust,
By God be number'd with the just.
And they that heard him this declare,
Cry'd, (conscious of the gen'ral care)
Who can be sav'd of all mankind?
But he with lenity rejoin'd,
What is impossible with man,
Omnipotence both will and can.

PARABLE XXXI

The Good Shepherd

IN truth, in very truth, I say,
The man that comes another way,
And enters not the door, his will
Is God's good sheep to fleece and kill:
But the true shepherd of the flock
Comes by the door-way; at his knock
To him the porter opes by choice,
And his sheep know the welcome voice:
And his own flock by name he hails,
And leads them out to verdant vales;
And when he puts them forth to feed,
He does his own good sheep precede,
Which follow, as his voice they know;
But after strangers will not go,
But flee away from such in fear,
As for their voice they have no ear.

893

This parable our Saviour spake,
Nor could the twelve his meaning take;
He therefore said to them again,
His gracious purpose to explain,
'Tis truth, the very truth direct,
I am the door-way in effect
Of my own sheep. Who came of old,
Were thieves and robbers of the fold;
But them the sheep did not revere.
I am the door, who enters here,
He shall be sav'd, and to his mind
Free passage and sweet pasture find.
To steal, to kill, and to destroy,
Are a thief's errand, and his joy:
But to give life my mission's seal'd
At large, eternal, unreveal'd.
I am the shepherd good and true,
Who gives his life for sheep like you.
The hireling, to the flock unknown,
Whereas the sheep are not his own,
Sees the wolf come in search of prey,
And leaves his charge, and flies away;
The wolf then seizes on the best
Secure, and scatters all the rest.
The hireling (ev'n as such) recedes,
Nor cares he for the sheep he feeds:
My sheep, the shepherd true and good,
I know, and I am understood.
Me as the Father knows, ev'n so
I him reciprocally know:
And I, his covenant to keep,
Lay down my life, and save my sheep.
And I have other sheep, beside
This fold, for which I must provide;
They, by my voice, shall be controul'd
At length one shepherd and one fold.
Here is my Father's love intense,

Because I willingly go hence,
And die the death to live again,
No man I charge, that I am slain:
But, so empower'd my life resign,
(To yield and to resume is mine)
This is the Father's great behest
Giv'n to my soul's supreme request.

PARABLE XXXII

The True Vine

THE true and genuine vine am I,
The husbandman my Sire on high;
Each branch in me that grows in vain,
He will not suffer to remain:
But that which yields a plenteous store,
He purges to increase the more.
From your offence you now are clear'd
By those pure words, which you have heard.
Abide in me, and I in you;
For as the branch no fruit can shew,
Unless it cleave unto the tree,
So ye are nothing but in me.
Ye are the branches, I the vine,
Much fruit you bear whene'er you join
Your Saviour, and abide in one;
But without me is nothing done.
And if a man do not abide,
As a dead branch he's cast aside;
And men, for such have no desire,
But for the fuel of the fire.
If you in me shall make abode,
Nor are my words in vain bestow'd,
Ye then shall ask for what you will
Secure of my compliance still.

Your fruitfulness to God confirms
The glory; on no other terms
Ye my true followers can be.
And as the Father's love's to me;
So are you all to me most dear:
In mine affections persevere.
Ye in your love shall surely stand,
By giving heed to my command,
As I, while I to God's incline,
Continue in the love divine.
These things I've said, that ye might dwell
In joy, which shall to fullness swell—
Obey me—to each other shew
That love, which I have shewn to you:
And there's no love this love transcends,
That a man die to save his friends.

PARABLE XXXIII

The Good Samaritan

A CERTAIN councellor arose,
And, tempting him, did this propose,
What duties, master, must I do,
To gain eternal life with you?
'What's in the written law decreed?'
The Lord reply'd, 'how dost thou read?'
He answer'd, 'Thou shalt love the Lord
Thy God with all thy heart's accord,
With all thy soul to him inclin'd,
And all thy strength, and all thy mind,
And as thyself and special end
Thy neighbour and his wealth befriend.'
The Lord replies, 'Thou answer'st well;
This do, thou shalt in safety dwell.'
But he, desirous to evade,

And justify his practice, said,
'O Lord, and out of all mankind,
Pray, where must I my neighbour find?'
Then Jesus answer'd,—'On a day
A certain trav'ller took his way,
Bound from Jerusalem to go
A journey far as Jericho,
And thieves encount'ring in his course,
They stripp'd him of his cloaths by force,
And, when with many wounds he bled,
Departed, leaving him for dead.
By chance there came unto the place
A priest, who when he saw the case,
Pass'd over on the other side:
A Levite in like wise espy'd,
And pass'd off from the wounded man.
But, haply, a Samaritan,
As he was trav'lling where he lay,
With pity did his case survey,
And where he maimed was and bruis'd,
Bound up, and oil and wine infus'd;
Then mounting on his beast he leads,
And to an inn with caution speeds:
And on the morrow when he went,
He took out two pence to content
The host, and gave him charge, Take care,
Whatever more in this affair
Thou spendest, I will thee repay
Whene'er I come again this way.
Which person, therefore, can'st thou tell,
Was neighbour unto him that fell
Amongst the thieves?'—The man (he cries)
That saw his wounds with pitying eyes.
Then Jesus answer'd, 'Get thee hence,
And imitate benevolence.'

PARABLE XXXIV

The Children in the Market-Place

To what (says Christ the prince of grace)
Shall I compare this froward race?
What are they like in word and way?
They're like to little folk at play,
Which in the market-place commun'd
With one another, 'We have tun'd
Our pipes, and ye no measure kept,
We've mourned, and ye have not wept.'
For, first, the way John Baptist lead,
Not drinking wine, nor eating bread,
And you all cry'd, he was possess'd.
The Son of Man became your guest,
And him to reprobate ye join,
'Behold, a glutton, giv'n to wine,
Of publicans and vice the friend.'
But wisdom's children shall defend
Their parent working various ways,
And bring her off for endless praise.

PARABLE XXXV

Christ and Mary Magdalen at the Pharisee's Entertainment

A PHARISEE the Lord implor'd,
To come and bless his social board:
The Lord accepted of his treat,
And went and sat him down to meat;
When, lo! a woman of the place,
Fall'n by her sins into disgrace,
And knowing that the Lord was there,
Did to the Pharisee's repair,

And brought a box of sweet perfume,
And stood behind him in the room,
There bath'd his feet the while she cry'd,
And with her locks dishevell'd dry'd;
Then with her lips she kiss'd his feet,
And pour'd thereon her ointment sweet.
This, when the Pharisee, that made
The entertainment, had survey'd,
He thus within himself agreed,
If this man was a seer indeed,
He would have known, that she, who came
And touch'd him, was of evil fame.
But Christ unto his thought reply'd,
'Simon, there's something to decide,
Which I shall speak to thee anon.'
And Simon answer'd, Lord, say on.
'A certain creditor from two
Had got a sum of money due,
The one five hundred pence he lent,
The other fifty—in event,
When neither had a mite to pay,
He both forgave. Now, therefore, say,
Which of the twain shall love and bless
The most?'—Says Simon, as I guess
The person whom the most he spar'd.
Says Christ, 'Thou rightly hast declar'd.'
Then turning from his seat aside,
Seest thou this object here, he cry'd:
When I came in thy house to greet,
Thou gav'st me nought to wash my feet;
But she for that her tears has us'd,
And wip'd them with her hairs diffus'd.
Thy welcome no kind kiss endear'd,
But ever since I first appear'd,
This woman here has been profuse
To kiss my feet. From out thy cruse
Thou pourd'st no oil upon my head,

But she her precious balsam shed:
Wherefore, I tell thee, I think fit
Her sins, though many, to remit.
For much she lov'd, as much she ow'd:
But she that has the grace bestow'd
Of mercy for a small concern,
Will love but little in return.
Thou from thy sins (he cries) art free.
Then certain of the company
Said in themselves, 'Who's this, forsooth,
That pardons sins?' But God the truth
Did his poor penitent release,
'Thy faith has sav'd thee, go in peace!'

PARABLE XXXVI

The Kingdom of Christ compared to a Little Child

WITH little children certain went
To Christ our Saviour, to th' intent
That he should touch them and should bless,
To whom the twelve deny'd access,
And those that brought them there, aggriev'd.
Which, when the Lord himself perceiv'd,
It did his anger much provoke,
'Permit (he cry'd) the little folk
To come to me, and check them not,
For to such vot'ries I allot
The honour of Christ's blest demain.
For of a truth I tell you plain,
The man, whoe'er shall not receive
(In strict attention to believe)
Christ's kingdom, as 'tis preach'd by me,
With all a child's simplicity,
Shall in that kingdom find no place.'

The children then did he embrace,
And on their heads his hands impress'd,
And with divine good-nature bless'd.

PARABLE XXXVII

The Disciples the Salt of the Earth, &c.

YE are the salt (the Prince of worth
So call'd his followers) of the earth;
But if that salt of savour fail,
What can the damage countervail?
It from that time ev'n to the end
Answers no purpose we intend:
But to the dust devolves, and then
Is trampled under foot by men.
You're to the world a light reveal'd.
A city cannot be conceal'd,
That's built on a commanding site;
Nor do mere men a candle light
Beneath a bushel to convey,
But on a candlestick display,
And so of course its beams shine out
To all the family about.
Let your light shine before the face
Of men, that they your works may trace,
And, as their goodness they admire,
Give glory to your heav'nly Sire.

The name of ev'ry thing express'd
By Christ was consequently bless'd;
Thence render'd better for its use,
Thence consecrated from abuse.
He therefore oft his proverb brings
From lowly life and common things,
That they (whom high-flow'n thoughts offend)

The vulgar might attention lend:
And, while their sov'reign source they seek,
Wit, learning, genius, might be meek.

PARABLE XXXVIII

The Beam and the Mote

JUDGE not, lest ye be judg'd for pride:
For with what judgment you decide,
Ye shall be censur'd like for like;
And the same measure that ye strike,
That shall be measur'd you again.
And why beholdest thou with pain
The mote that's in thy brother's eye,
And thine own beam canst not descry?
Thy brother, how canst thou reprove,
'From thee let me that mote remove,
That I may set thy vision right';
When, lo! a beam obstructs thy sight.
Thou hypocrite with canting tone,
First cast the beam from out thine own:
And then shalt thou distinctly note
Thy brother's eye, and clear the mote.

Men, with regard to mental light,
Are wilfully depriv'd of sight;
With others crimes themselves amuse,
Lest their own hearts they should peruse,
And, irksome talk! all joy forbear,
Urg'd to tears, temperance, and pray'r.
This the worst men the most will grudge,
For ev'ry Judas is a judge,
And all that deviate from God's way
The great accuser must obey.

PARABLE XXXIX

Pearls not to be cast before Swine

To dogs present not things divine,
Nor cast your pearls before the swine;
Lest wrath should crush, what filth disdains,
And rend the donor for his pains.

   CHRIST here his conduct to ingrates,
By precept clears, and vindicates;
For he did oftentimes refuse
Plain doctrine to the rebel Jews.
For there are incidents and times,
When criminals affect their crimes
In such, that they advisers scorn,
Still hated more, the more they warn.
Thus Christ, nor word, nor works, they own'd,
But for his merit would have ston'd.

PARABLE XL

A Stone not to be given for Bread, nor a Serpent for Fish

Ask! God shall grant it without doubt;
Go, seek! and thou shalt find it out;
Knock! they shall open for thy pains.
For every one that asks, obtains;
Who seeketh, finds; who knocks, comes in.
For which, ev'n of the sons of sin,
Will give his child requiring bread
A stone for nurture in its stead;
Or if he should a fish demand,
Will put a scorpion in his hand?
If you, thus evil as ye be,
Can give things with propriety,

And for your children good select;
How much more, in the like respect,
Shall God your Father in the height
Give good things to th' importunate?
Then what you'd have your neighbours do,
In your ownself th' example shew:
The case your own you cannot err,
For laws and seers the same infer.

PARABLE XLI

The Strait Gate

To hardship and to many a strait
Inur'd, affect the narrow gate.
For wide the door, and broad the way,
That leads to horror and dismay:
But fond of ease, and chusing wrong,
There multitudes together throng.
For strait's the gate, and hard the road
That leads to life's sublime abode,
And few there be of all mankind
That can th' obstructed passage find.

*The Champion's evangelic life
Is contest and predestin'd strife,
We're christen'd soldiers of the Lord,
And must by hardship claim reward.
Up hill by land our steps we guide,
By sea we row 'gainst wind and tide:
Below we lose above to win,
And scorn all peace that's link'd to sin:
Thro' straits and thorns the Lord obey,
And leave the wordlings to their way.*

PARABLE XLII

The Wolves in Sheep's Clothing

BEWARE of prophets in pretence,
That come with seeming innocence
Like sheep, but both in will and pow'r
They're wolves to worry and devour:
These by their fruits you shall detect.
Do men from thorns the grapes collect,
Or figs from thistles? Even so
On the good tree good fruit will grow:
But when once damag'd in the root,
The tree's corruption mars the fruit.
A tree that's good, with proper care,
An evil fruit will never bear;
Nor can a tree that's naught at heart,
By any means good fruit impart:
And all (not such as we require)
Are fell'd and cast into the fire.
On men too thus your judgments pass,
And by their fruits their merit class.

PARABLE XLIII

The House built upon a Rock

NOT they that merely cite my name,
Lord! Lord! but those heav'n's bliss shall claim
Which by my Father's will have stood,
Who dwells in heav'n for actual good.
In that day many shall apply,
'Lord! Lord! did we not prophecy,
And in thy name the dev'ls eject,
And marvels in thy name effect?'
To whom I will again profess,
Depart, ye sons of wickedness:

I know not or your works or you.
Wherefore the men that hear and do
My words, I liken to a man,
Who taking wisdom for his plan,
Upon a rock his house did frame;
Rains fell, and inundations came,
And tempests blew, and could not shock
The building founded on a rock.
And these my words who will not hear,
And do them in religious fear,
I liken to a fool that plann'd
And built his house upon the sand;
Rains fell, and inundations came,
And tempests blew upon the same,
'Till down it tumbled, roof and all,
And great and grievous was the fall.

The Lord himself's the corner-stone,
Which we depend upon alone:
By whom all eminence ascends,
Which all perfection starts and ends.
The blasts of envy, floods of vice,
In vain attack our edifice,
Which still all violence shall mock,
As founded on the Lord our rock.
Dissenters from the holy law
Build upon stubble and on straw;
And as the ground-work that they place,
Such is the building, free from grace,
Alike unhallow'd and uncouth,
As void of permanence as truth.

PARABLE XLIV

A House divided against itself

To Jesus with a man they come
Who was possess'd, both blind and dumb,
And him he cur'd to that degree,
That he could both converse and see;
And all were struck at what was done,
And question'd, 'Is this David's son?'
But when the Pharisees had heard
This mercy, they blasphem'd and sneer'd,
'This fellow does not dev'ls expel
But by the very prince of hell.'
But Jesus knew their thoughts, and said,
Where'er division makes a-head,
That kingdom to confusion falls;
And ev'ry house, within whose walls
Intestine feuds begin to reign,
Can never for long time remain.
If satan then himself eject,
He is divided in effect,
And how can his dominion hold?
And if, by Beelzebub controul'd,
I cast out devils, by what name
Do these your children do the same?
Wherefore for this, when you're arraign'd,
They shall your judges be ordain'd:
But if I dev'ls themselves command
By God the spirit of my hand,
Then is Christ's kingdom come indeed.
For how can any one succeed
To force a strong man's house, and spoil,
Unless he first his prowess foil?
And when h' has bound him on the spot,
Shall pillage all that he has got.
Whoe'er from me himself withdraws,
Declares against me and my cause:

Who gather not with me, are seen
To scatter all they reap or glean.
Wherefore believe my word express,
All blasphemy and wickedness,
Which men commit at any time,
Shall be forgiv'n, except the crime
Against the Holy Ghost alone,
For which no sinner shall atone.
And whatsoever man shall frame
His speech against my word and name,
The Son of God shall that remit:
But him he never shall acquit,
Who shall the Holy Ghost offend,
Nor now, nor in the latter end.
Let things be as they are. The tree
If good, the product good must be;
Or make the tree corrupt, at best
The fruit's the same—that is the test.
O race of vipers! bad in grain!
How can ye righteousness maintain?
For from the fulness of the heart
The mouth does all its speech impart.
The good, as from a wise man's hoard,
Shall riches of the heart afford:
The bad, as in a miser's hole,
Shall treasure things against the soul.
For ev'ry word which indiscrete,
(I say) ye for the nonce repeat,
The talkers all must stand aghast
Before Christ's judgment-seat at last:
For words well-weigh'd, or misapply'd,
Thou shalt be judg'd, or justify'd.

This sin (tho' horror of offence)
Does not exclude fair penitence.
For had the monsters, whose conceit
Did strive Christ's mercy to defeat,

908

And interrupt his ghostly pow'r,
But pleaded guilty the same hour,
And faithful promis'd to amend,
They'd made an injur'd God their friend.
For vipers from beneath, that lurk
To thwart God's love about its work,
Are more Christ's hate, and satan's prey,
Than actual sin in open day.

PARABLE XLV

The Whole need no Physician

ONE day when Christ had took his seat
In his own house his food to eat,
Then also publicans came in
With sundry branded for their sin,
And with Christ Jesus sat in view,
With his disciples not a few:
(For having for a little space
An home, his flock increas'd apace)
But as the Scribes, and sect severe
Of Pharisees, beheld him here,
They ask'd of his disciples then,
With publicans and sinful men
His bread why has your master broke?
When Jesus thus in answer spoke,
'The healthy no physician seek,
Who's needful to the sick and weak;
Not for the righteous was I sent,
But for the sinners to repent.'

PARABLE XLVI

The Children of the Bride-Chamber

SAINT John's disciples, and the sect
Of Pharisees, did much affect
The use of fasting certain days,
They, therefore, in familiar phrase,
Ask'd, 'Why do John's disciples use
Strict abstinence, and thine refuse?'
Then Jesus thus himself express'd,
'Can children, of the bridal bless'd,
Themselves with abstinence chastise
In joy before the bridegroom's eyes?
Long as the nuptial feast shall last,
In very truth, they cannot fast:
But soon enough the days arrive
That shall from them the bridegroom drive,
And then they shall their food forego
In downright bitterness and woe.
So, likewise, no man sews a patch
Of an old cloth, that will not match,
Upon a vestment that is new:
For otherwise the thing you sew
Will make the cloth contract and purse,
Until the rent be made the worse.
So no one will new wine infuse
In old and tainted jars to chuse;
Else the new wine will burst the clay,
And or be marr'd or waste away:
But wine that's just fin'd off and new,
Should have fresh receptacles too.'

Both purposes you will destroy,
Or gladd'ning grief, or damping joy.
But here the Lord's good-nature shines,
Who suffers by high-fed DIVINES,
'Why could not we cast out the fiend?'

910

Because you have yourselves demean'd.
For miracles so great and rare
Come but by fasting and by pray'r.
But after all it was not right
To give up to each hypocrite
His own true servants to the last,
Whose food was better than their fast.

PARABLE XLVII

The Bearing of the Cross

AND having bade the throng draw near,
His doctrine with the twelve to hear,
He said, 'Whoever would apply
To me, he must himself deny,
Take up the cross where'er I go,
And be my follower in woe.
For who his precious life would spare,
Shall lose it for his over-care:
But for the gospel's sake and mine
Whoever shall his life resign,
The same shall save it at the last.
For when a man's account is cast,
What shall it profit, if he win
The world, and lose his soul in sin?
Or what exchange can counterpoise
His soul and heav'n's eternal joys?
Whoever, therefore, in this age
Of vice, and rank adult'rous rage,
Shall be asham'd of me and mine,
And of the doctrine I injoin,
Him too the Son of Man shall spurn
In like contempt at his return,
With all his Father's glory crown'd,
And all th' angelic host around.'

PARABLE XLVIII

The Necessity of Self-denial

SAINT John did thus the Lord address,
'We saw a person dispossess
In thy blest name th' infernal pow'rs,
And we forbade him, as not ours,
Nor following where thou goest before.'
But Jesus said, Forbid no more;
For who does marvels in my name,
Will never lightly Christ defame:
And whosoe'er with hand and heart
Is not against us, takes our part.
And whosoe'er shall bid you take
A cup of water for my sake,
Because you're servants of the Lord,
In no wise shall escape reward.
But whatsoever man offends
The least of these my little friends,
Which rest their confidence in me,
Better he fell into the sea,
A mill-stone tied to plunge him in.
For if thy hand offend in sin,
Off with it: for 'tis better mead,
If maim'd, to lively grace you speed,
Than with two hands to go to hell,
Where fiends in fire eternal dwell;
Yea, where the worm shall never die,
And fiends unceasing flames supply.
And if thy foot offending slide,
Off with it: for 'tis on thy side
Rather that halt to life you speed,
Than with two feet to sink indeed,
There where the worm shall never die,
And fiends unceasing flames supply.
And if thine eye offence should see,
Out with it: for 'tis well for thee,

Rather God's kingdom to obtain
One-ey'd, than go to hell with twain;
Yea, where the worm shall never die,
And fiends unceasing flames supply.
For ev'ry man provoking ire,
Must be detain'd in salt of fire;
And ev'ry sacrifice that's pure
Is of the salt that makes endure:
The salt is good; but if it lose
Its savour, who that salt shall use?
The salt of my pure word imbibe,
And to each other peace prescribe.

PARABLE XLIX

The Reed shaken with the Wind

JOHN Baptist having chosen two
Of his disciples, with a view
Of proving Jesus, sent them out
To put the matter out of doubt:
'Art thou Messias, God's elect,
Or some one else must we expect?'
(And many a plague he in that hour
Did cure, and sickness, by his pow'r:
He cast out devils in their sight,
And to the blind restor'd the light.)
Then Jesus answer'd, 'Go your way,
Tell what you have seen and heard to-day:
The lame do walk, the blind do see,
The lep'rous are in purity,
The dead arise, the deaf give ear,
And all the poor the gospel hear:
And great his blessing and his praise,
Who takes no umbrage at my ways.'
And when the messengers of John

Were by the Lord's commandment gone,
He to the people then began
To speak of this amazing man,
'What went you out in such a press
To seek for in the wilderness?
A man that wavers in his mind,
Like reed, when shaken by the wind?
Again, I say, what sought ye there,
A man soft-clad in camel's hair?
For dainty folk the court's the place,
And such as gorgeous vestments grace.
But still what went you to explore,
A prophet? Yea, and something more.
For this is he of whom 'tis penn'd,
Behold, my messenger I send
Before my face, who shall fore-run,
The way adjusting for my Son.
For know, 'mongst those of women born,
No greater seer did e'er adorn
The world than John—and yet I say,
The man that owns my word and way,
The Christian in the least degree,
Is of more eminence than he.'

John own'd our blessed Saviour first,
And should have follow'd him at worst,
Not for himself disciples made,
But been his master's, and obey'd.
This in the infant church did tend
To schism, and his untimely end.
But in Christ's kingdom he shall reign,
Who quick as thought shall Christ maintain,
Nor hope, nor charity shall want,
Whose faith's implicit from the font.

914

PARABLE L

Leaving all for Christ

IT happen'd, as they went along,
A certain man from out the throng
Cry'd, 'Lord, I will thy steps attend,
Where'er your painful course you bend.'
And Jesus said, 'Without an home,
Forlorn the Son of Man must roam,
Though foxes are of holes possess'd,
And ev'ry bird has got his nest.'
And to another Jesus said,
'Come, follow me.' But he delay'd,
And cry'd, 'Lord, suffer me to go
And first my father's corse bestow.'
But Jesus, 'Leave the conduct free
Of dead men for the dead to me:
But thou the living God maintain,
And preach Christ Jesus, and his reign.'
Another made an offer too,
'Thy steps, O Lord, will I pursue;
But first permit me, where I dwell,
To bid my family farewel.'
But Jesus to the man rejoin'd,
'Not they that plow, and look behind
Unto the world and its deceit,
Are subjects for Christ's kingdom meet.'

Behold, a cruel hardship here,
Most worthy of a poor man's tear!
The God Supreme of human race,
The Lord of pity, love, and grace,
Had neither dwelling-place, nor bed
To house a friend, or lay his head.
Sure, those that saw were dead indeed,
Who gave him neither help nor heed.
Observe too, when a man sets out

In Christ, he must have done with doubt,
From carnal cares divorce his soul,
And press directly for the goal.

PARABLE LI

The Leaven of the Scribes and Pharisees

TAKE heed (said Christ the Word of heav'n)
To shun the Pharisaic leav'n,
Ev'n hypocritical disguise:
For nothing's veil'd from human eyes,
Which shall not in due time be shewn,
Nor hid, but shall be fully known.
Wherefore whate'er you've spoke by night
In darkness, shall be heard in light;
And closet-whispers shall resound
Upon the house-tops all around.
And, friends, let me exhort you all,
Let not such men your hearts appall,
That can the human body kill,
Without more pow'r to evil will.
But I'll forewarn you whom to dread,
Ev'n him, who when h' has smote you dead,
Has pow'r to cast the soul in hell;
Fear him, and tremble to rebell.
Are not five sparrows brought and sold,
If ev'n two farthings be but told?
Yet is there not a single bird
By God forgot, the Life and Word.
And ev'n the very locks you wear
By God are number'd to a hair.
Fear not; your lives in God's account
The worth of sparrows far surmount.

His tenderness to human kind,
As Jesus shews, he would remind

His flock, that he has still a care
For animals in earth and air,
And those beneath the rolling tide
For all by sparrows are imply'd.
It is a most accepted thing
Before the Maker and the King,
To imitate God's goodness here.
For 'tis a truth as day-spring clear,
That brutes to kindly treat and feed
Is love to Christ in very deed.

PARABLE LII

Humility recommended

CHRIST did this parable repeat
To certain bidden to a treat,
When he remark'd each eager guest
To chuse his place out for the best.
'Invited to the bridegroom's cheer,
In his chief room do not appear,
Lest some great man of nobler race
Be bidden to the self-same place,
And he that bade thee, come and say,
To your superior, friend, give way;
And thou begin with shame to burn,
And to the lowest place return.
But when thou'rt ask'd, do not presume,
And sit thee in the meanest room,
That he who bade thee there to sup,
May call thee, friend, come higher up;
And thou shall have respect with those,
Who next to thee their seats dispose.
For whoso will himself exalt,
Shall be abas'd for his default:
But men who're mean in their own eyes,
Shall from humiliation rise.'

917

PARABLE LIII

The Necessity of Forecast

CHRIST to the multitude, that press'd
Around him, thus himself address'd,
'They that affect the gospel-life,
And hate not father, mother, wife,
With brethren, sisters, children, all
That they their property can call,
Yea, who shall not ev'n life decline
In my behalf, cannot be mine.
And who do not their cross sustain,
And follow me in woes and pain,
Cannot with my disciples band:
For which of you shall take in hand
To raise the structure of a tow'r,
And not first estimate his pow'r,
If he can with convenience spare
The cost to bring the whole to bear;
Lest, haply, after he has made
Th' attempt, and his foundation laid,
And cannot his design defray,
The people see, and mocking say,
This builder with a tow'r began,
But could not execute his plan.
Or what king, who would war declare
Against his foe, does not take care,
And sit him down and weigh the case,
If with ten thousand he can face
A king full twenty thousand strong:
Else while his armies march along,
He sends an embassage to sue
For peace, and its conditions too.
So none but who himself contents
To give up all at all events,
Can ever my disciple be—
Then mark the end, and follow me.'

PARABLE LIV

The Advent of Christ's spiritual Kingdom

CHRIST, by the Pharisaic train
Requir'd to shew them of his reign,
And at what time it should commence,
Thus answer'd their impertinence:
'That great event comes not about
By observation from without:
Lo! here, lo! there, they shall not cry,
And point it to the human eye;
For, as the Lord his grace imparts,
The heav'nly kingdom's in your hearts.'
Then said he to the twelve again,
'The time shall come when ye would fain
Behold a glorious day, like this;
But then ye shall have no such bliss.
And if, See here! See there! they say,
Attend them not or word or way.
For as in heav'n the light'ning shines
From one side to th' opposing *signs*;
So shall the SON, array'd in light,
On his own day, divinely bright,
Shine quicker than a mortal's thought,
And be by no observer caught.'

PARABLE LV

The Harvest and Labourers

AND Jesus journey'd to survey
Each town and village in his way,
And did in synagogues maintain
And preach the gospel of his reign,
And did all pain and sickness cure
Amongst the people rich and poor:

But when he saw their throngs so great,
He did the men compassionate,
As sheep that wander'd far and wide,
And had no shepherd for their guide:
Then to his followers he cries,
In truth, we have before our eyes
An harvest which does much abound,
But how few labourers are found!
Press then the Lord by pray'r and song,
(To whom both toil and fruit belong)
That he more labourers would send
With you to reap, and make an end.

REDEMPTION! how immense the plan
Which first the Lord with twelve began!
But soon he seventy men ordain'd,
Yet ordination was restrain'd
Until the Holy Ghost was sent,
When ev'ry where th' apostles went,
They bishops, priests, and deacons made;
But some deserted, some betray'd
The Lord, ev'n in the purer times,
When wond'rous grace enhanc'd their crimes.
O Lord! we pray, by thy command,
Send thou more lab'rers to thy land.
Let us not spare to spread thy name
Abroad; nor brook the mighty shame,
That the poor infidel and blind
Are still the more part of mankind.

PARABLE LVI

Perseverance in Christ encouraged

BEHOLD! I send you all away
Like sheep amongst the wolves of prey;

Then be ye like the serpents keen,
But doves, as harmless and serene.

Yet of the carnal world take heed:
For at their bars they shall implead,
And scourge you in the house of pray'r,
And to their chiefs you must repair,
And dragg'd before each earthly prince,
Both Jews and Gentiles shall convince.
But, when giv'n up to pow'r, be meek,
And take no thought what ye shall speak:
Ye shall be prompted in that day
In ev'ry thing you ought to say.
Ye speak not but as God controuls
Your spirit, working in your souls.
And brothers brethren shall forsake,
And sire his son, when life's at stake;
Children against their parents rise,
And ev'n tormenting deaths devise;
And all shall hate you, and defame,
Because you're called by my name:
But they that to the last endure,
Shall make their own salvation sure.

PARABLE LVII

Adherence to the Doctrine of Christ

THEN to them all our Saviour cries,
Beware lest you apostatize,
Or to the Pharisees ye make,
Or leav'n of Sadducees partake.
They thereupon conferr'd and said,
It is because we've took no bread.
But Christ observing them, exclaim'd,
O scant of faith, most rightly nam'd!

Why do you tax yourselves with wrong,
Because you brought no bread along?
Do sense and mem'ry fail you still,
How five loaves did five thousand fill,
And what the baskets that remain'd?
And how sev'n thousand were sustain'd
By four, who did sev'n baskets leave?
How is it, ye do not perceive,
I spake not touching daily food,
But that ye should yourselves exclude
From that same leav'n whose horrors please
The Pharisee and Sadducees.
Then by them it was clearly seen,
The leav'n of bread he did not mean,
But to the doctrine did object
As held by each dissenting sect.

PARABLE LVIII

The Stability of Christ's Church

CHRIST thus did his disciples try,
As, Who do men alledge that I,
The Son of Man, on earth am come?
Some say, John Baptist; other some,
Thou'rt Jeremias, or a seer.
'But whom to you do I appear?'
Thou'rt Christ (did Peter then declare)
The living God's immortal heir—
To him then Christ himself address'd,
Simon Bar-Jona thou art bless'd:
This flesh and blood could not unfold,
But thee my heav'nly Father told.
And unto thee again I tell,
That Peter I have nam'd thee well,
And on this rock my church shall tow'r,
'Gainst which hell gates shall have no pow'r:

And I will give to thee the keys
Of heav'n, and whatsoe'er you please
To bind on earth, in heav'n shall stand,
Or loose, be loos'd at thy command.
Then did he charge them, (as a test
How far their zeal would brook behest)
That they should not their Lord proclaim,
That he was Jesus Christ by name.
Thenceforth the Lord began to show
His foll'wers, how he needs must go,
And at Jerusalem sustain
From priests, scribes, elders, scorn and pain,
And him tho' they to death should doom,
He the third day would life resume.
But Peter took him up, and chid
His master, crying, 'God forbid!
Such things shall never thee betide.'
But turning to him, Christ reply'd,
Satan recede, and get thee hence!
For thou to me art much offence:
Thou dost to carnal things incline,
And savour'st not the things divine.

When Peter found that he was prais'd
By Christ, and o'er his brethren rais'd
In his esteem, he in that hour
Began to dream of wealth and pow'r:
For satan, at his elbow, said,
Thou of the church art sov'reign head;
And all mankind, as thou think'st fit,
Thou shalt condemn, or shalt acquit;
In costly garbs thou shalt be drest,
And feast on viands of the best;
Thou shalt from kings exact renown,
And make thyself a triple crown—
But Jesus bade the dev'l recede,
Or Peter had been Pope indeed.

923

PARABLE LIX

The Easiness of Christ's Yoke

CHRIST JESUS thus his thanks address'd
To God, 'O Father, be thou bless'd,
Thou Lord of heav'n and earth below,
Because these things thou would'st not show
To carnal men or worldly wise,
But taught to babes thy mysteries:
Ev'n so, my God, for that is right
Whate'er is seemly in thy sight.
My Father leaves to me, his Son,
All things. Nor is there any one
Can know me, saving him alone:
Nor is the Father truly known
To any man, but Christ, and those
To whom I shall his will disclose.
Come all, o'er-laden and opprest,
Come here, and I will give you rest;
Unto my yoke your necks submit,
And taught of me yourselves acquit.
My heart is lowly and resign'd,
Hence for your souls ye rest shall find:
For easy is my yoke to wear,
And light the burden ye shall bear.

Not any wretch in want and woe
Bears half what Christ must undergo
In pain and anguish for his soul:
So all our suff'rings, on the whole,
Are light, and easy, if compar'd
With what the Lord himself has shar'd;
Or glory, which shall be reveal'd
To such as God, through Christ, has seal'd.
Observe too—that the Lord gives praise,
That truth her intellectual rays,
Beam'd on the simple, were deny'd

To wit and philosophic pride.
The more unlikely are the means,
Whene'er God's prowess intervenes,
To bless and strengthen human race,
The more the marvel and the grace.

PARABLE LX

The Sign of the Prophet Jonas

THE Scribes and Pharisees, to thwart
Our Saviour Christ, did this retort,
We would a sign from thee behold:
But he the wilful atheists told,
'A wicked and adult'rous seed,
Require a sign, but shall not speed,
Except in that which Jonas writes.
For as that seer three days and nights
In the whale's belly did reside,
So shall the Son of Man abide
In earth's recess an equal space.
Ev'n Nineveh's rebellious race
Shall try this people at the last,
And on fair evidence shall cast.
They turn'd their hearts, by Jonas warn'd,
But you've a greater prophet scorn'd.
The queen from forth the south shall rise,
And cast this nation when she tries,
Which did from farthest earth appear,
The lore of Solomon to hear:
But, lo! the man ye will not heed,
Is greater far in word and deed.'

In public, and before the sun,
Ten thousand miracles were done
Each day by Jesus Christ, to cure
925

The pains and ailments of the poor:
Yet Scribes and Pharisees must join
To tempt our Lord, and ask a sign.
They saw his works: but his discourse,
These works were mighty to inforce,
They heard not, or broke off by hate,
By sneer, by question, and debate.

PARABLE LXI

Spiritual Affinity

WHILE yet the people he detain'd,
As he his blessed will explain'd,
Behold, his mother stood apart,
And brethren, who had set their heart
A joint-petition to declare,
Which was to speak with Jesus there.
Then certain did the Lord remind,
Behold, thy mother stands behind,
And brethren, something have to say.
But he th' informer kept at bay,
And ask'd, 'My mother, who is she,
And brethren in the first degree?'
And then his blessed hands he spread
To his disciples, and he said,
'My mother and my brethren view;
For who my Father's will shall do,
Are mothers, brethren, sisters, all
That truth and tenderness can call.'

Connections form'd with God above,
Are not by carnal claims, but love,
And to the Lord, through goodness, dear
Saints soul to soul in heav'n adhere.

PARABLE LXII

The Woman of Canaan

WHEN Jesus did from thence depart
To Tyre, and that Sidonian mart,
Behold, a Canaanitish dame
From the same coasts directly came,
'O Lord, thou son (it is most sure)
Of David, father of the poor,
Thy mercies on my daughter show'r,
Now in the fiend's vexatious pow'r.'
But he reply'd not to her speech.
Then did the twelve the Lord beseech,
Dispatch that woman to her own,
For after us she makes her moan.
I am not sent, he answ'ring said,
But to the sheep from Israel stray'd.
Then fell she meekly at his feet,
'Lord Jesus! help me, I intreat.'
But he return'd, 'It is too dread
To give the dogs the children's bread.'
And she again, ''Tis true, O Lord;
But then ev'n dogs have their reward,
Which is the scraps and crumbs of all
That from their master's table fall.'
Then Jesus in conclusion saith,
'O woman, mighty is thy faith!
Thy suit is heard.'—And it befell,
That at the word the maid was well.

Our Lord's original intent
Was for the Jews salvation meant,
The first fruits of his wond'rous plan,
Then all the nations, man by man,
But Abr'ham's seed, the good and great,
Had satan made adulterate,

To thwart the Lord's peculiar grace,
And introduce the heathen race.
This Jesus grudg'd in a degree,
In zeal for tribe and family:
But ·yet determining for good,
He in this case the fiend withstood.
Observe we here the woman's praise,
So humbly apposite of phrase,
Our end we gain, and wrath defeat,
When once our answers are discrete.

PARABLE LXIII

The two Sons of Zebedee

THE spouse of Zebedee, that bare
The sons of Thunder, made a pray'r,
As she to Christ adoring came;
And Jesus said, What would the dame?
'Grant me, O Lord, that either son
Be with thee in thy kingdom; one
Upon thy right hand to appear,
The other on the left as near.'
But Jesus answer'd their desire,
'Ye know not what ye would require.
Do ye yourselves of strength believe
The cup I drink of to receive?
And in that baptism be baptiz'd,
Which is for Christ himself devis'd?'
O Lord, we do, they answer make.
'Ye shall indeed my cup partake,
Be baptiz'd in my baptism too;
But 'tis not of my gifts to you,
On right or left to place, but theirs
For whom my heav'nly Sire prepares.'
But when this thing was told the ten,

They were enrag'd at both the men:
But Jesus call'd them all, and said,
'Ye know the Gentiles chuse a HEAD,
And that great prince that holds the reins,
Will plead a merit for his pains:
But with you it shall not be so;
Who would be great, he shall be low,
And he th' aspiring chief of all
A lord at ev'ry servant's call.
'Tis with the Son of Man the same,
To serve, and not be serv'd, he came;
A minister of no esteem,
Which dies the myriads to redeem.'

When Christ the multitudes had fed
With God's good fishes and his bread,
At once so great was his renown,
The people proffer'd him a crown,
From which in haste the Lord withdrew
To better points he had in view.
Christians must honour and obey
Such men as bear the sov'reign sway:
But, in respect of each to each,
The Lord and his apostles teach,
That we should neither load nor bind,
But be distributive and kind.

PARABLE LXIV

The Head-Stone in the Corner

THE Lord did thus bespeak the throng,
'Have ye not read in David's song?
What scoffing builders could disown
Is of the church the corner-stone,
The work of God, supremely wise,

And is stupendous in our eyes.
Therefore I to you all aver,
God shall his heav'nly reign transfer
To nations that shall grow in grace,
And rend it from the Jewish race:
And whoso on that stone shall dare
To fall, he shall be broken there;
But on the man that stone shall fall,
'Twill grind him as the powder small.'

The rebel Jews, perverse of will,
New plans of faith projecting still,
Deny'd the very law they read,
And brought tradition in its stead:
Thus did they spurn the corner-stone,
And laid foundations of their own.
Now Christ has built the church in pow'r
At once her basis and her tow'r;
And who shall stumble in offence,
Though with a plea of innocence,
Must seek to pray'r, must weep apart
In broken and a contrite heart.
But sins of an enormous cry
Force Christ in vengeance from on high;
But mercy glories to adjourn,
And bear affront, and wait a turn.

PARABLE LXV

Tribute payable to Cæsar

THE Pharisees did council take,
How they might trap him, as he spake;
And to the Lord their sect'ries sent,
With Herod's crew, to that intent,
Who said, 'We know that thou art true,
And teachest us God's work to do

In truth, nor dost thou stand in fear
Of any man, or rank revere;
We, therefore, would that thou declare
What is thy thought in this affair,
Is it a lawful thing to pay
To Cæsar tribute or gain—say?'
But Christ their craft did instant see;
'Ye hypocrites, why tempt ye me?
Let me the tribute-money view.'
A penny to the Lord they shew—
'Whose superscription and whose head
Is on this piece of coin? he said.'
They answer, It is Cæsar's face
And title. Then the Prince of grace,
'To Cæsar Cæsar's things assign,
And to the Deity divine.'

PARABLE LXVI

The Woman and her seven Brethren

THEN came the Sadducees, whose sect
The resurrection reject,
And ask'd him, 'Moses has decreed,
If a man die and leave no seed,
His brother then his wife must wed,
And raise up issue in his stead.
Now with us from one father rose
Sev'n brethren: and the eldest chose
A wife, whom childless he resign'd,
And to his brother left behind;
This to the second, and the third,
Ev'n to the seventh man occurr'd.
The woman likewise died at last.
Now, at the trump's reviving blast,
Which with the woman shall be bless'd?

For of all sev'n she was possess'd.'
Christ answer'd, 'Ye have all mistook,
Blind to God's pow'r and to his book.
For when again they shall arise,
They do exchange no marriage-ties,
And are in such a state of bliss
As angels. But, to clear up this,
Have ye not read what was imply'd
When thus the great Jehovah cry'd,
I am the God of Abraham's seed,
The God of Isaac bound and freed,
The God of Jacob still alive,
For death in him all souls survive.'

PARABLE LXVII

The Hypocrisy of the Scribes and Pharisees—The straining out a Gnat—The white Sepulchres—The Hen gathering her Chickens, &c.

WOE to the Pharisaic pride,
And woe dissembling Scribes betide!
For ye shut up God's heav'nly grace,
And such as would Christ's reign embrace,
Ye not permit to enter in,
Nor will yourselves the work begin.
Woe to the Pharisaic pride,
And woe dissembling Scribes betide!
For widows houses ye devour,
And make long pray'rs, pretending pow'r,
For which ye, therefore, shall receive
The sentence that has no reprieve.
Woe to the Pharisaic pride,
And woe dissembling Scribes betide!
For over sea and land ye stray
To make one proselyte your prey,

And he becomes by twofold more
Hell's child, than you yourselves before.
Woe be to you, ye leaders blind,
That say, whoe'er himself shall bind
Ev'n by God's temple, 'twill not hold:
But whoso swears him by the gold,
That gilds the temple, he must rue.
Ye fools and blind! for of the two,
Which has it, gold? or God's own home
That sanctifies the gilded dome?
And by the altar who shall swear,
Does nothing, but the off'ring there
Who shall adjure, his oaths remain.
Ye fools and blind! which of the twain
Is great, what for acceptance lies,
Or what receives and sanctifies?
Who then adjure the altar dares,
By that and all thereon he swears;
And who attests the church, attest
Both that and him that's in it blest;
And whoso swear by heav'n, imply
God's throne and Him that sits on high.
Woe to the Pharisaic pride,
And woe dissembling Scribes betide!
For tithe of anise, mint, ye pay,
And cummin, but ye do not weigh
The greater points God's laws propose,
As judgment, mercy, faith—all those
Ye should have honour'd every one,
Nor your own trifles left undone.
Blind teachers! that the gnat strain out,
And gorge the camel without doubt.
Woe to the Pharisaic pride,
And woe dissembling Scribes betide!
For ye make clean th' exterior part
Of cup and plate with care and art,
Which yet contain, o'er-charg'd within,

Exaction and excess of sin.
Blind Pharisee! first make thou clean
What in the cup and plate are seen,
And so thou shalt of course provide
To purify the outward side.
Woe to the Pharisaic pride,
And woe dissembling Scribes betide!
For whited tombs your lives be like,
Whose form and gloss th' observer strike:
But inwardly with filth are fraught,
With dead men's bones, and all things naught.
Ev'n so you outwardly appear
To men as righteous and sincere:
Yet your false hearts belye your smile,
Full of hypocrisy and guile.
Woe to the Pharisaic pride,
And woe dissembling Scribes betide!
Because the prophets vaults ye paint,
And deck the graves of ev'ry saint:
And living in your fathers time,
Ye cry, ye had not known their crime,
Nor been in prophets blood imbru'd;
Wherefore ye of yourselves conclude,
That you're the seed of murd'rers base:
Fill up the measure of your race.
Ye serpents! vipers! one and all!
How shall ye 'scape a second fall?
Wherefore, behold! I send you down
Seers, prophets, scholars of renown,
And ye shall murder some, and some
Shall nail on crosses, when they come,
Some shall in synagogues be scourg'd:
So that against you may be urg'd
The blood of all men shed on earth,
That boasted any plea of worth,
Ev'n from the cry of Abel's veins
To holy Zachary's remains,

'Twixt fane and altar who expir'd,
All of this race shall be requir'd.
   O Salem! Salem! whose fell rage
Assassins each prophetic sage,
And stones God's servants from on high
Sent for thy peace! How oft would I
Have gather'd all thy race again,
Ev'n as th' officious hen is fain
Beneath her wings her brood to call?
But ye would not attend at all.
Behold! your house is left forlorn:
For of this truth your tribes I warn.
Me shall ye see again no more,
'Till ye shall say, as ye adore,
'All benediction, and all fame
On him that comes in Christ his name!'

PARABLE LXVIII

The Ax laid to the Root of the Tree—The Lord's Fan

JOHN thus the multitudes appriz'd
That came of him to be baptiz'd,
O race of vipers! who is he
That warns you future wrath to flee?
Bring fruit that's for repentance meet,
And do not thus each other greet,
'We from the patriarch Abraham came.'
For this I to you all proclaim,
That God from forth these stones ashore
Can seed to Abraham restore.
And now the ax, so oft defy'd,
Is to the trees their root apply'd;
And that on which no fruit is found,
Is fell'd and burnt upon the ground.

What means, these terrors to avoid,
(The people ask'd) must be employ'd?
He says, Two garments do you wear,
Give one away to him that's bare;
Let him too that abounds with food,
Be thus distributive and good.
Then also to the baptism go
The publicans, and pray to know,
What, master, would you have us do?
'Exact no more than is your due.'
The soldiers too would understand,
How they should honour his command?
He said, 'All violence refuse,
Nor falsely any man accuse,
And be contented with your pay.'
Now all th' expecting people stay,
And reason in their hearts, if John
Be Christ?—he answ'ring thereupon
To all in general replies,
With water I indeed baptize,
But one, far mightier than I,
Comes after me, and now is nigh,
The latchet of whose blessed shoes
I am not worthy to unloose;
He shall baptize your inward parts,
Whose ghostly pow'r shall purge your hearts:
In whose right hand the fan is seen,
And he his threshing-floor will clean,
In barns collect the wheat intire,
And burn the chaff with ceaseless fire.

PARABLE LXIX

The Temple of the Lord's Body

WHEN Christ had purg'd his house of sin,
And those that sold and bought therein,

The Jews requir'd a sign to see
To warrant his authority.
'Lay (says the Lord) this temple waste,
In three days it shall be replac'd.'
'Twas six and forty years, they cry,
Ere this house rear'd its head so high;
Shall three days cause the like event?
But he his blessed body meant.

The Lord did usually refuse
Such satisfaction to the Jews:
Nor is there any sign, ev'n here,
But that of Jonas, it is clear.
Yet from this place th' accusers built
Their hopes to tax the Lord with guilt,
Because they knew nor word, nor cause,
Nor what he spake, nor who he was.

PARABLE LXX

The Second Birth

THERE was a man of high degree
Amongst the Jews, a Pharisee,
The same to Jesus Christ repair'd
By night, and thus his mind declar'd:
Rabbi, we perfectly descry,
That thou'rt a teacher from on high;
For no man can so far transcend,
Unless his God his deeds attend.
To him Christ Jesus made reply,
In deed, in very deed, say I,
Except a man be born again,
He sees not Jesus in his reign.
Then Nicodemus, In what sense
Can man in age new birth commence!

Can he return him to the womb,
And there his childhood re-assume?
Then Jesus thus th' objecter press'd,
'Tis truth, the very truth profess'd,
No man can Christ in pow'r confront,
But by the spirit and the font:
Then marvel not that I maintain,
Ye must indeed be born again.
Where the wind listeth it can blow,
Thou hearst the sound, but dost not know
Whence comes it, or what point to touch;
Men in the spirit born are such.
Then said the ruler, still in doubt,
How can these myst'ries be made out?
Then Christ, Art thou a master here
To whom these things do not appear?
In truth, in very truth direct,
We plainly speak from intellect,
And still bear witness from our eyes,
And ye our evidence despise.
If earthly things ye not receive
At telling, how will you believe
If heav'nly things should be display'd?
For no man heav'n's ascent has made,
But He, the Son of man, profess'd,
That came from heav'n of heav'n possess'd.
For in the desart, as appear'd,
The serpent Jethro's son had rear'd:
Ev'n in such wise, on such a plan,
They shall lift up the Son of man,
That whosoe'er their hearts ally
To him, thro' faith, may never die,
But be to endless life consign'd.
For God so greatly lov'd mankind,
That he gave up his Son and heir,
That whoso plac'd affiance there,
Should not in jeopardy be cast,

But be to life eternal pass'd.
For God did not his Son degrade,
That all men should be convicts made,
But that they should thro' him be sav'd,
For he has condemnation stav'd,
Whoe'er on him their trust repose:
But condemnation waits on those
Already, who deny the name
Of God's begotten Son that came.
And this is guilt, because the light
Illum'd the world divinely bright;
But men did rather love their gloom
Thro' evil deeds in dread of doom.
For men, whose ways are all unclean,
Hate light, nor chuse they to be seen,
Lest their foul deeds should be reprov'd:
But he, that did as best behov'd,
Seeks light, to have his workings known,
That they were done in God alone.

PARABLE LXXI

The Woman of Samaria

CHRIST in a certain town remains,
Call'd Sichar, in Samaria's plains,
Near to that spot, the patriarch bless'd
For Joseph, in his will express'd.
Now Jacob's well was where he went,
And Jesus, with his journey spent,
Sat down at ease upon the brink
(The hour was then the sixth) to drink;
When from Samaria thither came
A woman—Christ address'd the dame,
'Give me to drink.' (For his co-mates
For meat had sought the city-gates.)

How comes it, Sir, to pass, said she,
That you should ask to drink of me,
A woman of Samaria's place,
And thou a man of Jewish race?
For with Samaritans the Jews
All kind of intercourse refuse.
Then Christ, 'Didst thou but understand
God's gift, and him that asks thy hand,
Thou'dst offer'd of thine own accord,
And hadst receiv'd for thy reward
From life's eternal well a draught.'
Sir, says the woman, thou hast nought
Wherewith to draw, and deep the spring,
Whence living water canst thou bring?
Canst thou afford more pow'rful aid
Than father Jacob, he that made
This well, whence for himself he drew,
His children, and his cattle too?
Then Christ, 'Who to this water makes,
Shall thirst again; but whoso takes
The quick'ning water that I give,
Shall never thirst, but ever live.
For what I give to him in peace
Shall be life's well-spring not to cease.'
Lord, with this water me suffice
That I nor thirst nor draw, she cries.
Says Christ, 'Go call thy husband here,
And with him at this place appear.'
No husband in the world have I—
'I have no husband, is no lie.
I have no husband, is well said:
For five thou hadst; but art not wed
Unto the man you now receive.'
Sir, thou'rt a prophet, I believe.
Our fathers worshipp'd in this mount:
But in respect to your account,
Jerusalem's the place of pray'r,

And we should only worship there.
The Lord returns, 'You may rely,
O woman, that the hour is nigh,
When neither here, as heretofore,
Nor there you shall your God adore.
Ye worship that ye do not know:
But with the Jews it is not so,
From where salvation comes in pow'r.
For now arrives the very hour,
When faithful men, divinely meek,
In spirit and in truth shall seek
The Father; 'tis the Father's will,
That such their homage should fulfill.
God is a Spirit, we confess,
In truth and spirit must we bless.'
The woman answers, I am clear,
Messias, call'd the Christ, is near,
Whose coming all things shall explain.
Then said the Lord to her again,
'I that speak with thee am the Man.'
At which forthwith the woman ran,
Without her water-pot, and calls
Unto the men within the walls,
Come, see the Man, that did the tale
Of all my life at once unveil;
Is not this Christ himself indeed?
Then went the citizens with speed.
But mean time his disciples pray'd,
And urging, Master, eat, they said.
But he return'd unto their pray'r,
'Eat must I when you're not aware.'
Then 'mongst themselves they ask'd, and
    sought,
Has any man some victuals brought?
'My meat, he cries, is to fulfill
My Father's word, and do his will,
Do ye not say, four months remain,

And then arrives the time for grain:
Behold! I say, lift up your eyes,
And look up to the crops that rise,
Which stand upon the fields around,
Already whit'ning all the ground,
And he that reaps shall earn his hire,
And life's eternal fruit acquire.
That they that sow, and they that reap,
With joy one harvest-home may keep:
And herein a true proverb's shown,
One reaps what was by others sown.
I sent you to be reapers there
Of that, in which ye took no care:
Their labour other men bestow'd,
And you upon the spoil abode.'

   And many of Samaria's race
Believed on the Prince of Grace,
For that the woman said, 'The tale
Of all my life he did unveil.'
So when the city came to greet
The Lord, they did his stay intreat;
And two days did he there abide:
And many persons more beside
Believ'd through faith in his own word,
And with the woman thus conferr'd,
'Now we believe that he is true,
Not for the words he spake to you;
For we have heard him with our ears,
And to us all the truth appears;
And in his words and deeds we find
The Christ and Saviour of mankind.'

PARABLE LXXII

The Bread of God

WHEN the great concourse, newly fed,
Beyond sea to Christ Jesus sped,
Rabbi, how cam'st thou here? they cry'd;
Then to them all the Lord reply'd,
'In very truth the Lord ye sought,
Not for the miracles he wrought,
But for the loaves, your ample treat,
When rank'd upon the grassy seat.
Toil not for perishable food,
But that which is a lasting good,
Which Christ unto you all shall deal,
For him did God the Father seal.'
What must we do, and what decline,
(They say) to work the works divine?
Christ answer'd, 'This shall God content,
That ye believe in Him he sent.'
They say, What sign then do'st thou shew,
That we may see? What do'st thou do?
Our fathers in the desert waste
Did of celestial manna taste,
According to the word express,
He gave them bread from heav'n to bless.
'In very truth (the Lord pursu'd)
'Twas Moses gave you heav'nly food;
But God my Father in his love
Gives truer bread from heav'n above:
For God's good bread that feeds the heart,
Is He that could from heav'n depart
To quicken a lost world.'—They cry,
Lord, evermore this bread supply.
'I am the bread (the Lord repeats)
Of life. Whoever me intreats,
Shall never know fierce hunger's pain,
Nor can the faithful thirst again.

But I have told you, ye have view'd,
Yet not believ'd the things I shew'd.
I came to do and to enjoin
My Father's pleasure, and not mine.
And this is his great will at large
Which sent me, That of all my charge
I should have nothing cast away,
But raise it at the latter day:
And thus too shall his will be done,
That ev'ry man that sees the Son,
And owns him, wins th' immortal prize,
And at my judgment shall he rise.'
The Jews then murmur'd one and all,
That he himself the bread should call
That came from heav'n. And is he not
The son the carpenter begot,
Joseph by family and name?
How is it that from heav'n he came?
To them then did the Lord retort,
'Do not yourselves by murmurs thwart.
No mortal can embrace my cause,
Save whom th' Almighty Father draws,
And I will raise him in the end.
It thus is in the prophets penn'd,
And they shall all of God be taught.
Each man then that has *heard* in *thought*,
And has internal eyes to see,
Will by my Father come to me.
Not that there's any man can view
The Father, save the faithful few
That are of Him, they see indeed.
In truth, in very truth, his creed,
Who trusts in me, secures his bliss :
I am the bread of life for *this*.
Your sires eat manna, and are dead:
This is the true celestial bread,
That a man eat, and never die:

I am such nurture from the sky:
Whoe'er shall live on this repast,
His life shall through all ages last.
My flesh I give, the bread of grace,
To save for life all human race.'
The Jews then 'mongst themselves did strive,
How can we eat this man alive?
'In very truth (says Christ afresh)
Unless you eat your Saviour's flesh,
And drink his blood, ye have no lives.
Who then shall eat and drink revives:
For him I finally will raise,
Since meat for grace and drink for praise
My flesh and blood sincerely be.
Who thus shall fare, must dwell in me,
And I in him. With such intent
As me the living Father sent,
And I by him exist; ev'n so
Who eat me in my grace shall grow.
This is that bread from heav'n supply'd,
Not what your fathers eat, and died:
For he that of this bread shall feed,
Must live for ever in his deed.'

PARABLE LXXIII

Many Mansions in God's House

LET not your hearts be sunk with grief:
In God you rested your belief:
Believe likewise in me. Above
In God's great house of peace and love
Are many rooms for souls inspher'd;
If 'twere not so, ye should have heard.
I go your mansions to prepare;
And if I find you places there,

945

I will come after my decease,
And take you to myself in peace:
And where I am about to go,
And how to follow me, ye know.
Lord, (Thomas saith) thou doest not say,
Where goest thou, can we know the way?
To him then Jesus made reply,
'The way, the truth, the life am I:
None but by me can have access
Unto my Father's happiness.
Of me, had your conceits been true,
You would have known my Father too:
But henceforth ye shall have the grace
To know and see him face to face.'

[Though the following Passages of the New Testament be not Parables, yet as they are altogether per-
tinent to our present Design, we have not scrupled to
insert them.]

CHRIST disputing amongst the Doctors

Now when the Lord was twelve years old,
The customary feast to hold,
His parents to the city went;
And when the festal days were spent,
The child, as they went home again,
Did at Jerusalem remain.
But this they did not understand,
And rather thought he was at hand
Amongst the trav'lers by the way:
They therefore journey'd for a day,
And of each neighbour and each friend,
When they had sought him to no end,

They to the city turn'd about
Determining to find him out;
And this was the event at last,
That, after full three days were past,
Him in the temple plac'd they found
With learned doctors all around,
Whom he did hear by turns debate,
And from his seat interrogate:
And all admir'd a child so wise,
Struck with his reas'ning and replies.
And when his parents came in view,
They were in great amazement too.
And Mary said unto him, Son,
What is this thing that thou hast done?
Behold, thy father here, with me,
Has sought thee in anxiety.
And he, 'What is it that you sought?
Had ye not yet so much of thought,
That I must needs with care pursue
The work my Father bids me do?'

CHRIST to the church did first repair,
And open'd his commission there;
Before the elders of the Jews
The tendency of grace he shews,
And with their best divines conferr'd
About the beauty of his WORD.
Mean time in vain his earthly sire
And mother after him inquire:
For his great work he must begin,
Promulge the GOSPEL, *silence sin,*
With all his heart and mind ABOVE,
And all his labour that of LOVE.

The Disciples pluck the Ears of Corn on the Sabbath-day

CHRIST JESUS on a certain morn
Went through a field of standing corn;
This happen'd on the Sabbath-day,
And his disciples on the way
Were hungry, and began to eat
From the rubb'd ears the ripen'd wheat.
The Pharisees, when this they saw,
Said, thy disciples break the law,
And on the Sabbath act amiss;
But he his answer made to this,
'What, have ye never read the place,
How David did in such a case,
As he was hungry, with the band,
That then was under his command,
How to the house of God he sped,
And from the altar took the bread,
That bread not ever lawful known
To eat but for the priests alone?
Or have ye not read this at least,
That in the temple every priest
May still the Sabbath-day profane,
And yet in innocence remain?
But to you all it shall appear,
One greater than the temple's here.
And had ye known what this implies,
I mercy choose, not sacrifice,
Ye had been tempted to relent,
And not condemn'd the innocent:
For, know, the Son of Man bears sway
Ev'n sov'reign of the Sabbath-day.'

Pilate and the Galileans

AND some in company relate
Th' unhappy Galileans fate,
Whose mingled off'rings Pilate burn'd
With their own blood.—The Lord return'd,
'Think ye, they sinn'd in a degree
Beyond all men of Galilee,
That they were doom'd to undergo
Such cruelties? I tell you, No.
But if you do not soon repent,
Ye all shall share a like event.
Or those eighteen on whom there rush'd
Siloam's falling tow'r and crush'd,
Think ye, they did the crimes outweigh
Of all the Jews? I tell you, nay,
But if ye do not soon repent,
Ye all shall share a like event.'

Men never God's resentment feel
More fierce, than when they dare to deal
In judgments. 'Tis the Lord alone,
By whom all circumstance is known:
How force impells, how treach'ry lurks,
How wrath, and how temptation works;
How fiends approach, when grace withdraws,
What boldness, or abashment cause;
How wealth puffs up, how hardships drive,
How worldlings punish, or connive.
Then inward turn thy conscious eyes,
And self-condemn'd, be meek and wise.

Christ delivereth the Woman taken in Adultery

CHRIST to the mount of olives fled,
And early in the morning sped

Back to the temple yet again,
And all the folk, a numerous train,
Did to his residence repair,
And he sat down and taught them there.
Then came the Pharisaic band,
And Scriv'ners, having in their hand
A woman in adult'ry found,
And shewing her the Lord, they sound,
'Lord, this is an adult'ress base,
And far too evident the case.
Now Moses, that we might atone
For such, commanded us to stone:
But what say'st thou?'—The wily Jews
Thus press'd him, that they might accuse.
But Jesus stoop'd upon the spot,
And with his finger something wrote,
Making as though he nothing heard:
So when they ask'd, and persever'd,
Recov'ring of himself, said he,
Whoso from carnal vice is free
Amongst you all, let him begin
To stone this woman for her sin.
And then again, his body bent,
He wrote upon the ground intent.
This when the multitude had heard,
(Not one by his own conscience clear'd)
Sneak'd man by man from Christ and truth,
Ev'n from the eldest to the youth:
So that they left the Prince of Grace,
And woman standing in the place.
When Jesus then himself anew
Had rais'd with nothing in his view,
Except the woman, he inquir'd,
'Woman, where are thy foes retir'd?
Art thou by none a convict made?'
Lord, not by any one, she said.
Then answ'ring her again, said he,

'Thou art no convict made by me:
The Lord most merciful adore,
And go thy ways, and sin no more.'

The Story of Zaccheus

THROUGH Jericho as Jesus came
A man (Zaccheus was his name)
Chief of the Publicans for gold
And pow'r, sought Jesus to behold;
But could not for the press his eyes
Indulge by reason of his size.
He therefore hasty ran before,
And climb'd upon a sycamore,
That he his passing Lord might see,
Who when he came beside the tree,
Look'd up, and saw him o'er his head,
'Zaccheus, haste, come down, he said;
For in thy house this very day
Thy Lord has purposed to stay.'
He therefore coming down in haste,
With joy his holy Guest embrac'd:
Which when observ'd by all the rest,
They murmur'd, that he went a guest
With one so much immers'd in sin.
Mean time Zaccheus stood within,
And said unto the Lord, 'Behold,
The half of my ill-gotten gold
I give the poor; and if by theft,
Or falshood, any I've bereft,
Four-fold the same I will replace.'
Then answer'd Jesus, This day grace
Is come upon this house; for he
Is also Abraham's progeny.

Praise-worthy in a high degree
Is godly curiosity;
To search the Lord, above, around,
If haply he may yet be found.
Short-sighted reason, dwarf desire,
Are faith and zeal when lifted high'r.
Then on the Tree of Life sublime
With hands and knees devoutly climb;
Catch mercy's moments as they fly,
Behold! the Lord is passing by.

The poor Widow commended

CHRIST saw some men of wealth and rank
Throw money in the public bank,
And saw a needy widow'd dame
Cast in two mites into the same:
He then this observation made,
And unto those around he said,
'This widow, needy and oppress'd,
Has done far more than all the rest.
For these from their abundance deal
To God and to the common-weal:
But she from an impoverish'd lot,
Has cast in all that she had got.'

Much is requir'd, where much is giv'n,
And in proportion as they've thriv'n,
Men should the Lord with wealth adore.
But when from a contracted store
You by small means attain great ends,
Then virtue tow'rs, and grace transcends.

952

The Transfiguration

CHRIST JESUS on a certain day
Upon a mountain went to pray,
Commanding Peter to be there,
And John and James to join in pray'r:
When, lo! the fashion of his face
Was alter'd through exceeding grace,
And all his garments glist'ring white
By far outshone the morning-light:
And, lo! two men talk'd with them there,
Which Moses and Elias were,
Who came in glory from their peace,
And spake to him of his decease,
To happen in a certain space,
And nam'd Jerusalem the place.
Peter mean time and th' other twain
Slept sound, and when they woke again,
The bright appearance that he made,
And two men with him they survey'd:
Now haply as they went away,
The elder saint began to say,
'Lord, it is pleasant to abide,
And in this place let us provide
Three tabernacles for the three,
Elias, Amram's son, and thee.'
This spake he on that great event,
Not understanding what he meant.
A cloud descended over-head,
And cover'd them, as this he said;
And now their hearts began to quake,
As in the cloud they entrance make:
And from the cloud a voice there broke,
Which thus the trembling saints bespoke,
'This is my best beloved Son,
Attend that his commands be done!'
When those disciples heard the sound,

They straight fell prostrate to the ground.
But Christ approaching to their aid,
And touching them, 'Be not afraid,
(He cry'd) 'but instantly arise.'
And when they lifted up their eyes,
No man they either see or hear,
Save Jesus only standing near:
And as the mountain's brow they leave,
From Christ they this command receive,
'This vision to no man explain,
Till Christ your Lord be ris'n again.'

Our Saviour's want, and friendless state,
Which all the race of wordlings hate,
Were one great cause the restif Jews
Did his blest ambassage refuse:
Hence ev'n the very twelve were prone
To flee and leave the Lord alone.
He therefore shew'd this glorious sight,
Transfigur'd into ghostly light,
To fortify the faith of those
Which from the chosen he had chose.
The caution giv'n, that they should hide
This vision, till their Master died
And rose again, was on this wise,
Lest envy 'mongst the nine should rise;
Or drive the Jews by crime on crime,
To cut off Christ before his time.

The fiery Disciples

Now when the time was near compleat
When Christ must re-assume his seat,
He sat his face with stedfast view
The way tow'rds Salem to pursue,

And messengers before him sent,
Who to a certain village went,
By the Samaritans possess'd,
And there provision would have dress'd,
But they deny'd the Prince of Grace,
Because towards that hated place,
Jerusalem, his course he steer'd;
Which James and John no sooner heard,
But to Christ Jesus they apply,
'Lord, shall we summon from the sky
Upon their heads consuming fire,
As did Elias in his ire?'
But Jesus turn'd, and in offence
Rebuk'd them for their vehemence,
And said, 'Ye know not, in your zeal,
What spirit wakes the wrath ye feel;
For Christ his mission's not design'd
To sacrifice, but save mankind.'

All bold opposers to consume
In the true stile of modern Rome,
These zealots were for fire and sword,
To make Christ's holy name ador'd.
But he against such zeal PROTESTS,
His peaceful sway no wrath infests;
But all his reign, and all his race,
Are truth and mercy, love and grace.

Martha reproved

Now haply in their way they came
Unto a certain village-dame,
Call'd Martha, who did entertain,
And make them in her house remain;
And with her was a sister dear,
Nam'd Mary, who was glad to hear

The word of Christ with heed discreet,
And sat obsequious at his feet.
But Martha was perplex'd with care,
Eager to serve and to prepare,
And she with her complaints drew nigh,
'Lord, dost thou not regard that I
Am left to serve alone? she said,
Bid Mary that she lend her aid.'
But, 'Martha, Martha, Christ return'd,
For many things thou art concern'd;
But one thing needful is profess'd,
And Mary's part is far the best,
Which she has chosen here this day,
And I shall never take away.'

All worldly work and carnal cares
Are little to the soul's affairs:
Laborious man would make pretence,
And challenge heav'n by diligence;
And while he's hoarding for the moth,
Thinks he shall 'scape eternal wrath.
No.—Ghostly toil and mental pain,
For blest incorruptible gain,
Are that which Christ our hope desires,
And dread necessity requires.

Our Saviour washing his Disciples Feet

FROM supper when the LORD arose,
Aside his garments he bestows,
Then with a towel girt about
His loins, he pours some water out
Into a bason, and began
To dip their feet in man by man,
And straightway with the towel dry'd,
The which his girded loins supply'd.

Then he to Simon Peter came,
Who with anxiety and shame
Cry'd out, 'Lord, do'st thou wash my feet?'
Then Christ, in condescension sweet,
'Thou know'st not what these things imply
At present, but shalt bye and bye.'
O Lord, (did Peter then rejoin)
Thou shalt not wash these feet of mine.
Christ answer'd, 'If I wash thee not,
With me thou hast no part or lot.'
Lord, not alone my feet (he said)
But wash my hands, and wash my head.
Says Christ, 'Whose feet I wash to-night,
They're pure and holy in my sight,
And for their body have no call:
Thus are ye cleansed: but not all.'
(He knew by whom he was betray'd,
And therefore this exception made.)
So after he had wash'd their feet,
And took his garments and his seat,
He then did question every one,
'Know ye how much for you is done?
Me Lord and Master ye revere,
And ye say well. The truth is clear.
If then your Lord and Master deign
To wash your feet, 'tis very plain
In likewise that ye ought to do,
And wash each man his fellow's too.
The truth, the very truth I say,
His Lord the servant must not sway,
Nor does the poor man, sent on earth,
Exceed the sender's endless worth.
If all these things ye comprehend,
You're bless'd to goodness if they tend.'

The Lord, e'er yet they drag him hence,
Did this last charity dispense,

957

Thus his Apostles feet prepare
News evangelical to bear.
But mark what time he makes his claim,
Avouching his majestic name,
Ev'n when humility was great,
And meekness, meekness at the height.
'Me Lord and Master, as ye greet,
I serve your board, and wash your feet.'
Much too for their eternal use
From hence all Christians should deduce,
That brother brother should attend
As kind assistant, guide, and friend,
To help to purge all filth away,
And every long laborious day,
To lend a hand to speed the plough,
Or shoulder to the burthen bow.
Respect the pattern set on high,
And learn of CHRIST *to live and die.*

RELIGIOUS
AND DEVOTIONAL POEMS

*Hymns
for the Amusement
of Children*

HIS ROYAL HIGHNESS PRINCE FREDERICK, BISHOP OF OSNABRUG.

H Y M N S

Lydia FOR THE *Heaton*

A M U S E M E N T

O F

C H I L D R E N.

By CHRISTOPHER SMART, M. A.

THIRD EDITION.

L O N D O N:

Printed for T. CARNAN, at Number 65,
in St. Paul's Church-yard. Price 6d.

MDCCLXXV.

TO

HIS ROYAL HIGHNESS

PRINCE FREDERICK,

BISHOP OF OSNABRUG,

THESE

H Y M N S,

COMPOSED FOR HIS AMUSEMENT,

ARE,

With all due Submission and Respect,

HUMBLY INSCRIBED TO HIM,

AS THE BEST OF BISHOPS,

BY

HIS ROYAL HIGHNESS's

Most Obedient and

Devoted Servant,

Christopher Smart.

HYMN I

Faith

I

THE Father of the Faithful said,
    At God's first calling, 'Here am I';
Let us by his example sway'd,
    Like him submit, like him reply,

II

'Go take thy son, thine only son,
    And offer him to God thy King.'
The word was giv'n: the work begun,
    'The altar pile, the victim bring.'

III

But lo! th' angelic voice above
    Bade the great Patriarch stop his hands;
'Know God is everlasting love,
    And must revoke such harsh commands.'

IV

Then let us imitate the Seer,
    And tender with compliant grace
Ourselves, our souls, and children here,
    Hereafter in a better place.

HYMN II

Hope

I

Ah! Hannah, why should'st thou despair,
  Quick to the Tabernacle speed;
There on thy knees prefer thy pray'r,
  And there thy cause to mercy plead.

II

Her pious breathings now ascend,
  As from her heart the sighs she heaves;
And angels to her suit attend,
  Till strong in hope she now conceives.

III

Then Samuel soon was brought to light
  To serve the Lord, as yet a child—
O what a heart-reviving sight!
  Sure Cherubims and Seraphs smil'd.

IV

Thus yet a child may I begin
  To serve the Lord with all my heart;
To shun the wily lures of sin,
  And claim the prize, or e'er I start.

HYMN III

Charity

I

O Queen of virtues, whose sweet pow'r
Does o'er the first perfections tow'r,
Sustaining in the arms of love,
All want below, all weal above.

II

With thee, O let my thoughts conceive,
For all the very best believe;
Predict, pronounce for all the best,
And be by bearing all things blest.

III

To suffer long, and still be kind
In holy temperance of mind,
Rejoice that truth is on my side,
As free from envy as from pride.

IV

Both tongues and prophecies shall cease,
And painful knowledge cede to peace;
And time and death o'er all prevail,
But Charity shall never fail.

V

Then guide, O Christ, this little hand,
To deal thy bounties round the land;
To clothe and feed the hungry poor,
And to the stranger ope my door.

VI

My cup of water, Christ, is free,
For all that love and thirst for thee;
With wisdom many a soul to win,
And loose the irksome bonds of sin.

VII

Make me, O Christ, tho' yet a child,
To virtue zealous, errors mild,
Profess the feelings of a man,
And be the Lord's Samaritan.

HYMN IV

Prudence

I

O BEST œconomist of life,
Tho' all the passions were at strife;
Yet thou, fair Prudence, could'st assuage
The storm, and moderate its rage.

II

With Dove and Serpent at thy call,
As caution'd by the Lord of all,
Thou art in Christ full well aware,
Of open force or secret snare.

III

To check thy thoughts divinely meek,
To weigh thy words before you speak,
To make the day's demand secure,
To be the treas'rer of the poor.

IV

All these, Prudentia, these are thine;
And God thro' Christ shall make them mine:
To do my best till life shall end,
Then on futurity depend.

HYMN V

Justice

I

O LET not fraud 'gainst me prevail,
My God, my Christ avow'd;
Which weigh'st the mountains in thy scale,
And ballancest the cloud.

II

And still peculiar on my side,
　Keep me from rigour free;
Make me forgive, in manly pride,
　All that exact on me.

III

Pay my demander more than due,
　With measure heap'd and press'd;
And rather welcome than pursue,
　My brother when distress'd.

IV

O give me sense and grace to know
　Thy will, and check my own;
In heav'n above, in earth below,
　The Lord is judge alone.

HYMN VI

Mercy

I

O SWEET—attentive to the pray'r,
Ye forward hope and stave despair;
Thro' Christ his blood divinely spill'd,
Tremendous ruin to rebuild.

II

Tho' high above the great and just,
Yet thou descendest to the dust;
Both to the sovereign and the slave,
Nor quit'st the monument and grave.

III

O let me like the righteous die;
And so I shall if thou art by!
The viol in thy hand uprears,
My Saviour's blood, my Saviour's tears.

IV

Come, Cherub, come, possess my soul,
All wrath and bitterness controul:
If thou thy charming pow'rs bestow,
I'll shew thee to my veriest foe.

HYMN VII

Temperance

I

FOR forty days the Lord abstain'd.
   (The subtle tempter near)
And greatly every bait disdain'd,
   Self-aw'd and self-severe.

II

This is the pattern that I set,
   To keep the flesh in awe:
I will not gross desires abet;
   Withdraw, foul fiend, withdraw!

III

The fiend withdrew, the Angels came,
   And worshipp'd at his feet;
'O great Jehovah, word and name
   Inestimably sweet!

IV

'How cou'd that cursed serpent dare
   Thine honour to offend?'

Says Christ, a little while forbear,
    'Tis for a glorious end.

V

O may I keep the body cool,
    By fasting on my knees;
And follow strict religion's rule,
    Those days the church decrees.

VI

Keep, keep intemp'rance far away
    'Tis duty and 'tis love;
Or how shall I my breast display,
    To nest my Saviour's dove.

HYMN VIII

Fortitude

I

STAND fast, my child, and after all,
Yet still stand fast, says holy Paul;
Thy resolution be renew'd,
For this is Christian Fortitude.

II

Repeat the Lord's own pray'r for grace,
At ev'ry hour, in ev'ry place;
Spring up from human to divine,
For strength invincible is thine.

III

Then, as the great Apostle saith,
'Bove all things take the shield of Faith,
Salvation's helm, and for thy sword,
E'en God's good Spirit and his Word.

IV

And now in dang'rous giddy youth,
Your loins begirt about with Truth;
Your feet with Gospel-peace be shod,
Your breast-plate Righteousness from God.

V

When to the ghostly fight alarm'd,
Know, soldier, thou'rt completely arm'd,
And free from terror or dismay,
March on, engage, and win the day.

HYMN IX

Moderation

I

Tho' I my party long have chose,
    And claim Christ Jesus on my side,
Yet will I not my peace oppose,
    By pique, by prejudice, or pride.

II

Blessed be God, that at the font
    My sponsors bound me to the call
Of Christ, in England, to confront
    The world, the flesh, the fiend and all.

III

And yet I will my thoughts suppress,
    And keep my tongue from censure clear;
The Jew, the Turk, the Heathen bless,
    And hold the plough and persevere.

IV

There's God in ev'ry man most sure,
    And ev'ry soul's to Christ allied:
If fears deject, if hopes allure,
    If Jesus wept, and pray'd and died.

HYMN X

Truth

I

'TIS thus the holy Scripture ends,
    'Whoever loves or makes a lie,
On heav'n's felicity depends
    In vain, for he shall surely die.'

II

The stars, the firmament, the sun,
    God's glorious work, God's great design,
All, all was finish'd as begun,
    By rule, by compass, and by line.

III

Hence David unto heav'n appeals,
  'Ye heav'ns his righteousness declare';
His signet their duration seals,
  And bids them be as firm as fair.

IV

Then give me grace, celestial Sire,
  The truth to love, the truth to tell;
Let everlasting sweets aspire,
  And filth and falshood sink to hell.

HYMN XI

Beauty. For a Damsel

I

CHRIST, keep me from the self-survey
  Of beauties all thine own;
If there is beauty, let me pray,
  And praise the Lord alone.

II

Pray—that I may the fiend withstand,
  Where'er his serpents be:
Praise—that the Lord's almighty hand
  Is manifest in me.

III

It is not so—my features are
  Much meaner than the rest;
A glow-worm cannot be a star,
  And I am plain at best.

IV

Then come, my love, thy grace impart,
    Great Saviour of mankind;
O come and purify my heart,
    And beautify my mind.

V

Then will I thy carnations nurse,
    And cherish every rose;
And empty to the poor my purse,
    Till grace to glory grows.

HYMN XII

Honesty

I

I HAVE a house, the house of prayer,
    (No spy beneath my eaves)
And purring gratitude is there,
    And he that frights the thieves.

II

If I of honesty suspend
    My judgment, making doubt,
I have a good domestic friend,
    That soon shall point it out.

III

'Tis to be faithful to my charge,
    And thankful for my place,
And pray that God my pow'rs enlarge,
    To act with greater grace.

IV

To give my brother more than due,
    In talent or in name;
Nor e'en mine enemy pursue,
    To hurt or to defame.

V

Nay more, to bless him and to pray,
    Mine anger to controul;
And give the wages of the day
    To him that hunts my soul.

HYMN XIII

Elegance

I

'Tis in the spirit that attire,
    Th' investiture of saints in heav'n.
Those robes of intellectual fire,
    Which to the great elect are giv'n.

II

'Bring out to my returning son
    The robes for elegance the best';
Thus in the height it shall be done,
    And thus the penitent be blest.

III

'Tis in the body, that sweet mien,
    Ingenuous Christians all possess,
Grace, easy motions, smiles serene,
    Clean hands and seemliness of dress.

IV

Whoever has thy charming pow'rs,
　　Is amiable as Kidron's swan,
Like holy Esdras feeds on flow'rs,
　　And lives on honey like St. John.

HYMN XIV

Loveliness

I

GOOD-nature is thy sterling name,
　　Yet loveliness is English too;
Sweet disposition, whose bright aim,
　　Is to the mark of Jesus true.

II

I've seen thee in an homely face,
　　Excel by pulchritude of mind;
To ill-form'd features give a grace,
　　Serene, benevolent and kind.

III

'Tis when the spirit is so great,
　　That it the body still controuls,
As godly inclinations meet
　　In sweet society of souls.

IV

It is that condescending air,
　　Where perfect willingness is plain,
To smile assent, to join in pray'r,
　　And urg'd a mile to go it twain.

V

To grant at once the boon preferr'd,
  By contrite foe, or needy friend;
To be obliging is the word,
  And God's good blessing is the end.

HYMN XV

Taste

I

O GUIDE my judgment and my taste,
  Sweet SPIRIT, author of the book
Of wonders, told in language chaste
  And plainness, not to be mistook.

II

O let me muse, and yet at sight
  The page admire, the page believe;
'Let there be light, and there was light,
  Let there be Paradise and Eve!'

III

Who his soul's rapture can refrain?
  At Joseph's ever-pleasing tale,
Of marvels, the prodigious train,
  To Sinai's hill from Goshen's vale.

IV

The Psalmist and proverbial Seer,
  And all the prophets sons of song,
Make all things precious, all things dear,
  And bear the brilliant word along.

976

V

O take the book from off the shelf,
    And con it meekly on thy knees;
Best panegyric on itself,
    And self-avouch'd to teach and please.

VI

Respect, adore it heart and mind.
    How greatly sweet, how sweetly grand,
Who reads the most, is most refin'd,
    And polish'd by the Master's hand.

HYMN XVI

Learning

I

COME, come with emulative strife,
To learn the way, the truth, and life,
    Which Jesus is in one;
In all sound doctrine he proceeds,
From Alpha to Omega leads,
    E'en Spirit, Sire, and Son.

II

Sure of th' exceeding great reward,
'Midst all your learning, learn the Lord—
    This was thy doctrine, Paul;
And this thy lecture should persuade,
Tho' thou hadst more of human aid,
    Than thy blest brethren all.

III

Humanity's a charming thing,
And every science of the ring,
    Good is the classic lore;

For these are helps along the road,
That leads to Zion's blest abode,
   And heav'nly muse's store.

IV

But greater still in each respect,
He that communicates direct,
   The tutor of the soul;
Who without pain, degrees or parts,
While he illuminates our hearts,
   Can teach at once the whole.

HYMN XVII

Praise

I

THO' conscience void of all offence,
   Is man's divinest praise,
A godly heart-felt innocence,
Which does at first by grace commence,
   By supplication stays:

II

Yet I do love my brother's laud,
   In each attempt to please;
O may he frequently applaud,
'Good child, thou soon shalt go abroad,
   Or have such things as these.—

III

'This silver coin'd by sweet queen Anne,
   This nosegay and these toys,
Thou this gilt Testament shalt scan,
This pictur'd Hymn-book on a plan,
   To make good girls and boys.'

IV

O may they give before I ask,
    Suggest before desire,
While in the summer-house I bask,
The little lab'rer at his task
    Is worthy of his hire.

HYMN XVIII

Prayer

I

PRAY without ceasing (says the Saint)
Nor ever in the spirit faint;
With grace the bloom, and faith the root,
The pray'r shall bring eternal fruit.

II

When the great Seer sad news did bring
To Ahab, e'en that wicked king!
Hear what the word of mercy says,
Spare thou the man, 'behold he prays'.

III

Our hopes Christ Jesus to elate,
Has bid us be importunate,
And with the bustling widow vie,
That triumph'd over tyranny.

IV

'Tis peace, 'tis dignity, 'tis ease,
To bless the Lord upon our knees;
The voice and attitude of fear,
For God's own eye, for God's own ear.

V

Christ Jesus, when the Twelve besought
His aid, the PATER NOSTER taught;
By giving glory we begin,
And end in deprecating sin.

VI

Then give the glory yet again,
For who wou'd be in grief or pain,
Or brook anxiety and care,
When the quick remedy is pray'r.

HYMN XIX

Patience

I

BY sin and Satan un-intic't,
JOB, type of our Emanuel Christ,
With all the gems he had in store,
None half so bright as Patience wore.

II

Job, son of Issachar, at length
Proves Patience is the child of Strength;
Yet Jesus could new pow'rs create,
And e'en in weakness made her great.

III

Long-suff'ring God, whose goodness can
Bear with and bless provoking man;
Let us, like thee, attempt our parts,
And 'gainst false brethren arm our hearts.

IV

Teach us in sickness to adore
Thine hand, and all our ills restore:
Or let us meditate in death,
On Thee—poor man of NAZARETH.

V

Teach me in poverty to think
Of him who drank on Cedron's brink;
But had nor mansion-house nor bread,
Or to repose him or be fed.

VI

Teach me 'midst all the griefs below,
This transient state, this world of woe,
Submissive on my bended knee,
To take my cross and follow Thee.

HYMN XX

Watching

I

At every tempter's first essay,
Be sure to watch, be sure to pray;
For this great requisite the Lord
Has strongly urg'd upon record.

II

Yea this he strongly urg'd to all,
A warning common as his call;
Then who can his behest revere,
And not obey in heed and fear.

III

Had the good man been on his guard,
His doors and windows duly barr'd,
He wou'd not, by the Lord advis'd,
Have lost his all, and been surpriz'd.

IV

Had this command been fully weigh'd,
Peter his Lord had not betray'd;
But, spite of all his mighty boast,
He fail'd and slept upon his post.

V

Sleep not—but watch the chamber well,
By sleeping Holofernes fell;
And Jael's memorable nail
Did o'er a sleeping king prevail.

VI

'Behold, I come'—come quickly then,
Thou Saviour of the souls of men;
For pray'r and hymns are mine employ,
Who long for ever-wakeful joy.

HYMN XXI

Generosity

I

THAT vast communicative mind,
That form'd the world and human kind,
   And saw that all was right;
Or was thyself, or came from Thee,
Stupendous generosity,
   Above all lustre bright.

II

'Not for themselves the bees prepare
Their honey, and the fleecy care,
   Not for themselves are shorn:
Not for themselves the warblers build,
Not for themselves the lands are till'd,
   By them that tread the corn.'

III

The Lord shed on the Holy Rood
His infinitely gen'rous blood,
   Not for himself, but all;
Yea e'en for them that pierc'd his side,
In patient agony he died,
   To remedy the fall.

IV

O highly rais'd above the ranks
Of Angels—he cou'd e'en give thanks,
   Self-rais'd and self-renew'd—
Then who can praise, and love, and fear
Enough?—since he himself, 'tis clear,
   Is also gratitude.

HYMN XXII

Gratitude

I

I UPON the first creation
  Clap'd my wings with loud applause,
Cherub of the highest station,
  Praising, blessing, without pause.

II

I in Eden's bloomy bowers
  Was the heav'nly gardner's pride,
Sweet of sweets, and flow'r of flowers,
  With the scented tinctures dy'd.

III

Hear, ye little children, hear me,
  I am God's delightful voice;
They who sweetly still revere me,
  Still shall make the wisest choice.

IV

Hear me not like Adam trembling,
  When I walk'd in Eden's grove;
And the host of heav'n assembling,
  From the spot the traitor drove.

V

Hear me rather as the lover
  Of mankind, restor'd and free;
By the word ye shall recover
  More than that ye lost by Me.

VI

I'm the Phœnix of the fingers,
  That in upper Eden dwell;
Hearing me Euphrates lingers,
  As my wondrous tale I tell.

VII

'Tis the story of the Graces,
  Mercies without end or sum;
And the sketches and the traces
  Of ten thousand more to come.

VIII

Lift, my children, lift within you,
  Dread not ye the tempter's rod;
Christ our gratitude shall win you,
  Wean'd from earth, and led to God.

HYMN XXIII

Peace

I

THE Mount of Olives was thy seat,
  O Angel, heav'nly fair;
And thou, sweet Peace, didst often meet
  Thy Prince and Saviour there.

II

But now abroad condemn'd to roam,
  From Salem lov'd and bless'd;
A quiet conscience is thine home,
  In every faithful breast.

III

Thou didst Augustus first inspire,
  That bloody war should cease;
And to Melchisedec retire,
  The Sov'reign of our peace.

IV

O come unto the Church repair,
    And her defects review;
Of old thou plantedst olives there,
    Which to redundance grew.

V

Sustain the pillars of the state,
    Be health and wealth conjoin'd;
And in each house thy turtles mate,
    To multiply mankind.

HYMN XXIV

Melancholy

I

O PLUCK me quick the raven's quill,
    And I will set me down,
My destin'd purpose to fulfil,
But with this interrupted skill,
    Of thought and grief profound.

II

How to begin, and how depart,
    From this sad fav'rite theme,
The man of sorrow in my heart,
I at my own ideas start,
    As dread as Daniel's dream.

III

As soon as born the infant cries,
    For well his spirit knows,
A little while, and then he dies,
A little while, and down he lies,
    To take a stern repose.

IV

But man's own death is not th' event,
    For which most tears are due;
Wife, children, to the grave are sent,
Or friends to make the heart repent,
    That it such blessings knew.

V

O thou, which on the mountain's brow,
    By night didst pray alone;
In the cold night didst pay thy vow,
And in humiliation bow,
    To thrones and pow'rs thine own.

VI

Tell us, for thou the best can tell,
    What Melancholy means?
A guise in them that wear it well,
That goes to music to dispel
    Dark thoughts and gloomier scenes.

VII

Say, didst thou solitude desire
    Or wert thou driv'n away,
By rank desertion to retire,
Without or bed, or food, or fire,
    For all thy foes to pray.

VIII

Yet thou didst preach of future bliss,
    Peace permanent above,
Of truth and mercy's holy kiss,
Those joys which none that love thee miss,
    O give us grace to love.

HYMN XXV

Mirth

I

IF you are merry sing away,
    And touch the organs sweet;
This is the Lord's triumphant day,
Ye children in the gall'ries gay,
    Shout from each goodly seat.

II

It shall be May to-morrow's morn,
    A field then let us run,
And deck us in the blooming thorn,
Soon as the cock begins to warn,
    And long before the sun.

III

I give the praise to Christ alone,
    My pinks already shew;

And my streak'd roses fully blown,
The sweetness of the Lord make known,
    And to his glory grow.

IV

Ye little prattlers that repair
    For cowslips in the mead,
Of those exulting colts beware,
But blythe security is there,
    Where skipping lambkins feed.

V

With white and crimson laughs the sky,
    With birds the hedge-rows ring;
To give the praise to God most high,
And all the sulky fiends defy,
    Is a most joyful thing.

HYMN XXVI

Mutual Subjection

I

SOME think that in the Christian scheme
    Politeness has no part;
That manners we should disesteem,
    And look upon the heart.

II

The heart the Lord alone can read,
    Which left us this decree,
That men alternate take the lead
    In sweet complacency.

III

When his Disciples great dispute
    Christ Jesus reconcil'd,
He made their sharp contention mute,
    By shewing them a child.

IV

If I have got the greater share
    Of talents—I shou'd bow
To Christ, and take the greater care
    To serve and to allow.

V

This union with thy grace empow'r
    More influence to supply;
Hereafter, he that lacks this hour,
    May be as great as I.

HYMN XXVII

Good-Nature to Animals

I

THE man of Mercy (says the Seer)
    Shews mercy to his beast:
Learn not of churls to be severe,
    But house and feed at least.

II

Shall I melodious pris'ners take
    From out the linnet's nest,
And not keep busy care awake,
    To cherish ev'ry guest.

III

What shall I whip in cruel wrath
  The steed that bears me safe,
Or 'gainst the dog, who plights his troth,
  For faithful service chafe.

IV

In the deep waters throw thy bread,
  Which thou shalt find again,
With God's good interest on thy head,
  And pleasure for thy pain.

V

Let thine industrious Silk-worms reap
  Their wages to the full,
Nor let neglected Dormice sleep
  To death within thy wool.

VI

Know when the frosty weather comes,
  'Tis charity to deal
To Wren and Redbreast all thy crumbs,
  The remnant of thy meal.

VII

Tho' these some spirits think but light,
  And deem indifferent things;
Yet they are serious in the sight
  Of CHRIST, the King of kings.

HYMN XXVIII
Silence

I

BEFORE thy betters with suspence,
　　Into thyself withdraw;
Silence denotes superior sense,
　　And shews superior awe.

II

Keep blessing still within thy heart,
　　In meditation meek;
Thus thou'rt prepar'd to act thy part,
　　When urg'd at length to speak.

III

When words break forth not duly weigh'd
　　From out the babler's tongue,
Full many a mournful mischief's made,
　　Full many a conscience stung.

IV

Then pray with David, that the Lord
　　Wou'd keep himself the door;
And all things from thy lips award,
　　That make thy brother sore.

V

But if there be a point to praise
　　Some godly deed of price,
With all thy might thy plaudits raise,
　　Here silence were a vice.

HYMN XXIX
Long-suffering of God

I

ONE hundred feet from off the ground
 That noble Aloe blows;
But mark ye by what skill profound
 His charming grandeur rose.

II

One hundred years of patient care
 The gardners did bestow
Toil and hereditary pray'r
 Made all this glorious show.

III

Thus man goes on from year to year,
 And bears no fruit at all;
But gracious God, still unsevere,
 Bids show'rs of blessings fall.

IV

The beams of mercy, dews of grace,
 Our Saviour still supplies—
Ha! ha! the soul regains her place,
 And sweetens all the skies.

HYMN XXX
Honour

I

IN man it is the truth affirm'd,
 Mean craft and guile withstood,
And variously by various term'd,
 Is both by grace and blood.

993

II

Courage and patriot zeal thou art,
 An ardour for the whole,
At once munificence of heart,
 And magnitude of soul.

III

In women 'tis that jealous fear,
 Which tends to parry shame;
It is their Chastity's barrier,
 And bulwark of their fame.

IV

It is sweet dignity and ease,
 Reserve without disdain;
Pleasing, tho' negligent to please,
 Bearing, not giving pain.

V

Then kneel, ye little prattlers down,
 I'll bless, if you will pray,
And one shall wear the laurel crown,
 And one be Queen of May.

HYMN XXXI

Immortality

I

'BE of good cheer, for I, ev'n I,
 Have overcome the world':
The wind and tide are yours—apply
 Your oars with sails unfurl'd.

II

Sure Immortality was known
  To few, but very few,
Before I came, the corner-stone,
  To build my work anew.

III

But now ye know it in your hearts,
  Ye hear it with your ears;
Not by dark visions, or by starts,
  Its evidence appears.

IV

Sheep, blessed sheep, ye shall be brought
  To pleasures how divine!
To joys surpassing human thought,
  And such as equal mine.

V

How brilliant past conceit each star
  Shall shine before the Lamb:
'Tis bliss to know not what ye are,
  By knowing what I AM.

HYMN XXXII

Against Despair

Old Ralph in the Wood

I

A RAVEN once an Acorn took
   From Bashan's tallest stoutest tree;
He hid it by a limpid brook,
   And liv'd another oak to see.

II

Thus Melancholy buries Hope,
   Which Providence keeps still alive,
And bids us with afflictions cope,
   And all anxiety survive.

HYMN XXXIII

For Saturday

I

Now's the time for mirth and play,
Saturday's an holiday;
Praise to heav'n unceasing yield,
I've found a lark's nest in the field.

II

A lark's nest, then your play-mate begs
You'd spare herself and speckled eggs;
Soon she shall ascend and sing
Your praises to th' eternal King.

HYMN XXXIV

For Sunday

I

ARISE—arise—the Lord arose
   On this triumphant day;
Your souls to piety dispose,
   Arise to bless and pray.

II

Ev'n rustics do adorn them now,
   Themselves in roses dress;
And to the clergyman they bow,
   When he begins to bless.

III

Their best apparel now arrays
   The little girls and boys;
And better than the preacher prays
   For heav'n's eternal joys.

HYMN XXXV

At Dressing in the Morning

I

Now I arise, empow'r'd by Thee,
   The glorious Sun to face;
O clothe me with humility,
   Adorn me with thy grace.

II

All evil of the day foresend,
   Prevent the tempter's snare;
Thine Angel on my steps attend,
   And give me fruit to pray'r.

III

O make me useful as I go
　My pilgrimage along;
And sweetly sooth this vale of woe
　By charity and song.

IV

Let me from Christ obedience learn,
　To Christ obedience pay;
Each parent duteous love return,
　And consecrate the day.

HYMN XXXVI

At Undressing in the Evening

I

THESE cloaths, of which I now divest
　Myself, ALL-SEEING EYE,
Must be one day (that day be blest)
　Relinquish'd and laid by.

II

Thou cordial sleep, to death akin,
　I court thee on my knee;
O let my exit, free from sin,
　Be little more than Thee.

III

But if much agonizing pain
　My dying hour await,
The Lord be with me to sustain,
　To help and to abate.

IV

O let me meet Thee undeterr'd,
  By no foul stains defil'd!
According to thy holy word,
  Receive me as a Child.

Pray Remember the Poor

I

I JUST came by the prison-door,
I gave a penny to the poor:
Papa did this good act approve,
And poor Mamma cried out for love.

II

Whene'er the poor comes to my gate,
Relief I will communicate;
And tell my Sire his sons shall be
As charitably great as he.

Plenteous Redemption

I

DAVID has said, and sung it sweet,
That God with mercy is replete:
And thus I'll say, and thus I'll sing,
In rapture unto Christ my King.

II

King of my heart and my desires,
Which all my gratitude inspires,
Bids me be great and glorious still,
And so I must, and so I will.

The Conclusion of the Matter

I

FEAR God—obey his just decrees,
And do it hand, and heart, and knees;
For after all our utmost care
There's nought like penitence and prayer.

II

Then weigh the balance in your mind,
Look forward, not one glance behind;
Let no foul fiend retard your pace,
Hosanna! Thou hast won the race.

THE END

NOTES
AND INDEX

NOTES

Page 385. *The Psalms of David*. The temptation to emend, overwhelming in these pieces, is to be resisted. Smart's syntax is elliptical but not illogical. It is a kind of mental shorthand which shews how far the originals had become part of his poetic consciousness, and it gives a peculiar and personal strength to his renderings. For instance, *Without my fault* (p. 535) is a condensed phrase for 'through no fault of mine'; *season'd corn* (p. 534) for 'corn that comes in due season'; *Least but in love* (p. 543) for 'least (*i.e. smallest or youngest*) except in being the best beloved'. Sometimes a comma is inserted as a metrical or musical pause, and should be ignored in the syntax: for instance (p. 540), the sense of *His gracious covenant direct* runs straight on to the next line. At others the mental insertion of a comma removes the difficulty, as at (p. 583) . . . *in mercy supream*[,] *the just for unjust* . . ., where the sense is '[Christ] . . . the righteous (*just*) comes to live and die for the unrighteous (*unjust*)'. Such ellipses are part of the personal idiom and so of the poetic effect of these pieces, and the reader, once he has the way of it, should find no difficulty with them.

The following words may prove somewhat obscure:

Page 525 *canton*—apportion
Page 583 *rais'd*—raz'd
Page 590 *earning*—yearning (as on p. 642 and in *Jubilate Agno*)
Page 596 *chives*—stalks, stamens (as on p. 644)
Page 737 *travel*—travail
Page 826 [*ghostly*]—spiritual.

Page 963. *Hymns for the Amusement of Children*. This title was probably given by Carnan to be in keeping with the other books of the series, a list of which is printed at the end of the volume. The text here given is that of the third edition (1775) in the Bodleian Library.

INDEX OF FIRST LINES

Vol. I ends at p. 381

Vol. I ends at p. 381

Vol. I ends at p. 381

Vol. I ends at p. 381

Vol. I ends at p. 381

Vol. I ends at p. 381

Vol. I ends at p. 381

Vol. I ends at p. 381

Vol. I ends at p. 381

Vol. I ends at p. 381

Vol. I ends at p. 381

INDEX OF FIRST LINES

Vol. I ends at p. 381

Vol. I ends at p. 381

Vol. I ends at p. 381